DEVELOPING STRATEGIC THOUGHT:

Rediscovering the art of direction–giving

Also available in the McGraw-Hill Developing Organizations Series

THE ORGANIZATIONAL LEARNING CYCLE
How We Can Learn Collectively
Nancy Dixon
ISBN-07707937-X

THE WISDOM OF STRATEGIC LEARNING
The Self-managed Learning Solution
Ian Cunningham
0-07707894-2

ON INDIVIDUAL AND ORGANIZATIONAL TRANSFORMATION
The Time Challenge of Continual Quality Improvement
William R Torbert and Dalmar Fisher
ISBN 0-07707834-9

For further information on these titles and other forthcoming books please
contact

The Product Manager, Professional Books, McGraw-Hill Book Company
Europe, Shoppenhangers Road, Maidenhead, Berkshire SL6 2QL, United
Kingdom
Telephone ++44(0)628 23432   Fax ++44(0)628 770224

Developing Strategic Thought

Rediscovering the art of direction–giving

Edited by BOB GARRATT

McGRAW-HILL BOOK COMPANY

London · New York · St Louis · San Francisco · Auckland
Bogotá · Caracas · Lisbon · Madrid · Mexico · Milan · Montreal
New Delhi · Panama · Paris · San Juan · São Paulo · Singapore
Sydney · Tokyo · Toronto

Published by
McGraw-HILL Book Company Europe
Shoppenhangers Road, Maidenhead, Berkshire, SL6 2QL, England
Telephone 01628 23432
Fax 01628 770224

British Library Cataloguing in Publication Data
Developing Strategic Thought:
Rediscovering the Art of
Direction-giving. – (McGraw-Hill
Developing Organizations Series)
I. Garratt, Bob II. Series
658.4012

ISBN 0-07-707986-8

Library of Congress Cataloging-in-Publication Data
This data is available from the Library of Congress, Washington DC, USA.

1234 CUP 9765

Typeset by TecSet Ltd, Wallington, Surrey
and printed and bound in Great Britain at the University Press, Cambridge

To Sally
whose energy and commitment made this possible

Contents

Series preface   xi
Notes on contributors   xiii

1   **Introduction, by Bob Garratt**   **1**

PART ONE   THE CONTEXTS OF STRATEGIC THINKING

2   **From manager to director: developing corporate**
    governors' strategic thinking, by Bob Tricker   **11**
    Behind the boardroom door—what is the role of the
    board?   11
    Corporate governance—the exercise of power over
    companies   13
    What should the board be doing?   13
    The conformance and performance roles of the board   16
    On strategy and board structure   18
    The making of an effective board   20
    Developing directors with strategic skills   23
    From managers to directors—from management to
    governance   25
    Note   28
    References   28

3   **Preparing for turbulence: the changing relationship**
    between strategy and management development
    in the learning organization, by Max Boisot   **29**
    Introduction   29
    Strategic options   32
    The learning process   37
    Implications for management development   43
    Conclusion   45
    References   45

4   **Design as a strategic management resource, by**
    Christopher Lorenz   **47**
    The design paradox   47

Design's role in strategic thinking and operational
practice   50
Empirical evidence   53
The 'hard' side of design   56
The 'soft' side of design   56
Phases of corporate design evolution   57
From hard to hard/soft strategy   58
The design connection   58
Imagination versus visualization   59
Conclusion   61
References   62

PART TWO   THOUGHTS ON STRATEGIC THINKING

5   **Strategic thinking as 'seeing', by Henry Mintzberg**   **67**
    Note   70

6   **Hearing the baby's cry: it's all in the thinking,**
    by Colin Sworder   **71**
    Corporate visions   71
    The importance of information   73
    The importance of beliefs   73
    What is an attitude?   75
    Impacts on strategic thinking   77

7   **The processes of thinking strategically,**
    by Jerry Rhodes   **80**
    The role you give to thinking   80
    Characteristic thinking style   81
    Process and data   86
    Using *Thunks* for strategy   88
    The key *Thunks* for strategy   89
    Conscious awareness   94
    References   95

PART THREE   THE DEVELOPMENTAL PROCESSES FOR
STRATEGIC THINKING

8   **Strategic dilemmas occasioned by using alternative**
    scenarios of the future, by
    Charles Hampden-Turner   **99**
    Is strategy a viable concept?   99
    Visions of the future of capitalism   100
    Scenarios describing the dominance of three different
    capitalisms   100
    Describe three future worlds   102

Express their logics as a strategic calculus   114
Connect all three logics into a learning loop   116
Recommend a master strategy for accelerated
learning which could render all these futures
survivable and profitable   118
Describe the dilemmas which will have to be
reconciled in order for your organization to perform
effectively   119
Show how these dilemmas are fine-tuned   120
Towards a new creativity   136
Towards the value star   137
References   137

9 **The use of scenario thinking: can a scenario a day
   keep the business doctor away? by Bill Weinstein   139**
   Scenarios: what and why   140
   How scenarios are made and what is to be done
   with them   148
   Benefits and complications of scenario thinking   152
   The involvement and development of managers   155

10 **Developing director and executive competencies in
   strategic thinking, by Phil Hanford   157**
   Some comments on strategic thinking   157
   Developing your strategic thinking competencies   160
   'Tools for Thinking Strategically' programme   166
   Strategic thinking concepts   173
   Conclusion   182
   Notes   183
   References   183
   Further information on specific strategic thinking
   tools   184
   Recommended reading   185

11 **Strategic thinking in public service, by David
   Wilkinson and Mike Pedler   187**
   Introduction   187
   Key issues of strategy in public service   188
   Public sector or public service?   192
   The nature of strategic thinking in the public
   services   194
   Future scenarios   196
   The way ahead?   199
   Final words   203
   References   203

12 **International teams: avoiding the pitfalls and creating a source of international strategy, by Sue Canney Davison**   205
Cultural differences   206
Pitfalls in the development of international strategy teams   207
Effective approaches to developing international strategy teams   211
Best practice in development programmes   215
References   216

13 **Developing the international manager strategically, by Fons Trompenaars**   218
The international manager reconciles cultural dilemmas   219
The organizational context of the international manager's activities   230
How to develop the international manager   231
Summary and recommendations   239
References   240

14 **Helicopters and rotting fish: developing strategic thinking and new roles for direction-givers, by Bob Garratt**   242
Blockages to the direction-giving role   242
Coming to terms with the direction-giver's role: the learning board   243
Blockages to direction-giver development   245
Developing strategic performance-focused direction-givers   248
A three-stage approach   249
Four strategic thinking styles   251
The ten steps of strategic thinking   253
References   255

Index   257

Index of authors   263

Series preface

The McGraw-Hill *Developing Organizations* series is for people in the business of changing, developing and transforming their organizations. The books in the series bring together ideas and practice in the emerging field of organizational learning and development. Bridging theory and action, they contain new ideas, methods and models of how to get things done.

Organizational learning and development is the child of the organization development (OD) movement of the 1960s and 1970s. Then people like Schein, Beckhard, Bennis, Walton, Blake and Mouton defined a *change technology* which was exciting and revolutionary. Now the world has moved on.

The word 'technology' goes with the organization-as-machine metaphor. OD emphasized the *outside-in* application of 'behavioural science' which seems naïve in the context of the power-broking, influence and leverage of today's language. Our dominant metaphor or organizations as organisms or collective living beings requires a balancing *inside-out* focus of development and transformation of what is already there.

Learning is the key to our current dilemmas. We are not just talking about change. Learning starts with you and me, with the person – and spreads to others – if we can organize in ways which encourage it.

Learning is at a premium because we are not so much masters of change as beset by it. There is no single formula or image for the excellent company. Even the idea of 'progress' is problematic, as companies stick to the knitting and go to the wall. Multiple possible futures, the need for discontinuity almost for the sake of it, means that we must be able to think imaginatively, to be able to develop ourselves and, in generative relationships with others, to continually organize and reorganize ourselves.

Organizations are unique, with distintive biographies, strengths and opportunities. Each creates its own future and finds its own development paths. The purpose of these books is not to offer ready-made tools, but to help you create your own tools from the best new ideas and practices around.

The authors in the series have been picked because they have something to say. You will find in all of the books the personal voice of the writer, and this reflects the voice which each of us needs in our own organizations to do the best we can.

Bob Garratt is known for The Learning Organization *(Fontana 1985) in which he put forward the idea of the directors of the company being the 'brain' of the firm. Directing is different from managing, the processes of direction-finding requiring an outer scanning as well as an inner monitoring. In* Developing Strategic Thought, *Bob takes these ideas further and has assembled an impressive cast to help him do this.*

We are in the age of the organizational learning because, although strategic planning *can be a snare and a delusion, we have never had greater need of strategic* thinking. *In his introduction, Bob quotes a Fortune 500 analysis which shows the average life of major USA corporations at 45 years and falling. This is not coming about through an absence of strategic planning, and it is a statistic to concentrate the minds of those charged with leading the organization.*

I have known Bob for over 20 years, especially through his commitment to action learning. He is the editor of the Fontana 'Successful Manager' series and a moving force within AMED (the Association of Management Education & Development). He continues to make a significant contribution to the development of management education, in the UK and around the world. He is a natural leader for this series.

Mike Pedler

Notes on contributors

Max Boisot is Professor of Strategic Management at ESADE in Barcelona and Senior Associate at the Judge Institute of Management Studies at the University of Cambridge. He holds an MSc in Management from MIT as well as a doctorate in technology transfer from the Imperial College of Science, Technology and Medicine, London University. From 1984 to 1989, he was dean and director of the first MBA programme to be run in the People's Republic of China in Beijing. Max Boisot is currently completing a book on the strategic use of information in institutions and organizations.

Sue Canney Davison MA (Oxon) is the founder of Pipal International, a consultancy working on international integration and strategy. After working with an international team for six years in the Himalayas, Sue returned to the UK in 1986. Since then she has consulted and collaborated with businesses on intercultural communication and the development of senior international management programmes. Recent clients have included BP, ICI, Shell, Grand Metropolitan, Jardines Pacific, Fiat, Kone, and Daimler-Benz. Pipal International is also part of the PRC Consortium.

Sue's current research included in-depth doctoral research at London Business School using video analysis to elicit the dynamics of effective international teams in Europe and South East Asia. She has also just concluded a major research project for ICEDR (a worldwide consortium of top business school and companies) in which over sixty international teams have been surveyed and interviewed in depth to discover how these teams are contributing to global strategy, the current human resource practices to support these teams and the team skills necessary to create high performance.

Sue now acts as high level international team facilitator in companies such as Nokia and Wellcome and will be publishing the results of her experience and research over the next year. She hopes to share the findings of the corporate team research with intergovernmental negotiating bodies.

Bob Garratt is Chairman of Organisation Development Ltd in Hong Kong, and of Media Projects International in London. He has an international practice in director development and strategic thinking, with clients in the private and public sectors in Europe, Asia, North America, Australia and New Zealand. He is on the Professional Development Committee and

Fellowship Committee of the Institute of Directors, London; is a past chairman of the Association for Management Education and Development; and a member of the Guild of Management Consultants. He is a Visiting Fellow of the Management School, Imperial College of Science, Technology and Medicine, London University, and an Associate of the Judge Institute of Management, Cambridge University. His books include *Learning to Lead* (1991), *The Learning Organisation* (1987), *China Business Briefing* (1986) with Sally Garratt, and *Breaking Down Barriers: Priorities and Practice in International Management Education* (1980) with John Stopford.

Charles Hampden-Turner is a permanent visitor at the Cambridge University Judge Institute of Management Studies, and a professor on extended leave from the Wright Institute in Berkeley, California. He is the author of eleven books, most recently *Seven Cultures of Capitalism* (Doubleday, New York, 1993; Piatkus, London, 1994) *Corporate Culture: Vicious and Virtuous Circles* (Economist Books, London, 1990), and *Charting the Corporate Mind* (Basil Blackwell, Oxford, 1990). His best selling *Maps of the Mind* (Macmillan, New York, 1981) sold over 150,000 copies worldwide. His books have been translated into many languages.

He worked for Group Planning in the Shell International Petroleum Company from 1981 to 1985 and was Shell Senior Research Fellow at the London Business School from 1985 to 1990. Charles has a masters degree and a doctorate from the Harvard Business School.

He has consulted to Shell, BP, Digital Equipment, Apple, IBM, Analog Devices, Advanced Micro Devices, Motorola, Hanover Insurance, Barclays Bank, BZW, British Airways, US Air, ICI, Zeneca, the BBC, Nissan, Raychem, Clorox, Polaroid, Mercantile and General, the Auditor General's Office in Canada, SRI International, Coopers and Lybrand and many others.

He has been a visiting scholar to the Systems Dynamic Group at MIT, to the Ontario Institute for Studies in Education, to the Aspen Institute, to the Niagara Institute, and Visiting Professor at Erasmus University and the Roffey Park Management College. He was Visiting Scientist at the Tavistock Institute from 1979–1980. He is a winner of the Douglas McGregor Memorial Award and the Columbia University Prize for the Study of the Corporation.

Phil Hanford is an independent strategic management consultant based in Sydney. He assists executive teams in their formulation and implementation of an effective strategy aimed at developing both the organization's business and its culture. Thinking better and managing participatively are central themes in his work. He is particularly interested in helping directors and executives to develop their competencies in strategic thinking. In addition to Australia, he has worked in America, Africa and the South Pacific in a wide variety of roles: worker, manager, executive, consultant. His diversified career history together with formal studies in management bring both breadth and depth to his work. He has had numerous articles published and is currently completing a book on strategic management.

Christopher Lorenz has been Management Editor of the *Financial Times* since 1977, and an FT columnist since 1991. He specializes in corporate strategy and organization; the management of change; and product design and development. He has taught widely on in-company programmes for multinationals; at leading business schools in Europe and the US; and on a wide range of international management seminars and conferences. He has spent sabbaticals at Harvard, INSEAD and elsewhere, and has been a board member of both the international Strategic Management Society and the UK Design Council.

His books include *The Uneasy Alliance—Managing the Productivity-Technology Dilemma* (Harvard Business School Press, co-edited with Professors Robert Hayes and Kim Clark); *The Design Dimension* (Basil Blackwell, published in seven languages); and *The Financial Times on Management* (FT-Pitman, co-edited with Nicholas Leslie). In addition to the *Financial Times*, his articles have been published in the *McKinsey Quarterly*.

Henry Mintzberg is Professor of Management at McGill University in Montreal (and Visiting Professor at INSEAD, Fontainebleau, France), where he does research and writing on management and organizations—currently on the process of strategy formation, the design of organizations as well as the impact of design on organizations, and the roles of intuition, insight, and inspiration in a world of 'thin' management. His teaching activities at McGill are restricted to doctoral students; he now does all his management education with experienced practising managers, either in public seminars or within their own organizations. Much of this, together with his consulting activities, is conducted in Europe as well as North America. He is also currently co-chairing a McGill committee to redesign a degree programme in management education.

Henry received his doctorate and master of science degrees from the MIT Sloan School of Management and his mechanical engineering degree from McGill, working in between in operational research for the Canadian National Railways. The Universities of Venice, Lund, Lausanne, and Montreal have also granted him honorary degrees. He served as President of the Strategic Management Society from 1988-91, a worldwide association of 'thoughtful practitioners and insightful scholars.' He is an elected Fellow of the Royal Society of Canada (the first from a management faculty), the Academy of Management, and the International Academy of Management.

Henry is the author of *The Nature of Managerial Work, The Structuring of Organizations,* and *Power In and Around Organizations,* all published by Prentice-Hall in their Theory of Management Policy series. He has also published a textbook, *The Strategy Process,* with James Brian Quinn (in its second edition, also with Prentice-Hall), and, for a general audience, *Mintzberg on Management: Inside Our Strange World of Organizations* (with the Free Press in 1989). His articles number about ninety, including two *Harvard Business Review* McKinsey prizewinners, *The Manager's Job: Folklore and Fact* (first place in 1975) and *Crafting Strategy* (second place in 1987). He has recently completed a book on *The Rise and Fall of Strategic Planning.*

Mike Pedler, PhD, worked in marketing with Procter & Gamble before moving into industrial relations with the Workers Educational Association and then into management and organization development at Sheffield Business School. He is an independent consultant, writer and researcher and a partner, with Dr Tom Boydell and Professor John Burgoyne, in the Learning Company Project.

He is honorary Senior Research Fellow at the Department of Management Learning in the University of Lancaster and a non-executive director of Transform. He has written and co-authored a number of books and articles on management development and organizational learning including:
A Manager's Guide to Self-development (McGraw-Hill, 1978 and 1986), *Action Learning in Practice* (Gower, 1983 and 1991), *Managing Yourself* (Fontana, 1986 and Gower, 1990), *The Learning Company: a Strategy for Sustainable Development* (McGraw-Hill, 1991), *Self-development: a Facilitator's Guide* (McGraw-Hill, 1991). He is a past editor of *Management Education & Development* and Series Editor of the McGraw-Hill series *Developing Organizations*.

Jerry Rhodes founded his niche consultancy in 1975, to promote creativity and innovation in business. His life as a manager had been in Hoover, GKN, Rank Xerox and Kepner Tregoe UK. His first major project, with Philips in Eindhoven, originated the model of mind based upon the 25 Thinking-Intentions, or Thunks. Over some 20 years, he has put these 25 conceptual tools to work, improving management performance at many levels of several large client organizations. The result is a developed system for mapping and re-engineering the processes of management thought. Under the name of Effective Intelligence, this system is now licensed in Europe and Scandinavia, Canada and USA. Rhodes is the author of *The Colours of Your Mind* (HarperCollins, 1988) and *Conceptual Toolmaking* (Blackwell, 1991). He can be contacted at the Centre for Effective Intelligence, Cotswold House, Wotton-under Edge, GL12 7AR.

Colin Sworder is a co-founder and a director of Due Diligence Services Limited, a knowledge products and value-adding services company. He has over ten years' experience specializing in business performance improvement by enhancing the financial returns from human capital. His work with colleagues who specialize in increasing the effectiveness of business processes and in supply chain marketing is a novel approach to many of the challenges facing business managers in the Information Age. Educated in England, France and Germany, he lived in Johannesburg for ten years, where he owned a management services business.

Bob Tricker wrote *Corporate Governance*, the first book to use that title, in 1984. He was Director of the Oxford Centre for Management Studies (now Templeton College) throughout the 1970s and formed the Corporate Policy Group at Nuffield College, Oxford, to research the work of directors and boards. Earlier, after studying at Harvard Business School and Oxford University, he was the first Professor of Management Information Systems at Warwick University. He holds a doctorate for his work on information strategy and also qualified in the UK as a Chartered Accountant and a Chartered Management Accountant, serving on the Councils of both bodies. He is the founder Editor of *Corporate Governance—an international review* and has also written *The Independent Director*, *Harnessing Information Power* and co-edited *The Director's Manual*. For the past decade he has been a professor of the University of Hong Kong Business School and Director of the International Corporate Policy Group, which links professional directors and scholars around the world. He has served on many boards and governing bodies and consults and lectures worldwide on corporate governance, corporate strategy and board-level effectiveness.

Fons Trompenaars is a leading authority on cultural diversity and was recently identified by the *Financial Times* as a 'likely new star of the world's management seminar circuit'. He is Managing Director of the Centre for International Business Studies (CIBS) in The Netherlands, a consultancy and training organization for international management. In 1991 he was awarded the International Professional Practice Area Research Award by the American Society for Training and Development. His books include *Riding the Waves of Culture* (1993) and *The Seven Cultures of Capitolism* with Charles Hampden-Turner (1994).

Bill Weinstein is Professor of International Business at Henley Management College, UK and an independent management consultant. Prior to his post at Henley, he had been Fellow in Politics, Public Policy and Management at Balliol College, Oxford University. As a consultant, author and lecturer on company executive development programmes, he has focused mainly on the impact of the changing external environment on strategy and organizational structure, in both the market and public service sectors. He publishes annually, using scenarios, the *Executive Guide to Global Change*. His videos on scenario thinking, made with David Frost and Brian Redhead, are widely known in companies and management schools. His work in developing and applying a distinctive technique of economical scenario analysis has involved dozens of domestic and international organizations covering a wide range of businesses and public services. He also has experience as a non-executive director or chairman of several UK Stock Exchange listed companies.

David Wilkinson is a freelance consultant working with client organizations on developing strategic responses to change. He was formerly on the academic staff at Huddersfield Polytechnic and at Bradford and Ilkley Community College. He later became Assistant Director with Bradford Metropolitan Council and then special adviser on strategic change and organizational development to the Chief Executive.

Much of his current consultancy work is in the public arena, including both commissioning and provider organizations, and covering a wide range of public service activity. He is particularly concerned to help organizations chart realistic routes through the waves of short-term change initiatives in ways that link strategic imperatives to real long-term individual and organizational learning at all levels. A current focus is upon the development of multi-agency and cross-boundary working for both strategic and operational perspectives.

1   Introduction

Bob Garratt

Few books have been written on strategic thinking. Until very recently it has been assumed to be a rarely used part of management, a process with which few except those at the very top of an organization need concern themselves. In the Western world overconcentration on organizational efficiency, the short term and bottom lines has shown its limitations. The need for more long-term and reflective thinking linked to organizational effectiveness and creating alternative futures is beginning to be recognized. From this is emerging a simple but profound truth. 'Directing' an organization is very different from 'managing' one. This seemingly prosaic statement has great implications for those managers who are given, or aspire to, the role of directing their organizations, particularly in the way they *think* about formulating policy and strategy. The quality of such strategic thinking will also have profound effects on the way we regard, and our expectations of, the direction-givers of our governments, public and private corporations, health services, education systems and voluntary groups.

The 1970s and 1980s model of the 'top manager-as-action-hero'—crisis orientated, rapidly responding, opportunistic, pragmatic and ultimately ruthless—is now being put into a more balanced historical perspective. Their overconcentration on the short-term organizational efficiency often at the cost of long-term organizational effectiveness is understandable but not forgivable. It is becoming increasingly clear that such top management myopia with its crude interpretation of 'market forces' is unacceptable as we enter the challenges of the twenty-first century.

The international GATT Agreement of 1993, and the subsequent development of the World Trade Organization, has given us the possibility of massive increases in world trade as well as opportunities for political and economic cooperation which are unprecedented. How best does one rise to such truly global challenges? They demand strong visions of what the future could be and ingenuity about how to get there. This is certainly not through a reliance on 'bottom line' thinking. Having spent most of the 1980s in some form of recession, most Western managers will find this growth scenario, with its seemingly infinite combination of possible futures, difficult with which to come to terms. Those whose main role is to give direction to their organization will find the challenges doubly difficult if they do not accept that a significant amount of their time will be spent thinking and debating about these futures, rather than going out and managing current crises. I am sufficiently old-fashioned to believe that if you have the job title 'director', or perversely in US corporations 'president' or 'vice-president', then a significant part of your work is to give direction to your organization. This is currently unfashionable in management circles who tend to see the title as a reward at the end of a managerial career rather than the first step of a new one. This is likely to change rapidly when the understanding of the GATT Agreement percolates through.

This book reviews the international work of people—in business, government, consultancy and academia—who are leading the developmental processes in the underrated study of strategic thinking. All the contributors are involved in directing, or actively advising directors of, major organizations around the world and all the material has been used successfully for some years in such organizations.

'Strategic thinking' is the process by which an organization's direction-givers can rise above the daily managerial processes and crises to gain different perspectives of the internal and external dynamics causing change in their environment and thereby give more effective direction to their organization. Such perspectives should be both future-orientated *and* historically understood. Strategic thinkers must have the skills of looking both forwards and backwards while knowing where their organization is now, so that wise risks can be taken by the direction-givers to achieve their organization's purpose, or political will, while avoiding having to repeat the mistakes of the past.

Many readers will interpret strategic thinking as 'strategic planning'. I do not. I am with Henry Mintzberg in believing that 'strategic planning' is an oxymoron—a contradiction in terms like 'friendly fire', 'fun run' and 'military intelligence'. As this is dealt with elegantly in Mintzberg's book *The Rise and Fall of Strategic Planning* (Free Press, 1994) I will not over-egg the point here. However, this belief does permeate the pages of this book. This is not meant to demean planning. It is necessary at all levels of an organization and 98 per cent of peoples' work lives are dominated by it. But in terms of strategic *thinking* it is necessary but not sufficient. This book helps to explore what sufficiency might be, assuming that planning is a process *after* strategic thinking.

A look at most 'strategic planning' processes will show that this is rarely so. Let us take an example. A branch of an international bank is based in Bahrain. Each year it must produce a strategic plan for agreement by the top management at its international headquarters. At the start, an hour or two, certainly no more than that, is spent in a rather desultory search for ideas about what is affecting its external trading environment over the next 12–18 months. This couple of hours is regarded by the local managers as a bit painful as they are not used to thinking in this way. So they try to get it over with as quickly as possible and produce a simple SWOT analysis (organizational Strengths, Weaknesses, Opportunities and Threats) which is then put aside with a sigh of relief.

Then the 'real' work begins—constructing budgets and plans in line with headquarters' guidelines. This intensive piece of work, full of internal negotiations and emotions, takes about two weeks. The results, with the SWOT pinned to the back, are then sent to the regional headquarters. The Bahrain board is exhausted before the next round of negotiations, with the regional directors, begins. The regional folk study the budgets and plans for the whole Arabian Gulf region in line with their understanding of the international headquarters' guidelines and profit ratios. They adjust, with not much consultation, the Bahrain proposals to be in line with their understanding of international headquarters' needs. The amended figures then go to the international headquarters. Here they are adjusted on a global basis by the headquarters' staff, again with little consultation. The figures eventually arrive at the main board meeting where they are adjusted by the board members to fit their needs and information. From these they agree the next year's budgets and plans. Afterwards the chairman adds a few final adjustments to regions and countries about which he thinks he has additional information. The figures are then sent back to regional headquarters for fine-tuning and are finally sent to the Bahrain board. The board receives them in stunned silence each year. The final figures bear little relationship to what they proposed or assumed to be possible. 'How on earth are we to achieve these plans — they bear little resemblance to reality?' they ask, usually in rather stronger terms. The process has taken some three months and absorbed most of the senior managers' time internationally. If it is not seen as locally implementable, is it worth it?

I argue that it is not. This example is not a parody but a case taken from 1994 and in my experience is typical of many such 'strategic planning and budgeting' processes around the world. It shows clearly the very human tendency to cut short our thinking time when we feel that we cannot exercise the necessarily *divergent* thinking needed to begin to comprehend the disruptive and many-faceted changes in the external environment of the organization — the rates of political, physical environmental, economic, social, technological and trade changes (PPESTT). Instead we tend to use our more comfortable *convergent* thinking style. This gets us rapidly to what we know best — budgets and plans. This is a strength in managers but a liability in direction-givers in that it reduces dramatically any hope we have of ensuring that a board's rate of learning is equal to, or greater than, the rate of change in the external environment.

The SWOT analysis needs to be treated in depth and with rigour to become the key *intellectual* analytical tool through which ideas, alternative scenarios and risks are *debated* before plans are developed. Direction-giving is essentially an intellectual process, after all. If this is not done, then organizations are condemned forever to short-termism and repeating the mistakes of the past. It could be argued that because of the recession in the West already things are getting better, that top teams are beginning to think more strategically. I doubt it, and would cite the recent alarming analysis of the *Fortune 500* list of companies which showed that the average life of major US corporations is now 45 years and falling. This suggests little $L \geqslant C$. If that is already happening to the biggest companies, what is happening to the smaller ones?

I think that this trend emphasizes the need to develop strategic thinking capabilities in our direction-givers. They do not stop being action-orientated managers just by being given the job title 'director' or 'vice-president'. After all, they have invested twenty or thirty years of their career in being rewarded for doing just that. They do not suddenly become intellectually omniscient when given a directorship as a prize at the end of a long managerial career. Over 90 per cent of them admit that they cannot do the job and have had no training in thinking strategically. That they do not get such training is an indictment of the lack of importance we have given to strategic thinking. It is also an indictment of those chairmen and presidents of organizations who fail in one of their key roles—the development of their direction-givers.

In this book I have assumed that 'direction-givers' and 'strategic thinkers' are the same. I realize that some organizations seal off their strategic thinkers from those ultimately charged with direction-giving. I think this unwise, as do the authors of these chapters. The strategic thinking competencies—the specific attitudes, knowledge and skills outlined in this book—must be held by the direction-givers of any healthy organization. They are the ones who must take the policy and strategy decisions for their organization, and the wise risks or dangerous opportunities, which will determine their, and their organization's, future.

The need to develop the *future orientation* of direction-givers comes over strongly in this book. It is described in many ways—'designing the future', 'inventing the future', 'creating the future', 'being proactive to make the future happen'. The essence is that direction-givers cannot be fatalistic and wait for the future to happen to them. Their job is to try to make the future happen in their way. Even in the more fate-orientated societies of Asia this idea is beginning to be accepted as the 'little tigers' of Hong Kong and South-east Asia begin to determine, with China, the future of world economic development over the next quarter-century.

Aligned to being comfortable with future-orientation is the idea of being skilled at *mapping*. One could characterize managers as needing good road maps to work out where they are and how to get to where they want to be. There are plenty of maps and benchmarks to which managers can refer and lots of 'how to do it' books available. Direction-giving cannot be like that. There are few road maps to the future. Keeping the cartographic metaphor, direction-givers have only the use of a compass rather than a map in unknown territory. To maintain direction in such circumstances requires a strong sense of organizational purpose, or political will, and a vision about where one wants to be and why.

This is borne out through my research using Jerry Rhodes' Thinking Intentions Profile. The results highlight directors' strengths in Vision, Commitment and Judgement. However, this inventory also shows that of the direction-givers I have assessed, the type of thinking least preferred is that of Ingenuity—of making the future happen. This issue of 'implementability' is increasingly being taken seriously in organizations. As Max Boisot points out, until the 1990s it was considered normal to spend a lot of time working on strategic planning and then to hope that one had the capability to implement it. Effective organizations have reversed such thinking and spend time understanding organizational capabilities *before* getting into the planning phases. This gives a much higher probability of effective implementation.

Direction-givers often flounder during the early stages of such thinking. This is where the mapping of *possibilities*—scenarios—can be such a great help. The definite article explaining the use of scenarios in organizations is Arie de Geus's 'Planning as learning' in the *Harvard Business Review* in 1988. Scenarios investigate alternative futures and then use such maps to allow the direction-givers to track back to the present. This exercises their mental muscles: directing is, after all, an intellectual activity, and helps to get them into their role as the 'learning board' (the business brain) in a relatively risk-free way. However, as the future unfolds itself the intellectual disciplines derived from scenario thinking allow a more rigorous analysis and prognosis of what might happen. This develops what Max Boisot refers to as their 'strategic repertoire'. From such rigorous analysis and prognosis a future can be constructed which allows healthier organizational growth and development, despite the frequent disruptions from the external environment. The future can never be made risk free, but the risks taken are at least likely to be wise, and thoughtful, ones.

Scenarios also allow freer use of intuition. We all possess this but it is often censored by ourselves and our work groups. A key skill of the direction-giver is to be able to spot before others 'weak signals' among the background noise in the external environment and then to use this information creatively. If boards are sufficiently sure of what they want to achieve (their purpose or political will) then they become more sensitive to spotting weak signals and will give reasonable time and weight through debate to determining their meaning. This builds the direction-givers' confidence in monitoring and making sense of a turbulent external environment and so helps them to prepare for the future in a more constructive and ingenious manner than their competitors. Colin Sworder's metaphor of 'hearing the baby cry' is helpful here.

The book is designed in three sections. Part One looks at the developing organizational contexts for strategic thinking. Bob Tricker continues his excellent work on corporate governance and director development by extending the debate he, I and others have been having over the roles of directors. It is significant that this chapter comes from Hong Kong, where the director's role in twenty-first-century business is beginning to be taken seriously as the East Asian economy expands to become the world's largest by the second quarter of the twenty-first century. Max Boisot's chapter follows with an essentially historic piece looking at the development of the idea and practice of strategic thinking from the 1960s to the present. He argues that for nearly thirty years the argument has been that business strategy has driven an organization's management development. This has been turned on its head by some organizations who realize that now management development (through the capabilities of its direction-givers) is seen increasingly to determine achievable strategies. This is followed by Christopher Lorenz's chapter on 'Design as a strategic management resource'. He reminds us of the central role of the *design* of products and services in the strategic thinking and direction-giving processes.

Part Two reviews some thoughts on the research about strategic thinking itself. To many this will be the most difficult part of the book because a common language for describing 'thinking' is, curiously, only just beginning to emerge. I have adapted Henry Mintzberg's excellent, concise address to the Finnish Foundation for Economic Education's conference on Arenas of Strategic Thinking in 1990 to ensure that the idea of strategic thinking as 'seeing' is properly registered. Colin Sworder's 'Hearing the baby cry' is a necessary restatement of some basic truths about thinking, beliefs, objectives and organizations which many managers have knocked out of them during their long careers. Jerry Rhodes's contribution is a deep piece on the seven elements of thinking crucial to what he considers comprises 'strategic thinking'. I think that this is an important new contribution to the field which will repay careful study.

Part Three focuses on the developmental aspects of strategic thinking for both the individual and the organization. It starts with a significant piece from Charles Hampden-Turner on the creation of scenarios and then demonstrates skilfully their application to the seven classic dilemmas of direction-givers. This, too, will require careful study as it encompasses the key decisions, and hence risks, which all directors must face while acknowledging that none will ever be 'right' save for the briefest of moments. Bill Weinstein follows with a detailed piece on the construction of scenario thinking and its relationship to organizational health. Of particular interest is the emphasis on breaking out of managerial 'binary' thinking (either/or thinking) and into the creation of a wide range of possibilities for serious discussion, debate and monitoring over time. This notion is further developed by Phil Hanford through his Australian experiences. He demonstrates the outline of his own successful strategic thinking programmes and in so doing provides a useful map of the major developmental processes available today. Dave Wilkinson and Mike Pedler look at the particular issues of developing strategic thinking in the public sector in the UK, especially where the culture of business and public service clash. The reframing of what 'policy', 'strategy' and 'operations' mean in the new environment is clearly shown, as is the need for deeper thought on the meaning of 'customers' and 'citizens'. Resolution of these terms will have a major impact on the nature of our public organizations in the twenty-first century. Two contributions follow concerning the international development aspects of strategic thinking. Sue Canney Davison demonstrates the strengths and pitfalls of using multinational top teams to develop strategic thinking, while Fons Trompenaars looks deeply at the national cultural differences, and their likely effects, on international development for the direction-givers. Finally, I reflect on experiences of the development of strategic thinkers and address how such folk can become a true 'learning board' not only getting into role as the business brain but also as the business heart and soul, by developing four distinctive thinking styles and following a ten-step process for the board's development.

The book is not designed to give great emphasis to the *content* of strategic thinking. This is because strategic thinking is essentially a *process* to which we add our own content dependent on our capabilities. This process requires high levels of awareness of the changes in the external environment—to see, hear and use ingeniously the weak signals which can give competitive advantage. It requires the ability to create a 'holistic' view of the interconnections between apparently contradictory trends in that environment; and the ability to balance the internal and external dynamics of one's organization to balance organizational effectiveness against organizational efficiency. Most of all, it requires *time to reflect* on, and reframe, the current mindsets which you and your competitors hold. Budgeting time for reflection is the key to the synthesizing process. From such analysis wiser strategic decisions can be made. Ultimately, strategic thinking requires the direction-givers to create, develop and maintain the organization's brain, heart and soul—the sources of both emotional and physical energy which drive the organization forward. This is a role well worth the inevitable early discomfort involved in developing strategic thinking.

Bob Garratt

PART ONE THE CONTEXTS OF STRATEGIC THINKING

2 From manager to director: developing corporate governors' strategic thinking

Bob Tricker

Behind the boardroom door—what is the role of the board?

Amazingly, the most important strategic decision-making body in the company—the board of directors—does not appear on the typical organization chart, and the most significant decisionmakers—the directors—receive little or no training in strategic thinking. The deficiency increasingly shows.

> The boardroom at IBM's Armonk headquarters in New York State is large and impressive: so is their board of directors, with well-respected figures many of them CEOs and chairmen of major companies. Yet shareholders at the 1993 annual meeting, in Tampa, Florida, were vociferous in their criticism. A board whose 'attitudes, decisions and trusting manners have caused this company's recent demise', said one; a board that 'surely lacks the pertinent current knowledge, skills and visions to deal with, add value to and guide IBM' said another. Twelve of IBM's 18 directors at that time were over 60 (average age 61.3). By contrast, the average age of the board of Microsoft, a much smaller company, whose market capitalization had overtaken IBM's, was 50.5. It was not age that the shareholders were criticizing, but the apparent lack of strategic knowledge, ability and wisdom of the directors to foresee the pitfalls that had led the once great company to face a 50 per cent drop in market value in less than a year.

How could such a strategic failure have occurred? In this chapter we will explore the role of the board of directors, the field of corporate governance as it is increasingly called, review board-level activities and consider what can be done to increase board effectiveness, particularly the development of directors capable of strategic thinking.

What is the role of the board of directors? To answer this question we need to remind ourselves of the concept of the company. The joint stock company, with limited liability for its shareholding investors, was an elegantly simple and eminently successful development of the mid-nineteenth century. It facilitated the provision of capital, encouraged business growth secured employment, provided innovation in industry and commerce, and created wealth. The model was robust and adaptable. Indeed, its great flexibility has led to the huge proliferation, diversity and complexity of corporate types and structures today.

The essential notion was to incorporate the business as a separate entity, with a legal persona, able to do many of the things individuals in business can do—buy, sell, employ, own assets, incur liabilities, contract and sue and be sued. The liabilities and responsibilities of the shareholding members of the company were separated from those of the company. Ownership was the basis of power. The shareholders, meeting together, nominated and appointed the directors, who had a duty to report to them regularly on their stewardship over corporate affairs. The members also appointed auditors to report whether the directors' report and accounts showed a true and fair view of the state of affairs in the company. That was the original idea; and it remains the *de jure* underpinning. But today's reality is a different matter.

The concept of the corporation, derived from these early ideas and, incidentally, rooted in Western, Anglo-American ideology, has permeated the business world. Reflecting the outreach of the British Empire in the Victorian era, company law in Australia, Canada, Hong Kong, India, New Zealand, Singapore, South Africa and elsewhere grew from the same roots and, although in each jurisdiction laws have diverged, the essential concept remains. The development of the corporate form in the various states of the United States is, likewise, built on the ideology of corporate individualism. In Japan, company law and regulation was influenced by the Western-allied occupying forces after the Second World War.

But the original corporate idea has become swamped by the profusion and confusion of different corporate types—from small, proprietorial firms in which the owner is also manager and director, through sizeable, but still family-dominated firms to vast corporate groups with a multitude of subsidiaries held at many levels, with complex ownership chains and networks, further complicated these days by global strategic alliances and joint ventures.

Public concern over the exercise of power over the modern corporation has come to the fore in recent years. As ownership and management have become increasingly separate, so pressures have arisen for more control over the CEO and top management team. Complaints about loss of strategic direction, overdominant CEOs and excessive executive remuneration have all been raised. Institutional investors in the United States have been able to wield enough power to remove the chairmen/CEOs from a number of major companies and force strategic changes. Company regulators have increased the requirement for checks and balances at board level, including proposals for the disclosure of more corporate information, wider use of independent outside directors on boards and their involvement in audit committees, nominating committees and remuneration committees. This emerging area of interest has been called 'corporate governance'.

Corporate governance— the exercise of power over companies

What exactly *is* corporate governance? It is about the exercise of power over companies. Consequently, it concerns the processes of the board of directors. (The governing body of profit-orientated companies is typically called the board, but in not-for-profit entities it might be called the council, the committee, the senate or some other name—but essential governance issues remain very similar.) Corporate governance concerns the relationships between the board and the members (the shareholders in the profit-orientated company, whether they are close members of the family in a private company, the holding company in the case of a subsidiary company in a group, or the individual and institutional investors in the public listed company). It is also about the relationships between the board and the top management (some of whom may be the same individuals, as we shall see later), the board and the auditors and company regulators, and the board and other stakeholders (such as the employees, suppliers, customers, lenders, even society at large as calls arise for greater accountability and responsibility from corporate entities. Figure 2.1 reflects this perspective of corporate governance.

What should the board be doing?

Given the central role of the board of directors, shown overleaf, how do they go about their work? What do boards do? To answer this question, a simple framework was devised (see Figure 2.2) as the basis for discussions with directors about the

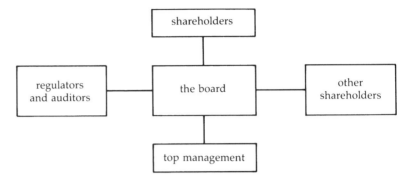

Figure 2.1   The relationships and boundaries of corporate governance

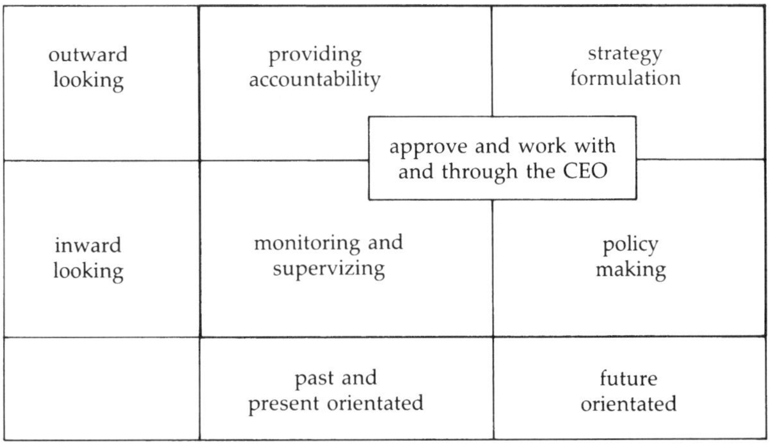

outward looking	providing accountability	strategy formulation
	approve and work with and through the CEO	
inward looking	monitoring and supervizing	policy making
	past and present orientated	future orientated

Figure 2.2   The framework for analysing board activities (from Hilmer and Tricker, 1991)

focus of board-level activity. The assumptions underlying this schema are that directors need to look inwards, as it were, at the management of the business(es) of the company and outwards on its competitive, strategic environment. They also need to look back at past events (particularly those of the recent past), at the present and over the future strategic time horizon of the firm.

On the one hand, in formulating strategy, the board is looking ahead in time and externally in direction, at the firm in its strategic environment. Strategies then need to be translated into policies to guide executive management within the firm. On the other hand, the board needs to monitor and supervise the activities of executive management, looking inwards at recent past performance and current management situations. Finally, accountability involves reflecting corporate activities and performance externally to the shareholders and any others with legitimate claims to accountability. The literature of strategy formulation is replete with 2×2 matrices. The only excuse for adding yet another is this one's claim to be comprehensive: in suggesting that directors should look internally and externally, in the past, present and future, they have nowhere else to look!

Some people, including Bob Garratt, the editor of this book, prefer to reserve the term 'policy making' for the activities in the top right-hand quadrant, arguing that this term more nearly reflects the popular use of the word 'policy', particularly in government circles, for example in reference to policy studies which then can lead to the strategies needed to carry them out. The author of this chapter prefers to use strategy in the sense used by the first commentators on the subject—like the great Chinese military strategist of the sixth century BC, General Sun, who wrote 'All men can see how the battle is won by the tactics I use: what no man can see is the strategy whereby victory is achieved'. Using this terminology, strategy formulation is the setting of direction for the company (why are we called directors, after all). Such strategies then need to be reflected in internal policy making to lay down the resultant pricing policies, labour relations policies, financial policies and so on.

In the studies, directors were asked, in the context of a company with which they were familiar, to describe the ideal balance of board-level effort between the four cells in the quadrant of Figure 2.2. Then they were asked to estimate the actual balance of time and effort devoted by the board to the four activities. A typical pattern emerged. Directors tended to report that, in their opinion, the board should be spending more time focusing attention on strategy and the business environment but that, in fact, the pressure on them was to focus internally and to emphasize the monitoring and control of management.

A smaller public company, in the British Midlands, made a special effort to ensure that the board spent sufficient time addressing strategic issues. They held a strategy workshop, away from the boardroom, every other year. The chairman developed a set of ground rules for these sessions. First, they were not to be extensions of the monthly, formal board meeting, so no conformance matters would be raised; indeed, no executive decisions would be taken during the workshop. Second, considerable effort was made beforehand to provide relevant data on the strategic environment of the business, on the customer and competitor context as well as the economic, political and social expectations in the countries in which they operated. Everyone was also expected to come briefed on strategic areas in which they were concerned. Third, an external facilitator was used to allow the chairman and the managing director to participate in the content of the discussions. He discussed the workshop individually with each participant beforehand, to ensure that everyone held similar expectations of the process and content. The facilitator then guided the workshop, ensuring that everyone contributed, that issues were pursued to the necessary depth and that, finally, a list of action points emerged, which could lead, with further work, to strategic decisions which the board would subsequently take. Confidentiality was, of course, vital. The company, which had originated in the textile industry, was able to build on its core competencies and, after some eight years of these strategic retreats, had repositioned itself as a world leader in special materials and coatings used in space, defence and firefighting applications, while many of their previous competitors in the textile industry were wound up.

Among the important challenges to the board of directors is the decision about where to put its effort, how to allocate its time and how much of the work is to be delegated to the CEO and the top management team. Wrong choices, in due course, will reverberate throughout the business.

The conformance and performance roles of the board

Figure 2.2 can be redrawn to provide a further insight into the exploration of board-level activities. The left- and right-hand sides of the matrix contain essentially different types of activity (see Figure 2.3). On the right, strategy formulation and policy making are activities that contribute to the *performance* of the firm; they are emphasizing the setting of direction whereas those activities on the left—supervision and accountability—are about ensuring *conformance* to policies and plans.

Much of the recent theoretical work on corporate governance (using the financial economists' ideas of agency theory), and the development of corporate regulation, have emphasized the conformance role of the board. For example, the proposals for outside directors on the board, the insistence of independence of outside directors, the separation of chairman and CEO, the use of audit, nominating and remuneration committees of the board with independent directors, greater disclosure, protection of minority rights, etc. are all conformance-led—focusing on the checks and balances needed over executive management and for appropriate accountability. The Cadbury Committee (1992)

	conformance roles	performance roles
outward looking		
inward looking		
	past and present orientated	future orientated

Figure 2.3   Further insights into board-level activities

proposals for the governance of UK listed companies, with its code of practice and emphasis on non-executive directors, audit committees and various forms of reporting on governance practices, with the ultimate threat of de-listing, totally reinforces the conformance perspective.

In Australia, the Hilmer Report (1993) took a different line, arguing that the primary role of the board is 'to ensure that corporate management is continuously and effectively striving for above-average performance, taking account of risk', with shareholder protection as a subsidiary role. Here, the primary emphasis is on the performance role, on adding value. The conformance role is subordinated.

In practice, of course, the conformance and performance roles need to be balanced, in the context of the contingent circumstances facing the company. Over time, as circumstances change, so must the focus of the board's attention. The great challenge is to have a board whose collective experience, knowledge and skill can cope with changing situations.

In a major British public company, the board had developed a strategy of growth through acquisition during the early 1980s, gearing up the company's finances and issuing shares to fund the substantial new investments. Some of the acquisitions took longer than expected to deliver the anticipated returns and rising financing costs and the developing world recession produced a funds-flow crisis. The board, which had appeared competent in developing aggressive growth strategies, proved to be less adept in handling a financial crisis. Eventually, pressures were brought for the CEO and chairman to resign. Now, reported one of the remaining non-executive directors, his role changed completely. Instead of responding to strategic ideas put up by the CEO and top management, they were expected to take the lead in finding suitable replacements for the CEO and chairman. The executive directors on the board, who previously had been so forceful, were powerless to act because the board was searching for their future boss.

Clearly, the structure and membership of the board play a significant part in the way the board works in practice.

On strategy and board structure

In the major corporations in the United States, the board of directors tends to delegate a great deal of responsibility for strategy formulation to the CEO and the top management team. The board, which is made up mainly of independent, outside directors, may ask penetrating questions about the implications of strategic proposals put before them by the CEO. But at the end of the day they have neither the information nor the time (most are CEOs or chairmen of other major corporations in non-competing fields) to formulate strategy at length themselves.

By contrast, the boards of large British companies tend to have more executive directors, who are often more directly involved in strategic planning (although under pressure to emphasize the importance of non-executive directors from institutional investors and the influential proposals of the Cadbury Committee report, British board structures are beginning to converge with the US position). In Germany, by contrast yet again, there are two levels of boards, with the management board responsible for setting the strategic direction and running the business, reporting to the supervisory board which approves corporate plans and strategic proposals, and monitors performance against them on behalf of the shareholders and the employees.

Since there are successful and unsuccessful companies in all three jurisdictions—Britain, Germany and the United States—it is not the structure of the board *per se* which leads to effective governance. Rather, it is the sum of the individual directors' abilities, their shared perceptions of the role of the board and the fusion of that board into an effective whole that distinguishes a mediocre board from one that can add long-term strategic value to the company.

Of course, directors make different contributions to strategic thinking and the strategy-formulating process. The experience of some will enable them to bring relevant knowledge and insights to the identification of strategic issues, and to the subsequent exploration, analysis and strategic decision. Some might have special skills and know-how on strategic issues directly relevant to the industry, markets, technology or financing of the business. Outside directors can be windows on the world—the source of external strategically valuable information, or may be able to connect the company to useful networks of contacts, for example in government, international business or finance. Such roles are, essentially, performance related.

To fulfil the conformance roles, the board also needs directors with appropriate conformance-related skills, such as the ability to assess performance, see issues from many perspectives and provide objective judgement, able to monitor top management, appraise executive ability and, if necessary, have the integrity to make changes. Some outside directors may also find themselves put in the position of being a watchdog for various interests, such as minority shareholders, lending bankers or other companies involved through strategic alliances: such nominee positions can be difficult.

It is very unlikely that most directors will have a combination of these attributes; it is also highly improbable that any one director will have them all. Moreover, the call on the various roles will be contingent on the situation facing the company and is likely to change as the board faces different issues. The challenge is to build a balanced board with the appropriate set of talents and to create a board level climate in which they will all be utilized to the full.

> A family company in the educational film and video business had been built up very successfully under the direction of the key owner–manager. As the rate of expansion called for additional capital, other shareholders invested in the company and joined the board. However, the original founder, who was still managing director and chairman of the board, found that now he had to report much more fully to the board on current business activities (the conformance roles) and, even more surprising to him, the non-executive directors wanted to be involved in the longer-term thinking of the business (the performance roles). One argued for a major diversification into a related business area; another came up with acquisition prospects. It took the chairman some time to adjust to these new expectations. But the situation was much improved when, on the suggestion of one of the major 'shareholder' non-executive directors, two additional outside directors were appointed, who would not have a major shareholding, but who could contribute from their business experience to the strategic discussions of the board.

The making of an effective board

What is needed for a board to be effective? Three things are vital—knowledge, time and board leadership. Let us review each briefly.[1]

Most companies provide routine papers for board meetings: in many cases, the content and presentation could be improved. Moreover, the focus of many board reports is on recent performance—on the conformance role. As corporate activities become more complex, the tendency is to increase the scope of the board reports. But at the end of the day, what is really needed is not more data but better informed directors and a more knowledgeable board. Directors derive the information they need from many sources—briefings, visits, casual conversations and so on. This is particularly the case in strategy formulation where directors need to understand the context in which strategy is being made—an appreciation of the subtle interactions between company, customers and competitors across the entire enterprise, and among volatile strategic alliances, together with a perspective on the broad economic, social and political expectations in the territories in which business is to be done.

The executive board of an international airline felt that they were inadequately briefed for strategic-level discussion in their regular board meetings. Although they received a mass of reports and financial information well before each meeting, these papers were all prepared from internal sources by the marketing, flight operations and accounting departments. The reports said nothing about competitor activities. Recently, the airline had been taken by surprise by a number of unexpected strategic alliances between competitors, including some agreements to share routes and pool frequent-flyer programmes. The directors wanted information, as the CEO said, 'to make us as surprise free as possible'. The outcome was the creation of a competitor-information system, in effect an intelligence-gathering system, which enabled information from many different sources to be collected, analysed, synthesized and made available to the board. Two major outcomes were reported. First, the executives were amazed at the amount of competitor and customer information that was already known within the organization but which had not previously been known to the directors. Second, that, in order to derive the full value of the new information, the directors themselves needed more knowledge of their industry and their markets: a programme of visits, briefings and networking contacts was set up. As a result, the directors now feel they have a better grasp on the strategic situation, and they now all share the same strategic perspective.

The time of board members seems always, perhaps inevitably, to be under pressure. Consequently, efforts made to maximize the effectiveness of board activities is likely to pay dividends. Careful planning of board meetings, well ahead of time, ensuring that everyone is properly briefed, that adequate time can be given to deliberations and that clear decisions are reached, minuted and acted on, is one solution. Another is the use of board committees. The use of conformance-style committees, comprising mainly or wholly outside directors, such as audit, remuneration and nomination committees of the main board, have been much discussed in recent years, to provide checks and balance mechanisms and to avoid the possibility of executive domination of board matters.

The delegation to board sub-committees of the performance activities, strategy formulation and policy making, has been less frequently discussed. Some boards have a 'chairman's committee' or an executive committee to relieve the board of some of the detail of planning and decision making for the board as a whole. The danger of board sub-committees on performance activities is that the other board members become less well briefed on important strategic issues and, thus, unable to make the contribution to strategy formulation that they should.

Faced with ever-increasing demands on their time, the board of a European-based multinational company adopted three proposals. First, they provided staff support to directors, for example to pursue issues and obtain information where members themselves did not have the time for investigations nor access to the necessary data. They had to overcome resistance from top management, who felt that these personal assistants to directors might encroach on their preserves. Second, they gave each director a 'portfolio' of one functional area (such as marketing, finance or R&D), one subsidiary company, and one international territory, as areas of particular interest on which they were to be fully briefed. Again, executive management expressed concern about infringement of their responsibilities, but found that it was actually beneficial to have a main board member taking a special interest in their area. Third, they instituted a strategy review committee, comprising the CEO and four of the outside directors, to consider and make proposals on strategic direction. This way, the board felt, all of the directors would be involved in the strategic deliberations about the future direction of the company, but on the basis of fuller discussions by the sub-committee, whose minutes went to all members of the board.

However, the most significant element in board effectiveness is board leadership and the resulting style or culture of the board. Where the roles of CEO and board chairman are combined, there is usually no doubt where the board leadership is going to come from. Where they are separated, the relationship between the CEO and the chairman becomes vital. The ability to work closely together, with an understanding based on trust and a clear appreciation of each other's role and responsibilities, is vital.

Under the influence of precedent, personality and power, boards can develop strikingly different styles of activity and behaviour.[1] Some were towards being a 'rubber stamp' for decisions already taken by top management. Indeed, this might be appropriate in the case of a wholly owned subsidiary company, where the decisions are being taken along the management organization responsibility/accountability chain. Other boards appear more in the nature of a 'country club', where the harmony among the members is more important than the achievement of tough-minded decisions. Others, yet again, become a 'representative body', more like the adversarial relations in a parliament with diverse interests; such boards typically have members representing different interest groups, such as joint venture partners. 'Representative board' styles are also frequently found in the governing bodies of companies limited by guarantee and other not-for-profit organizations, because board members have been elected by diverse interest groups.

The board of a company in the brewing industry, based in the British Midlands, had for three generations been dominated by two families. The company's progress might have been described as 'solid but slow'. When the company acquired another beverage manufacturer, the chairmanship was kept by the existing incumbent, but a new managing director was appointed from the acquired company. Predictably, the style of the board changed fundamentally. What had been a fairly comfortable, club-like atmosphere became a tough-minded professional style. Changes were seen in terms of the frequency of meetings, the subjects on the agenda, the 'chemistry' of the interpersonal relationships between the directors, the role played by the new managing director and his relationship with the chairman.

Having considered what it takes to make a board effective, we come to the main conclusions of this chapter: how to develop directors with the necessary strategic skills.

Developing directors with strategic skills

For many years, strategy formulation was thought of, at least in companies and business schools in the West, as part of the process of professional corporate planning. Both the textbook and the practice emphasized the need for a rigorous, analytical approach. First, determine the goals and objectives of the firm and then, in the light of a thorough analysis of the threats and opportunities in the business environment, make a realistic assessment of the strengths and weaknesses of the company's own situation. Corporate planners should identify possible strategic options, evaluate them and determine the appropriate plan, which would typically form the basis for resource-allocation decisions, budgetary planning and the management control processes.

Rigorous, analytical and professional: but company-centred, as though the firm were at the centre of the universe. No mention of competitors, except as potential threats. No concern with customers, except as a source of potential revenues. No thought of strategic alliances, except as a means of securing sources of supply or channels of distribution. In the business world of the 1960s and 1970s, when competition was limited, indeed when for many industries demand outstripped supply and competition was for materials, professional corporate planning was paramount. But as business became a battlefield as Japanese competition began to make inroads into market after market, so the quantification of corporate planning began to give way to the much less tidy, but far more innovative, creative approach of strategic thinking.

The Asian approach to strategic thinking had been different all along. Strategy was not making a plan: it was building the set of beliefs about the broad direction in which to go that emerged as part of a continuing consideration, just as General Sun (Tse), that great Chinese strategist, already quoted, realized. The idea is captured by Kenichi Ohmae (1986), writing about Japanese business strategists in *The Mind of the Strategist*, when he writes:

> They have an idiosyncratic mode of thinking in which the company, customers and competition merge in a dynamic interaction out of which a comprehensive set of objectives and plans for action eventually crystallizes.

With such a frame of mind, the business strategist recognizes that it is not possible to form strategies for one's own firm until you have taken a view on the strategies of the competitors, potential competitors and potential allies. A strategic perspective needs to know not only their current strategic direction but also their strategic strengths and vulnerabilities: otherwise it is not possible to foresee what strategic shifts on our part are likely to provoke the greatest reaction on theirs. Just as in a game of chess, the strategist needs to be able to think a number of moves ahead. Remember that chess is, essentially, a war game; but, unlike business, there are only two players! Moreover, strategic thinking needs a clear perspective on the emerging needs of the customers and potential customers—which probably means taking a view on their strategic positions, too.

There is another way of looking at the basic framework used in this chapter (Figure 2.2) which helps to portray this, rather Asian, perspective on strategy formulation. Instead of slicing the quadrant vertically (as in Figure 2.3, which separates strategy formulation and policy making, the performance roles, from executive supervision and accountability, the conformance roles), slice the quadrant horizontally (as in Figure 2.4).

outward looking	idiosyncratic strategy formulation and corporate guidance		
inward looking	business planning and management control		
	past	present	future

Figure 2.4   An alternative perspective on board-level thinking

Now we can see that, at the higher levels of board thinking, the whole enterprise is put in the context of the overall business situation. Thinking encapsulates past experiences, current information and expectations about the foreseeable future. It is an on-going process, not the creation of a specific plan. Strategy formulation is idiosyncratic, emergent, non-linear and provides guidance to the on-going activities of the enterprise.

Then, at a lower level of abstraction, the focus of the board and the top management can move to the group's businesses, on shorter-term plans, resource allocation and management control, keeping operational performance in line, while moving in the directions indicated by guidance from the higher planes of strategic thought.

Now we can turn to the crucial issue: how can directors be developed to be capable of making the strategically significant contribution described here? In the words of the title of this chapter, how are managers, who will have acquired considerable managerial experience before they are appointed to the board, be turned into directors, with the knowledge, skills and abilities to govern the company for the benefit of all concerned?

From managers to directors—from management to governance

Most directors have never received any formal training or development for their important role as a director. Even among those that have, the extent of their formal director-level education was probably limited to reading a book, or attending an occasional seminar on the role and responsibilities of company directors. Such approaches to director development, often from a legal perspective, certainly have their value, particularly as directors become increasingly exposed to regulation and litigation over their board-level responsibilities. But they will never develop people able to think strategically and govern effectively.

Indeed, the wisdom required by directors cannot be taught. It can only be learned, and learned mainly from experience. But that does not mean a continuation of the present hit-and-miss methods of development by immersion in board affairs over time. Over, say, ten years, directors will not automatically gain ten years of new, valuable experience: they may well get the same experience ten times over. Worse, experience that is now ten years out of touch with changes in outside practice.

Asked about the way directors on his board were developed, the chairman of the board of a major British company expressed surprise. 'We do nothing to develop our board members,' he said. 'We choose non-executive directors who already have a great deal of experience in running businesses, usually they are the CEO or chairman of a major group. Our executive directors only get promoted to the board when they have demonstrated that they can deliver the goods. We look for sustained management performance in their part of the company. They learn the tricks of the boardroom quickly enough. But, personally, I believe that they are little use for the first year or two: then, once they understand the way we do things, they begin to make a worthwhile contribution.' That chairman resigned last year and his successor has restructured the board and significantly changed its processes.

A wise chairman will realize that there are many ways in which directors can gain accelerated experience of board matters, and acquire strategic thinking skills in the process. For example, through

- The encouragement of discussions on strategic issues, insights and ideas during board meetings or strategy workshops. With suitable board leadership, such discussions enhance the idea of a learning board; one in which the entire process is recognized as an on-going opportunity to learn.

The incoming chairman of a major British public company that had seen its share price collapse over the past three years initiated a new agenda for board meetings. The reports from the divisions were provided in the board papers and only those that needed specific decisions were discussed. The CEOs of the divisions were then required once or twice a year to come to the board to make a full strategic presentation. The chairman also invited a speaker, sometimes from within the company, more often from the worlds of technology, international finance, business schools, research and so on, to make a presentation. Discussion continued over the board lunch. One of the long-standing directors, commenting on the changes introduced by the new chairman, said that in his opinion the efficiency of the board had been doubled and the effectiveness of the directors increased a thousandfold. 'We are at last beginning to understand the strategic reality of the industry, worldwide, and our place in it.'

- Membership, or better chairmanship, of a board committee, a board working party or task force on strategic issues. If the director is further asked to reflect on what has been learned from the experience, and to discuss this with his or her peers, the opportunity becomes a personal action learning project.

When Lord Caldecote was chairman of the Delta Group, a major UK listed firm, he briefed each new director privately. 'Remember,' he said to the executive directors, 'the danger of executives on the board is that you mark your own examination papers. I expect you to take off your executive hat in the boardroom and accept responsibility with me for the direction of the company.' Caldecote also invited directors to comment on his chairmanship, seeking ideas on matters that had not been on the agenda but that the board should be talking about.

induction

- The use of informal mentors, where longer-established members of the board accept a responsibility for the inception of new members to the board, initiating them into the way the board works and encouraging a regular discussion and review of the new member's development. Of course, the mentoring idea assumes that the structure, style and strategic thinking of the board is worth learning about!

The finance Director on the board of a joint venture company in a major transnational group, with the agreement of the CEO, accepted a personal responsibility for the induction and development of a new, younger member of the board. As part of the induction process, he arranged for her to travel around the group to see the vital units and talk with significant executives of the joint venture partner, to meet major suppliers, customers and competitors, and to meet the auditors. Then, he briefed her prior to board meetings, ensuring that she had sufficient and appropriate information and, after the meeting, discussed both the content and the process of the meeting. Over time, he also arranged some informal lunches at which he, and other directors and executives he invited, discussed developments of possible strategic significance. 'I shall always be grateful for that experience,' she was subsequently to say, 'it meant that I was able to start learning about the company and about strategy from the moment I became a director. I hope I shall have the opportunity to give the same insights and advice to someone else one day.'

The need for directors, in all types and size of company, who are capable of thinking strategically and of contributing effectively to the governance of the company, has never been so great. When business conditions are stable and slow to change, boardroom traditions that have 'stood the test of time' may well be suitable: in conditions of rapid and turbulent change, nothing short of a board that can learn and adapt will survive. Increasingly, the need is for directors, both executive and non-executive, whose mindset not only includes the industry—customers, competitors and allies—of the company but which is also global, sensitive to the strategic relevance of business cultures around the world.

In recent years there have been too many examples where the business has outgrown the board. Boards need the foresight to appreciate that it can happen and an ability to develop a strategy, structure and style that can do something about it. Hopefully, the ideas in this chapter will provide a stimulus to a review of board-level effectiveness and directors' strategic abilities. There are many other original responses waiting to be developed by those directors who think about the need to think strategically.

Note

1. It is inappropriate to develop this matter further in this chapter. For more information, see the chapters written by the present author in Taylor, B. and Tricker, R. I., *The Director's Manual*, London: Institute of Directors and Director Books, 1991, and by Hilmer, F. and Tricker, R. I. in *The Australian Company Director's Handbook*, Sydney: Prentice-Hall, 1991.

References

Berle, A. and Means, G. (1992) *The Modern Corporation and Private Property*, New York: Macmillan.

Cadbury, Sir Adrian (chairman) (1992) *Report of the Committee on the Financial Aspects of Corporate Governance*, London: Gee and Co.

Garratt, R. (1993) 'Directing and the learning board', *Executive Development*, **6**, No. 3.

Hilmer, F. G. (chairman) (1993) Strictly boardroom—improving governance to enrich company performance; a study facilitated by the Sydney Institute, Melbourne; Information Australia.

Ohmae, K. (1986) *The Mind of the Strategist*, London: Penguin.

Tricker, R. I. (1993) *International Corporate Governance—text, cases and readings*, Singapore: Prentice-Hall.

3 Preparing for turbulence: the changing relationship between strategy and management development in the learning organization

Max Boisot

Introduction

Strategy has always been considered the queen of the managerial disciplines. Like the mandarins in the Bureau of Astronomy in imperial China, strategists have the ear of those at the top of the organizational system. Their mystical pronouncements are greeted with a hushed respect that occasionally borders on the reverential and, if they do not have the face to launch a thousand ships, many certainly have the words to do so—and fees to match.

Alas for strategists, they are increasingly being asked to do more than merely give the magic word that will send vessels down the slipways; they are expected to get themselves involved in the detailed mechanics of the launching, ship by ship, ensuring not only that the vessels float when they hit the water but also that they perform as planned in their sea trials. Such humdrum commissioning activities are only partly redeemed by the cachet of their label: strategy implementation. The expression cannot conceal the fact that the strategist is now expected to spend less time on the bridge and more time in the boiler room.

Nothing 'routinizes charisma' as quickly and effectively, however, as getting one's hands dirty, and the move from strategy formulation to strategy implementation is gradually shifting the focus of strategy practitioners from a concern with elegant matrices—the *mappa mundi* of corporate navigators—to more practical day-to-day issues of management and organization development.

Welcome as this sudden infusion of 'reality testing' by strategists might be to practising managers, it nonetheless has continued to maintain management development at the service of strategy and, by implication, management developers at the service of strategists. Many who share Mintzberg's (1987) view of strategy as a partly emergent process, shaped as much by the capacity of people throughout the organization to respond to or create unexpected opportunities as by the strategic intentions of those at the top, might feel uneasy at the determinism implicit in a sequence that seems to proclaim a dubious distinction between those who think—i.e. strategists—and those who execute—among others, management developers. Such a distinction ignores the fact that strategy formulation is itself the outcome of organizational processes largely shaped by managerial ability and the culture it fosters.

The failure to treat strategy and organization processes interactively rather than sequentially has led to a growing divergence between 'espoused' theories of the strategy process and 'theories-in-use' (Argyris, 1977). The latter theories, however, have not as yet altered the existing balance between strategists and management developers, whose activities in the firm remain strongly subordinated to the strategic function. In recent years, the move by strategists downstream into implementation simply means that management developers can no longer exclusively serve the abstract ideals of, say, the human relations school or of humanistic psychology, as many of them had done in the days of OD. Instead, they are asked to mould the kind of executive specifically required by the chosen strategy and its implementation needs—human engineering, in effect, rendered palatable by a sweetening discourse on corporate culture.

This chapter argues that the relationship between strategists and management development is about to change. The environment to which strategy is called to respond has undergone a profound transformation in the past two decades and the corresponding evolution of strategic thought itself today challenges the nature of the links that traditionally bound it to the human resource development function as a whole and to management development in particular.

The major transformation in the strategic environment which strategy must deal with has been well documented and can be summed up in a single word: *turbulence*.

In the years following the Second World War, and up until the mid-1960s, economic recovery imposed its own dynamic on firms. Everything was scarce and, consequently, virtually anything that was produced could be sold. Competition was relatively muted as firms each concentrated on their own wedge of an expanding pie. They were playing in what game theorists call a 'game against nature', one in which the trick is to anticipate the future level of market demand and then to adjust the firm's productive operations to meet it (Ansoff, 1965). In such a game, the market, like the weather, is unaffected by the firm's own actions. The firm can only adapt to the market's estimated future level, it cannot influence it. The critical skills required to be an effective player in a game against nature are forecasting—i.e. anticipating future states— and strategic planning—i.e. formulating an adaptive response.

When the economic pie stopped growing in the late 1960s, firms began to be more selective about the markets they would invest in to maintain their own future growth. They also became much more aware that such growth might now have to come at the expense of other players. Highly impersonal games against nature, in which the moves of potential competitors could largely be ignored, were by degrees transformed into much more personal 'games against adversaries' who first had to be identified and then carefully watched. Suddenly, the mechanical forecasting and planning methods that had been used hitherto seemed insufficient. The moves and countermoves of adversaries now also had to be reckoned with and parried in an increasingly complex and potentially infinite regress. And in a game against adversaries, a passive adaptation to the moves of others could prove dangerous. To win, one had to become proactive. Strategy was transformed into a competitive process (Porter, 1980).

Having to cope with competitors as well as markets greatly increased the complexity of the firm's strategic task. Providing that competitors were not too numerous, however—in other words, that the industry was oligopolistically structured— some form of competitor analysis could be conducted by tracking the behaviour of key players in a given market. Unfortunately, a growing awareness of the importance of competitors hit strategic thinking at a time when the globalization of markets was either increasing the number of key players in many industries or making them less familiar and hence accessible to monitoring and analysis. For many strategists, competitor analysis under such circumstances seemed to be a counsel of perfection.

As if global competition in global markets were not enough, the experience of the past three years has confronted strategists with a radically new kind of turbulence—of the geopolitical kind. Global competition might be complex but at least the critical variables could still be identified: the size of markets, the number and size of competitors, the rules of the game in a given industry, etc. In the geopolitical upheavals that have overtaken both Communist and former communist countries—and that will continue to reverberate throughout the world for many years to come—the strategically relevant variables dissolve into a blooming, buzzing confusion. Are we still moving towards a global economic order as predicted by many strategy gurus, or are we reverting to competition in territorial units even smaller than the nation state itself, i.e. the Crimea, Serbia, Moldavia, Catalonia, Corsica, Scotland, etc.? Or, more perplexing still, are we moving towards both situations simultaneously? Underlying such questions are more basic ones. Of what strategic value is forecasting or competitor analysis in the face of geopolitical discontinuities of such seismic proportions as the disintegration of the former Soviet Empire? How helpful are these analytical tools in coping with turbulence?

In the next section we identify the strategic options available to firms confronting different rates of change and, in the third section, we interpret them as different manifestations of a learning process. The consequences of our analysis for the relationship between the strategy process and management development are discussed in the fourth section. A conclusion follows.

Strategic options

How have strategists responded to the phenomenon of increasing rates of change? How, for example, do they reconcile the need to feel in control of things that strategy making seems to express with control-sapping turbulence? One way of approaching these questions is to look how they cope with change as such, whether it is turbulent or not. From the literature, we can identify four basic types of response:

1. strategic planning
2. emergent strategy
3. intrapreneurship
4. strategic intent.

Obviously the field of strategy is more varied than these ideal types seem to indicate. But I believe that, as a response to different rates of change, any strategic activity can always be represented as a mixture of these four types. Each will now be briefly discussed in turn.

Strategic planning   Strategic planning expresses the belief that the strategically relevant environment is inherently predictable if a sufficient effort is made to understand and control it. Whatever turbulence is experienced by a firm, difficult as it may be to cope with, merely reflects our lack of understanding. With enough of the right kind of data and a judicious application of the appropriate analytical tools, the strategic environment can be adequately grasped and strategic planning can be used to give a sense of direction to corporate endeavours.

The thinking that underpins strategic planning is a legacy of more stable times when the environment was changing sufficiently slowly for an effective corporate response to emerge from methodical organizational routines. In this strategy regime, large quantities of data are collected on a periodic basis from the base of the corporate pyramid and sent towards the top for processing. The top extracts a pattern from the data that tells it what is going on both within the firm as well as in the external environment and, on the basis of the pattern it perceives, it then decides on a course of action that is subsequently transmitted downward towards the base of the organization for its implementation. Effective pattern making requires that all pertinent data be methodically processed. Since the top is in possession of all the relevant data, it is better placed than other parts of the organization to extract the right patterns from it, so that these therefore have little option but to rely on top management for their strategic direction. The process is hierarchical, methodical and rational.

Effective strategic planning is predicated upon two important assumptions. The first is that the rate at which environmental data are changing is slower than the rate at which they can be captured, processed and acted upon internally—not always a wise assumption in a bureaucratic organization. The second is that short-term fluctuations in external data mask a number of fundamentally stable and unchanging features that are both accessible to rational analysis and relevant to the strategic task. In other words, strategic planning is Parmenedian rather than Heraclitan; it treats turbulence as so much 'noise' in which an unchanging order can always be discerned if the required intellectual understanding is there. If it is, the intended strategies expressed in the corporate plan become realized with little loss of coherence (Figure 3.1) (Mintzberg, 1985). The skill of the strategist resides in the formulation of a course of action based on well-founded anticipation, more than on its implementation.

Figure 3.1   Strategic planning

Emergent strategy

Mintzberg

Emergent strategy is an expression coined by Henry Mintzberg to describe an organization-wide process of incremental adjustment to environmental states that cannot be discerned or anticipated through a prior analysis of data (Mintzberg, 1985). In such states, intended strategies do not get fully realized and realized strategies cannot solely confine themselves to the incorporation of top management's original intentions (Figure 3.2). The reasons that leakages occur between intention and realization is that the strategic level of the organization cannot act like an all-seeing central planner and that, in the course of a plan's implementation, unanticipated opportunities and threats will emerge which have to be dealt with incrementally in ways not originally foreseen by the strategy. Furthermore, the data needed for dealing with them will not necessarily be located at the strategic level but may be found at any location within the organization. If time does not allow for the upward transmission of data through the prescribed channels, an adequate response to it may have to be formulated and often in an *ad hoc* way, with the rest of the organization adjusting to such local behaviour only subsequently.

Strategy, then, cannot only be the rational elaboration of a single coherent picture constructed at the top of an organization; it must also be an emergent property of a cluster of fragmentary and partial understandings that

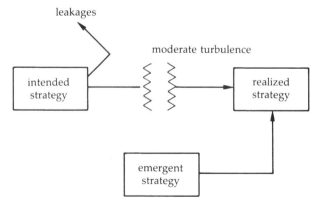

Figure 3.2   Emergent strategy

operate incrementally within the firm in response to events as and when they occur. An emergent strategy is a legitimation of Lindblom's 'disjointed incrementalism' operating at the strategic level as described and modified by Quinn (Lindblom, 1959; Quinn, 1980). Its effectiveness is predicated upon a cumulative process of learning by doing that is not disrupted or undermined by major discontinuities in the strategic environment. For this reason, it is suited to dealing with moderate rates of change, rather than with the more volatile conditions associated with turbulence.

Intrapreneurship

In situations where the perceived degree of environmental turbulence facing a firm is high and can neither be handled incrementally nor tamed by analysis, some management thinkers recommend a strategy of *intrapreneurship* (Pinchot, 1985). Rapidly changing external data does not effectively allow for any organizational integration of even partial perspectives; if anything, for the firm to be adaptive, it must formulate a series of *ad hoc* responses that move away from integration. Any understanding of the data now remains strictly local within the firm so that it becomes even more difficult to formulate a single coherent organizational response than it was under an emergent strategic approach. Emergent strategy then comes to dominate intended strategy to such an extent that it no longer makes sense for an integrated organization to speak of an *incremental* adaptive response to external change. (Figure 3.3). Threats and opportunities emerge that have to be dealt with locally, but now with little or no understanding of how they may affect the organization as a whole, and possibly no great concern either. Some of these local responses will be a source of future profits and growth, others will turn out to be a drain on scarce resources; none of this, however, can be discerned *a priori*.

Here, of course, we are at the polar opposite of the strategic planning process: not only can environmental turbulence *not* be reduced through analytical means, but action has to be taken at whatever point in the organization has the capacity and the willingness to act on very partial and ill-understood 'noisy' data. With intrapreneurship, the world is purely Heraclitan; all is flux and the top of the firm has no privileged insight into what to do since any intended strategy it may have pursued has all but been submerged. Of necessity, then, the firm must decentralize and operate as a loosely coupled system.

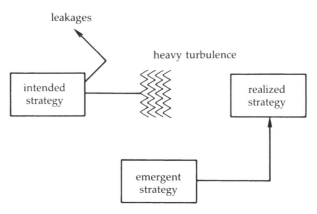

Figure 3.3   Intrapreneurship

Intrapreneurship can only be effective where the opportunistic behaviour it requires of particular individuals can be placed at the service of the firm as well as those individuals themselves. This is not always easy to achieve since an equitable matching of risks and rewards between individuals and firms cannot be ensured. Often intrapreneurship works at the expense of the firms that try to foster it. It requires a degree of *trust* between the players that cannot be taken for granted and that is continuously being placed under strain by the very turbulence for which it is designed to compensate.

Strategic intent

Strategic intent describes a process of coping with turbulence through a direct, intuitive understanding, emanating from the top of a firm and guiding its efforts. A turbulent environment cannot be tamed by rational analysis alone so that conventional strategic planning is deemed to be of little use. Yet it does not follow that a firm's adaptive response must be left to a random distribution of lone individuals acting opportunistically and often in isolation as in a regime of intrapreneurship. Strategic intent relies on an intuitively formed pattern or *gestalt*—some would call it a vision—to give it unity and coherence. Hamel and Prahalad (1989), in their *Harvard Business Review* article on strategic intent, cite as an example Komatsu's intuition that, if the firm was to grow, it had to 'surround Caterpillar' as well as Honda's that it had to 'beat Benz' for the same reason.

Strategic intent yields a simple yet robust orientation, intuitively accessible to all the firm's employees, an orientation which, on account of its clarity, can be pursued with some consistency over the long term in spite of the presence of

turbulence. Thus, whereas strategic plans get rapidly overtaken by persistent turbulence if they turn out to be the
abstract products of a faulty analysis, the objectives that are
derivable from the intuitions of strategic intent remain robust
in a regime of turbulence. Strategic intent thus apprehends
turbulence through a more intuitive rather than a purely
analytical understanding but, since such an understanding is
accessible to the firm as a whole, it can be used to energize a
coherent and sustained organizational effort. To counter the
centrifugal tendencies that plague the decentralized intrapreneurial firm, the one operating in a regime of strategic intent
can use a common vision to keep the behaviour of its
employees aligned with a common purpose when it
decentralizes in response to turbulence. Intended strategy
then gets realized in spite of any turbulence. It succeeds by
remaining simple and intelligible and by avoiding a level of
detail that might quickly be rendered obsolete by events
(Figure 3.4).

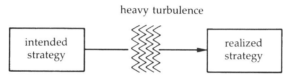

Figure 3.4   Strategic intent

Each of these strategic approaches to the problem of change
has its protagonists and its critics. Each also claims a high
degree of generality and exclusiveness. Perhaps too much. To
read Ansoff on strategic planning or Pinchot on intrapreneurship, for example, it is hard to imagine that the world is big
enough to accommodate both ways of handling strategy. And
yet in the next section we shall see that, far from being in
competition with each other, these four different approaches
to the strategy process are in fact complementary. Consequently, the relationship between strategy and management
development has to be a contingent one which must be
allowed to change and evolve as one moves from one strategy
regime to another.

**The learning
process**

Ross Ashby's (1958) *law of requisite variety* stipulates that, for a
system to preserve its integrity and survive, its rate of learning
must at least match the rate of change in its environment. We
can adapt this well-known insight to our own requirements by
equating a high rate of change with a high degree of

environmental turbulence, and a high rate of learning with a capacity to identify by intuitive or analytical means the critical parameters of the environment relevant to a system's survival—i.e. a capacity to extract useful information from 'noise' in a timely fashion.

Having done this, we can relate turbulence and under-standing to each other as in Figure 3.5. The law of requisite variety can then be interpreted as stating that an adaptive system only retains its integrity *qua* system by staying to the right of line A. To the left of the line, where the degree of turbulence exceeds the degree of understanding, the system confronts discontinuities that threaten its stability and cohesion. It may then either break up into autonomous sub-systems, each coping locally with a particular type of turbulence, or disintegrate altogether.

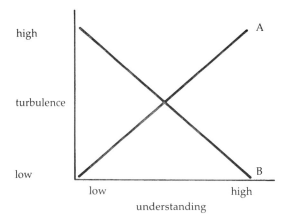

Figure 3.5   A learning environment

The traditional organizational response to turbulence has been either to steer clear of it as far as possible or to try to tame it by moving organizational processes diagonally downward along line B towards greater calm and greater understanding. In the lower regions of the diagram where turbulence is absent, the move from the left to the right can occur in an inductive fashion and at a quite serene pace: here learning is continuous and incremental and the past can reliably act as a guide to the future. A rational–analytical approach to strategy thus becomes possible when conditions are stable, the speed at which the leftward move occurs being dictated primarily by the quantity of data to be processed.

In the upper reaches of the diagram, by contrast, where turbulence is a major source of discontinuity, the move to the right itself becomes discontinuous and akin to a *'gestalt switch'* (Kuhn, 1962) in which new unforeseen patterns suddenly appear. Here the future can no longer be extrapolated from the past since it is likely to emerge from a *bifurcation*, an activation of one from among a set of unforeseeable possibilities that all remain latent in the evolution of a system but none of which can be predicted even if they could be identified as plausible scenarios (Laszlo, 1987; Thom, 1972; Prigogine, 1980).

There are many reasons why organizations habitually prefer travelling downward along line B rather than upward along line A. Two must be noted here.

The first is that turbulence is, for most people, a source of cognitive and affective discomfort. The myriad patterns discernible in a turbulent regime are hard to articulate and to communicate—they are uncodifiable (Boisot, 1986). By moving down line B, organizations move into calmer, more navigable waters. When everyone understands where the ship is heading, everyone can pull together in the same direction.

The second is that turbulence is also a source of organizational conflict. The alternative possibilities foreshadowed in the multiple patterns thrown up by turbulence attract different adherents within the organization and often pit them against each other. Consensus is then harder to achieve and the organization becomes paralysed. In sum, the move down line B helps to address problems of organizational coordination and motivation that are exacerbated by turbulence.

Yet, in spite of many firms' predilection for coasting down line B, if the expression *the learning organization* (Garratt, 1987), has any meaning at all it requires firms to confront the turbulence rather than avoid it, to *absorb* uncertainty rather than reduce it (Pascale, 1990). In short, a learning organization moves *upward* along line A, internalizing as it goes along a capacity to respond to any event or classes of events that occur under the line. Downward moves along B are not thereby excluded but they become a series of short-term consolidations, attempts to digest what has already been mastered and embed it in stable organizational routines. In a learning organization such moves do not compromise the firm's long-term thrust upward along line A, towards an even greater capacity to cope with turbulence.

How shall we characterize the strategic orientation of the learning organization? Figure 3.6 locates in the diagram the four strategic responses to change that we discussed in the preceding section. The conceptual scheme in the diagram now

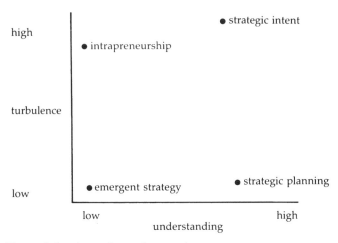

Figure 3.6   A typology of strategies

helps us to grasp the key ways in which these responses differ from and relate to each other.

For example, we see that both intrapreneurship and strategic intent are alternative ways of coping with turbulence but that, whereas in the first case a lack of corporate-level understanding of the strategic situation calls for a decentralization of the organizational response to the level of the individual in a loosely coupled system, in the second, a single intuitively apprehended vision can energize and orient the firm's efforts, thus maintaining a high level of organizational integration. An emergent strategy and strategic planning, by contrast, are both more likely to be appropriate in less turbulent environments where incremental adjustments to continuous change are possible. The two approaches are distinguished from each other by the more conceptual and analytical approach adopted by strategic planning; an emergent strategy is more likely to be guided by an accumulation of modest intuitions locally grounded in unconsciously acquired habits and skills.

Both lines A and B move strategic activity towards the right, that is, towards increased understanding and learning. Line B, however, traces out the more conventional path pursued by an organization as it grows and develops from a highly risky and uncertain entrepreneurial stance in the early days of its existence—reflecting a firm's fragility in its environment—to a more stable bureaucratic phase in which, following its early growth, a firm succeeds in routinizing and institutionalizing a good number of its organizational practices.

Our hypothesis now becomes clearer. A learning organization also moves to the right but exploits the organizational slack created by downward moves along line B to confront further turbulence by moving *simultaneously* along line A. One might think of line B as a wavefront progressing in the direction of A and activating any one of the four strategic responses that lie in its wake as circumstances require (Figure 3.7). None has any inherent claim to superiority since each reflects the amount of turbulence that the firm confronts at a particular moment or for a given task as well as the degree and type of understanding available to it in formulating its response. They thus form a *strategic repertoire* to be drawn upon according to the needs of the moment.

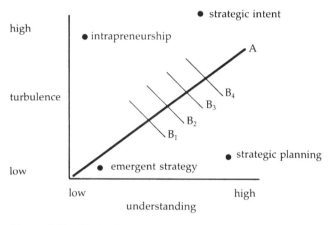

Figure 3.7   Strategic responses

The logic of our diagram, however, points to strategic intent being the distinguishing mark of the learning organization and, by implication, an essential component of its strategic repertoire. As the arrows of Figure 3.8 indicate, the vision or pattern that guides it can emerge either as an *intuition* from the intrapreneurial process—a move to the right—or as an *insight* derivable from an earlier analytical process. In both cases a cognitive discontinuity is involved: the energizing pattern or vision associated with strategic intent requires a leap that must be taken on faith.

If we think of strategy as the specification of tasks at the organizational level we discover a striking similarity between Figure 3.6 and Perrow's typology for the analysis of technical tasks (Perrow, 1967) (Figure 3.9). Perrow's characterization of tasks according to their routinizability and their intelligibility corresponds to the vertical and the horizontal axes of Figure

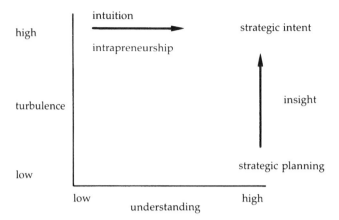

Figure 3.8   Intuition versus insight

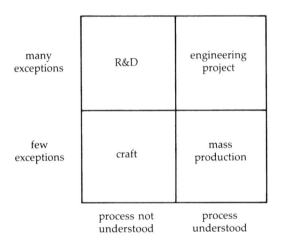

Figure 3.9   Perrow's typology

3.6. Tasks that are carried out under conditions of turbulence cannot be routinized and those that are not understood are not easily subordinated to the requirement of rational analysis and planning.

The basic difference between Perrow's approach and our own is that Perrow uses his typology statically to classify tasks whereas we use ours dynamically to operationalize the concept of learning at the strategic level. In effect, we are talking of *meta-learning*—Argyris (1977) calls it 'doubleloop learning'—an ability to move as required from one kind of strategic response to another that is distinguishable from the ability to elaborate and refine a single response. Meta-learning expresses an evolutionary orientation: it accommodates discontinuities in the environments encountered under turbulence by expanding the organizational variety of behaviour and insights that can help to cope with them. The evolutionary element can best be pictured as a simultaneous increase in turbulence-provoking energy inputs and knowledge-generating information inputs; together they move an organization's strategic capacity up line A. The increased energy inputs can be external to the firm—events over which the firm has no control but to which it must respond, as in a game against nature—or they can reflect the firm's own actions—as when, in a game against adversaries, it strives in some measure to enact its own environment (Weick, 1969). Increased information inputs then become necessary to 'tame' the turbulence, either by reducing it—the strategic planning solution—or absorbing it—through strategic intent.

Evolution, however, is not all turbulence. Like any system, organizations move through environments that at one moment are turbulent or 'chaotic' and at others are more stable. Meta-learning consists of recognizing when the regime is chaotic and when it is not and choosing the appropriate strategic response. Strategic intent, by moving up line A, expands the area within which appropriate responses are available, and hence the repertoire of strategic behaviours available to a firm; it thus expands the scope for meta-learning.

Implications for management development

What implications does all this have for the way that firms develop their managers? As indicated in the introduction, the traditional view of management development is that firms mould their managers to fit their strategic requirements. The link between an employee and the task he or she is assigned is usually mediated by plans and structures derived from the chosen strategy. A firm that diversifies its operations and then divisionalizes them will need a very different kind of manager from the one confined to a single industry and operation with a functional organization structure. In both cases, however, management development will remain subordinated to a strategic planning perspective and the management developer will continue to take his or her instructions from the strategist.

What happens, though, when articulated strategic plans are no longer available to guide the management developer? How is he or she going to justify his or her development budgets? Take, for example, the firm trying to foster a culture of intrapreneurship. Here, not only is the environment too turbulent to allow for anything like planning to take place, but people are being asked to act on the basis of personal hunches in the absence of full understanding.

In an intrapreneurial regime it is the managerial capacities of specific individuals that effectively dictate the firm's strategic orientation and not the other way round. The strategist, therefore, may well take his or her cue from the management developer. Once an intrapreneur has got a new business going, things may eventually settle down and the firm may well start travelling down line B into a more stable region. At that point, management development will once more place itself at the service of strategy. But, until then, a firm's strategic concerns will not be with plans and budgets; it will be trying to leverage the unique talent of key individuals to handle uncertainty and to persevere against the odds, where the odds are often nothing less than the organization itself and the inertia of its established routines. Subordinating the management development process to the strategy process under such circumstances could well kill intrapreneurship stone dead. Indeed, one of the reasons that intrapreneurship has enjoyed so few successes in large bureaucratic corporations is that it has been planted in cultures that are overwhelmingly committed to strategic planning or variants thereof. In other words, it has not been given enough organizational space to operate according to its own developmental logic.

What about firms that pursue emergent strategies? What role do they reserve for the management developer? The answer is as surprising as it is simple: none. Development in such firms is a process that involves *all* employees. The incremental response to new threats or opportunities can arise from any location within such enterprises whether or not such a location can be termed managerial. As with intrapreneurship, no synoptic view is required to guide the strategy process, and the more limited understandings that collectively shape the firm's overall response are as likely to come from the base of the organizational pyramid as from further up. Such an incremental approach can cope only with a limited degree of turbulence beyond which the consensus on which a collection of limited understanding can work together is liable to break down. An emergent strategy relies upon a horizontal information integration of pockets of 'local' knowledge (Hayek, 1945) and the development task is therefore framed primarily in terms of flexible networking throughout the system. Here management development gives way to development *tout court*.

Increase the level of turbulence and an emergent strategy moves towards intrapreneurship: adjustments no longer take place in a smooth, continuous fashion. If the forces that underlie the turbulence can be discerned, however, no matter how fuzzily, if they can be resolved into an intelligible pattern, then an organization can articulate a strategic intent—i.e. it can move up line A.

In a regime of strategic intent, management development once more puts in an appearance; but it now does so in partnership with strategy. Neither can afford to be dominant, for they mutually determine each other. The quality of the strategies pursued will depend on the quality of the people who make them and the quality of the people who are given the privilege of formulating strategies, which in turn reflect the effectiveness of the earlier strategies that selected them.

Conclusion

Organizations have been conceived of primarily as a device for reducing uncertainty (Simon, 1961; March and Simon, 1958). They achieve this by creating zones of stability—structures—that can maintain their identity over time in the face of external variations. Yet where the rate of external change increases excessively, stability can become ill-adaptive and threaten the firm's survival. Some balance, therefore, has to be struck between rates of external change and rates of internal adaptation to change. This requires that strategies for *reducing* uncertainty be complemented by strategies of *absorbing* it.

In sum, we can think of an organization enhancing its survival prospects not by seeking out *the* unique strategy or strategic approach that fits its circumstances but by expanding its strategic repertoire to cope with a broader variety of environmental contingencies. Developing managers to handle a repertoire of strategies, however, is quite a different matter from grooming them within the framework of a single strategy. To succeed in this task, people working in management development will need a much surer grasp of strategy than they have displayed until now and strategists will require a greater appreciation of what management development has to offer for the extension of their strategic repertoires.

References

Ansoff, I. (1965) *Corporate Strategy: an Analytic Approach to Business Policy for Growth and Expansion*, New York: McGraw-Hill.
Argyris, C. (1977) 'Double loop learning in organizations', *Harvard Business Review*, September-October.

Boisot, M. (1986) 'Markets and hierarchies in cultural perspective', *Organisation Studies*, Spring.

Garratt, B. (1994) 'The Learning Organisation', 2nd ed., London: HarperCollins.

Hamel, G. and Prahalad, C. (1989) 'Strategic intent', *Harvard Business Review*, May-June.

Hayek, F. (1945) 'The uses of knowledge in society', *American Economic Review*, **35**, 519-30, September.

Kuhn, T. (1962) *The Structure and Scientific Revolutions*, Chicago: The University of Chicago Press.

Laszlo, E. (1987) *Evolution: The Grand Synthesis*, Boston and London: New Science Library, Shamghala.

Lindblom, C. (1959) 'The science of muddling through', *Public Administration Review*, 59-88.

March, J. and Simon, H. (1958) *Organizations*, New York: Wiley.

Mintzberg, H. (1985) 'Of strategies deliberate and emergent', *Strategic Managerial Journal*, 257-72.

Mintzberg, H. (1987) 'Crafting strategy', *Harvard Business Review*, July-August.

Pascale, R. (1990) *Managing on the Edge*, Harmondsworth: Penguin.

Perrow, C. (1967). 'A framework for the comparative analysis of organizations', *American Sociological Review*, **32**, 194-208.

Pinchot, G. (1985) *Intrapreneuring*, New York: Harper and Row.

Porter, M. (1980) *Competitive Strategy: Techniques for Analysing Industries and Competitors*, New York: Free Press.

Prigogine, I. (1980) *From Being to Becoming: Time and Complexity in the Physical Sciences*, San Francisco, CA: Freeman.

Quinn, J. (1980) *Strategies for Change: Logical Incrementalism*, Home-wood, ILL: Richard, D. Irwin.

Ross Ashby, W. (1958) 'Requisite variety and its implications for the control of complex systems', *Cybernetica*, **1**, (2), 83-99.

Simon, H. (1961) *Administrative Behaviour*, New York: Macmillan.

Thom, R. (1972) *Stabilité Structurelle et Morphogenèse*, New York: Benjamin.

Weick, K. (1969) *The Social Psychology of Organizing*, Reading, MA: Addison-Wesley.

4 Design as a strategic management resource

Christopher Lorenz

The design paradox

The word 'design' means different things to different people. Depending on their point of view, it conjures up an image of women's fashions, designer clothing, furniture, fabrics and interior design, or even crafts. To some it suggests the creative side of engineering: design engineering. To others—most North Americans, but fewer Europeans—it embraces architecture. It has even crept into the world of chemicals and drugs.

To very few people does it suggest the activity which spans both the form and function of manufactured products—industrial design. Yet since the early 1980s a growing body of companies all over the world, from Tokyo to Detroit, Milan to Munich, Stockholm to Silicon Valley, has discovered that industrial design can be a much more powerful weapon—strategically as well as operationally—than they had ever suspected. In a succession of global markets, conventional means of differentiation—low cost and/or high levels of quality, technology and service—are becoming mere 'entry tickets' to the competitive battlefield. Instead, industrial design has become key to creating what Theodore Levitt calls 'meaningful distinction', in the sense not just of a product's shape and appearance but also of its entire character.

As a result, large multinational companies have begun to 'unchain' product designers capable of bridging and building upon the expertise of both marketing and engineering. Working at last as equal members of multidisciplinary teams, under the new kings of the product development process—'project', 'product', or 'programme' managers—industrial designers have begun to graduate beyond their traditionally subservient role to marketing and engineering.

The 'unchaining' of industrial design within Ford North America in 1980 gave priceless integrity and character to the design of the Ford Taurus which, by the late 1980s, had transformed the company's financial fortunes and went on to become the best-selling car in America, ahead even of the top Japanese model. A similar organizational unchaining of industrial design helped turn the Apple PowerBook portable computer into a remarkable success. In Europe, Philips and Rover cars were two obvious beneficiaries from the unchaining of design, in the 1980s and early 1990s, respectively. In Japan, company after company has learned to harness the commercial power of industrial design. The rest of South-east Asia, from South Korea to Singapore, Taiwan to Hong Kong, is now busily catching up.

Knowingly or otherwise, these companies are building upon the decades-old traditions of a handful of enterprises— Olivetti and Braun in Europe, Deere & Co. (John Deere) and IBM in the United States, Sony in Japan—whose founders or their successors pioneered the principle of powerful design, both within their organizations and in the external expression of their character: in their products, their communications and their buildings.

But behind the new organizational awakening of design lies a set of paradoxes. If its commercial power has been manifest since at least the 1930s, why do so many managements still fail to recognize it? Why, when they do, have so many not given it sufficient weight within their organization? Why, in spite of repeated design-led successes in the marketplace, have many of the design pioneers allowed their commitment to design to decay?

The problem is not merely the generic tendency of any established organizational philosophy or practice to decay over time, much as marketing has shrunk in many consumer goods companies from an imaginative, broad-lensed way of thinking to a narrow set of processes and procedures. Design's problem is very much greater for several reasons:

1. Design tends to be overlooked in the strategic concepts which most managers use, notably the 'business system' and the 'value chain'.
2. Academics and consultants have failed to develop a powerful model of the various constituents of design— the equivalent of marketing's '4 Ps'.
3. Design's traditional position within the corporate hierarchy as a junior function, buried deep under marketing or engineering, makes it hard for management to give it

sufficient weight alongside other functions. This is true even in the rapidly growing number of companies where product development has been reorganized from a traditionally sequential set of department-by-department activities into a parallel process in which specialists of all kinds work together in integrated teams.

4. Even in companies where design is at last being taken seriously, it tends still to be seen only as a 'soft', lightweight, right-brained activity by managers whose education has been largely left-brained, verbal, linear and analytical. As the value of 'soft' mental processes such as intuition becomes belatedly recognized as vital to corporate and business strategy, right-brained thinking is at last starting to be given its rightful place. But this alone is not enough to prompt companies to take design as seriously as they should. For that to happen, the 'harder' aspects of design also need to be recognized.

5. In countries—unlike Italy and Japan—where right-brained, visual, synthesizing skills carry a lower social status than left-brained analytical ones, designers are seldom taken seriously by the organizations for which they work. They tend to be seen as third-class citizens, rated even more lowly than the engineers.

6. Even when top management recognizes the potential power of design and the versatility of designers and tries to unleash their hidden potential, the way is often barred by turf warfare with engineers and/or marketing specialists.

Even among the corporate design pioneers, these inhibiting factors tend to assert themselves as the years pass, especially when the original top management gives way to a new generation. This has been true in recent years of Olivetti, Braun and IBM and, to some extent, of Deere & Co. For all these reasons, most companies need to undertake a voyage of 'executive discovery'—or rediscovery—about design's potential role in strategy.

Design's role in strategic thinking and operational practice

The business system

Design—including its 'soft' aspects—*was* included by McKinsey and Company in its original formulation in 1980 of its widely influential 'business system' concept, but it tends to be forgotten or omitted when the business system diagram is drawn in practice (Figure 4.1). The 'technology' and 'product design' elements of the system are often elided together into phrases such as 'commercialization of technology'. Moreover, the sub-sections of each element in the business system—including function, physical characteristics, aesthetics, and quality within the 'product design' element—tend to be omitted, again for reasons of simplicity. As a result, generations of managers develop skills in strategic thinking—or at least strategic planning—without paying sufficient, if any, attention to the different facets of product design.

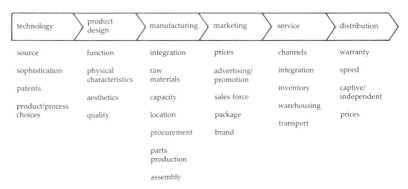

technology	product design	manufacturing	marketing	service	distribution
source	function	integration	prices	channels	warranty
sophistication	physical characteristics	raw materials	advertising/ promotion	integration	speed
patents		capacity	sales force	inventory	captive/ independent
product/process choices	aesthetics	location	package	warehousing	prices
	quality	procurement	brand	transport	
		parts production			
		assembly			

Figure 4.1   The business system

The value chain

Even more influential than the business system concept has been Michael Porter's value chain. It is in some senses more ambitious than the McKinsey business system since it distinguishes between primary activities and the 'support activities' which underpin them. But neither the original concept nor the ways in which it has been applied in business focus any attention on industrial design. For managers who know where to look—very much the minority—different aspects of industrial design are hidden away both in the support activity which Porter calls 'technology development' and in his 'primary activity' of marketing and sales. But Porter only mentions design specifically under the heading of 'technology development' and various aspects of 'operations', such as component and machine design. In every case, the emphasis is on the technological aspects of design.

The design mix

In marketing, the constituent elements of design *have* been recognized for some time by a small group of academics, but their work has not been sufficiently popularized. Philip Kotler (1984), who has influenced generations of thinking and expertise in marketing, is one of the few to have a clear view of design. He writes of companies needing to 'seek creatively to blend the major elements of the design mix, namely Performance, Quality, Durability, Appearance and Cost'. To complete his definition, he might have added 'Feel', 'Character' and what Clark and Fujimoto (1990) call 'Product Integrity'.

New product development styles

When products are developed by 'team rugby', 'simultaneous engineering', 'concurrent engineering' or integrated engineering—in place of the traditionally sequential relay-race approach—the importance of industrial design becomes obvious. It is no longer possible to think of industrial designers merely as people who 'wrap products in nice shapes and pretty colours', as one cynic described their traditional role. Instead, for the development process to be effective, they have to be equal members of the team almost from the start of the process (Figure 4.2). Clark and Fujimoto (1990) have written persuasively about the notion that product integrity can only flow from a product development organization which is itself integral—where every part of the process fits neatly with the other, just as every part of the product does or should. It is when they are given such a role that some designers show their ability to be far more than skin-deep 'stylists'. But their potential can only be captured fully if the organization and particularly the product, project or programme manager ceases to treat them as subservient to either marketing or engineering. Instead, they should be seen as separate from either function, but overlapping with them—as a bridge between them, and often as an informal integrator.

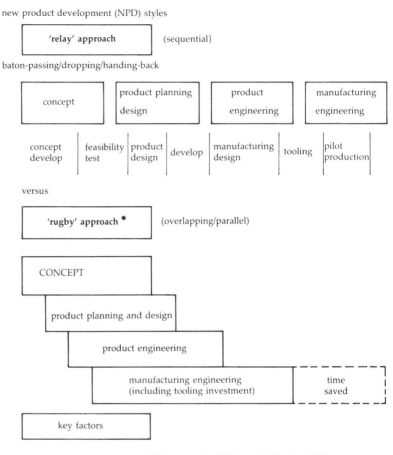

new product development (NPD) styles

| 'relay' approach | (sequential) |

baton-passing/dropping/handing-back

| concept | product planning | product | manufacturing |
| | design | engineering | engineering |

| concept develop | feasibility test | product design | develop | manufacturing design | tooling | pilot production |

versus

| 'rugby' approach * | (overlapping/parallel) |

CONCEPT

product planning and design

product engineering

manufacturing engineering (including tooling investment) — time saved

| key factors |

- project management (cf. HBS auto study (Clark and Fujimoto, 1990)
- task force
- multidisciplinary product/project team
- key involvement of industrial design throughout NPD process

Figure 4.2   The benefits of parallel development.
* *'Simultaneous/concurrent/integrated engineering'*

Team vision   This view of the place of industrial design in the development team, and as unofficial integrator, finds its clearest visual expression in a model developed at Philips in the early 1980s (Figure 4.3). It shows industrial design at one corner of a 'vision' triangle, being accorded equal weight with marketing and engineering (including both development and production engineering). The model also indicates the extent to which the industrial designer needs to at least understand, and often to supplement, marketing expertise and the various facets of engineering. Effective industrial designers not only need to possess deep aesthetic knowledge of form, colour and so on,

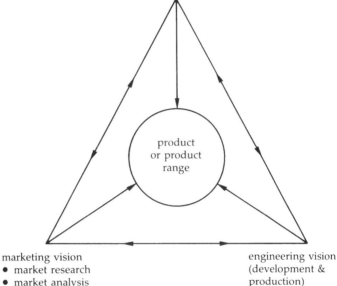

industrial design vision
- aesthetic knowledge (form, colours)
- social backgrounds, cultural backgrounds
- environmental relationships
- ergonomic requirements
- visual trends
- insight into aspects of marketing and engineering vision

product
or product
range

marketing vision
- market research
- market analysis
- economics
- distribution systems

engineering vision
(development &
production)
- technical research
- technical analysis
- economic targets
- production methods
- ergonomic research

Figure 4.3   Team vision

but must also understand social and cultural trends. They need to have considerable environmental knowledge, and must have experience in ergonomics, production and other technical skills. The 'team vision' model has proved a powerful lever within companies, helping managers understand the real potential of industrial design.

Empirical evidence

Lest any of the foregoing might seem merely enthusiastic theory, sceptics should note the growing body of evidence that experienced industrial designers can indeed act as described, provided they are permitted to do so by their organizations' cultures and their project managers. The author's own in-depth research has shown this in companies such as

Olivetti, Sony, Sharp, Ford, Philips, and Baker Perkins (a process engineering company which is now part of the APV Group) (Lorenz, 1990). Further evidence comes from fourteen companies, five each in Europe and Japan, and four in the United States, which were the subject of research for an international exhibition on 'Triad Design', organized by the Boston-based Design and Management Institute in 1989-90. (Several of them have since become business school case studies, used at Harvard and elsewhere.) That project expanded the research base considerably, by including multinationals such as Black & Decker, Canon, Digital Equipment, Texas Instruments, and Yamaha ('Designing for Product Success'; Lorenz, 1989).

The 'Triad' research confirms the potential power of design as both a source and a stimulus of competition through Levitt's 'meaningful distinction'—with the emphasis on 'meaningful', rather than just alternative shapes and colours. It also confirmed that design is being used in company after company as *much* more than styling: as a source of ideas in the new product development process. It plays this role in two main ways: by making new connections between customer patterns of behaviour, technology and various other aspects of a product's design; and by fostering the 'integrity' of the product.

Figure 4.4 indicates the different types of 'connections' which designers are capable of making between established or new consumer patterns of behaviour (or consumer 'needs'), and new or established technology. Reading clockwise from bottom left, the 'My First Sony' range of toy consumer electronics products connected an established consumer need—young children playing with radios and tape recorders—with established technology, but in a new way. The Sony Profeel component TV, which was the first TV system to be broken up into its component parts like an audio system, combined a new consumer need with established technology. On the other hand, the Sony 'Watchman' miniature portable TV combined new technology with a new consumer need or stimulated want. Sony's video camcorder range spanned both new technology for established consumer needs in its Video 8 format and an even more established technology in the Betamovie camcorder. Both types of camcorders can be classified as meeting an established consumer need because they replaced home film making by increasing the level of convenience and cost effectiveness (Lorenz, 1986). The more famous Sony Walkman series, in which industrial designers played only a supporting development role, was similar to the

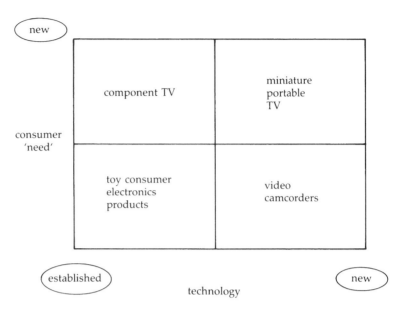

Figure 4.4   The 'design connection'

'Profeel' component TV, in being a new consumer need or activity using established technology. In a stimulating paper on 'design-based incrementalism', Susan Walsh Sanderson and Vic Uzumeri distinguish between 'technological' (new) innovations and what they call 'topological' ones: rearrangements of existing, well-understood components. In a detailed analysis of the full Walkman range they show that the initial Walkman product in 1979 was a 'topological' design. So have been most of its subsequent developments and refinements, with the exception of occasional major innovations such as several further miniaturizations of the basic design and the development in 1985 of a rechargeable version (Lorenz, 1986). In some cases, design acts not in a narrow functional way, but as a general integrating support for product planning and for product management/project management/programme management.

The empirical research cited above has also shown that 'design vision' sometimes acts not only as a support for Levitt's 'marketing imagination' but also as a substitute for it. Design's role is definitely not confined just to supplying its own vision, and providing its relatively mundane, though valuable, skills of sketching, shape and colour. This ability to act as a catalyst in the development of a team's 'product vision' rests on a designer's unusual combination of right- and left-brained skills, of communication skills, and of 'multi-linguality'. Effective designers contribute their own work, but also contribute to those of the other disciplines and stimulate, interpret and synthesize it. This involves 'hard' skills, systems and corporate structures as well as the designer's 'soft' skills.

The 'hard' side of design

In their work in product development teams designers do not always behave creatively. They sometimes act, more prosaically, as a communication channel between the other disciplines. As Bill Moggridge, co-founder of the IDEO engineering and design consultancy in California and Europe argues, 'design is always walking a tightrope between the linear (analytical) and the creative (synthetic)' (Lorenz, 1989). Henry Mintzberg, one of the few strategy academics to comprehend the power of design, nevertheless understates its power when he talks merely in terms of the match between design 'insight' and 'the intuitive or insightful process' of strategy making (Lorenz, 1989). Design is important not only to the 'soft' side of strategy but also to the 'hard'.

Forceful evidence of design's potential role is provided by Michael Smith, the former Deputy Chief Executive of APV-Baker Perkins. Although the company's business is heavy engineering, Smith, a marketing man who might have been expected to be hostile to design, says

> we gave the industrial designer a much greater role as the product planner, at a very early stage in the cycle. He no longer designed pretty guards to wrap our products in, but became the translator, the bridge, the catalyst. And he turned the marketing specification of a product into reality before the design, the materials or the manufacturing methods had been fully established (Lorenz, 1986).

Similar instances have occurred at Digital, Olivetti and many other companies.

The 'soft' side of design

The best-known case of a company allowing itself for the first time to use its designers' 'soft' skills—their insight and intuition as part of its broader process of 'crafting strategy' (Mintzberg, 1987)—is that of the Ford Motor Company, with its Taurus/Sable project in the early 1980s. In the words of Don Petersen, Ford's new chairman at the time, 'we decided to stop choking off the creativity of the very people whose job was to be creative. We gave them room to breathe' (Lorenz, 1988). Most business school case studies of the success of the 'Team Taurus' project understate the powerful role which design played in it. Within Ford itself, however, there is near-universal recognition of the role which design played in helping the company to recognize emerging consumer preferences and trends. This enabled it to abandon—or, at least, reduce—its traditional reliance on slavish consumer clinics. Petersen spoke of the vital importance of 'informed intuition' to the company's strategy. This comes very close to Mintzberg's use of the design process as an analogue for the process of 'crafting strategy'. Again reflecting the multi skilled power of design, Petersen spoke—unusually for a senior executive in such a large company—of 'the innate quest for harmony between analysis and emotion which each individual possesses, and every corporation also needs' (Lorenz, 1988). In different terms, he was reflecting one of the prime lessons which still applies from Peters and Waterman's *In Search of Excellence*: that management must constantly strike a balance between tightness and looseness and, in strategic terms, between analysis and emotion or intuition.

Phases of corporate design evolution

The conundrum why so many companies fail to apply design effectively within their organizations, and why a process of design decay is suffered even by those which do, is partly resolved by a model developed by Bill Moggridge and Arnold Wasserman, the former Design Director of Xerox and Unisys (Lorenz, 1989). Design-conscious companies all over the world have moved through several, ever deeper, stages of design management, according to this model. At the shallowest level—which does not mean that it cannot be effective for some years—some have relied mainly on a 'design person': either the company chief, such as Steve Jobs when he ran Apple and then Next Computer, or a charismatic design director, such as Dieter Rams of Braun, Gillette's German appliance subsidiary. Other companies, such as Apple and IBM, have moved on to 'design policy', institutionalizing design into a set of policies and procedures.

A third stage, called 'strategic design', and exemplified by Sony, Xerox and Unisys, integrates industrial design more deeply into the company. In such cases much of the design effort is devoted to such broad activities as lifestyle research, in order to anticipate product concepts ahead of competitors.

These are necessary but not sufficient phases for the substantiating of a company's commitment to design. IBM, Deere and Co., Olivetti and even Ford have not progressed sufficiently beyond stage three for sustainability to be assured.

But Sony certainly has. Dumas and Mintzberg (1989) rightly argue that, for design to be completely effective, it needs to 'infuse' an organization. To sustain the alliteration, this author's term 'permeate' is more appropriate. As Dumas and Mintzberg argue, 'it is insufficient merely to advocate that design should be put on an equal footing with other more conventional functions. Instead, it should infuse an organization, just like quality'. Drawing a parallel with accounting, Dumas recalls that accountants used to be tucked away in the corner of organizations before management accountancy developed. 'Now everyone in an organization does some accounting every day. The same is true of design—or should be', she says (Lorenz, 1989).

From hard to hard/soft strategy

If design is to be given its rightful place in an organization, it is vital to recognize that corporate and business strategy is not simply a 'hard' process, as was thought in the 1970s, but a combination of hard and soft, as Mintzberg has shown 1987, HBV etc.). Rather than classifying strategy as one of McKinsey's 'hard Ss', it should be placed in a new position, straddling hard and soft (Figure 4.5). Without that conceptual shift, the value of design is unlikely to be captured by the company. As Dumas argues, the 'soft S' of 'shared values' needs to include a broadly infused belief in design, as well as in the aspects of corporate culture which one normally associates with the term 'values'.

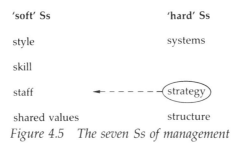

Figure 4.5   The seven Ss of management

The design connection

Industrial designers who act—however unofficially—as a form of integrator between engineering and marketing, require a combination of left- and right-brained skills. That means that they must be at least 'T-shaped' (Figure 4.6): design provides their skill-in-depth, but they also possess a broad horizontal 'bridge' comprising product and process engineering knowledge on the one side and marketing and

'THE DESIGN CONNECTION' (MULTIDIMENSIONAL)

- Between engineering and marketing (integrative)

- left brain   right brain
  (analysis)   (synthesis)

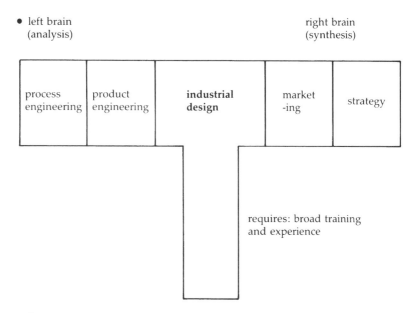

- Imagination versus 'visualizing what's not there'
  (cf. Galton, 1883; Levitt, 1983)

  i.e. 'creative' (Koestler)—synthesizing versus analysing

Figure 4.6   Making the design connection: 'T' shaped designers

strategic knowledge/insight on the other. That, in turn, requires designers to be very broadly trained and to develop experience not only in the design function—a need which few companies recognize. There is some evidence to suggest that the most effective designer in a manufacturing company may be the one whose first degree is in engineering or architecture but who has then gone on to develop an equally deep skill in industrial design. Rather than T-shaped, such people's skills are U-shaped, with two verticals.

Imagination versus visualization

In assessing the contribution which design can make to corporate strategy and operations it is important to distinguish between two concepts which are usually used interchangeably but which have very different meanings: imagination and visualization. Theodore Levitt (1983) provides an admirably clear definition of imagination: the construction of mental pictures 'of what is or is not actually present, what has never been actually experienced'. To exercise the imagination, as he says, requires 'intellectual or artistic inventiveness' (usually both). Levitt is right when he says that the exercising of imagination in business must involve not only the shedding of constraints such as convention and conviction but also the discipline to combine disparate facts or ideas into new amalgamations of meanings. He may also be right that a proportion of marketing executives is capable of exercising and channelling that imagination. So, for that matter, may some engineers.

But Levitt is on highly controversial ground when he claims that 'anybody can do it'. The odds are heavily stacked against much imagination slipping through the thick filters of formality and procedure that characterize the way most people think, and the way most organizations behave. By the time the majority of people reach adulthood, their imagination has usually been swamped by the imposition of conventional frameworks of thinking; this process is accelerated by the stifling bureaucracy of most companies.

As in marketing and engineering, there are, of course, exceptions to this rule in almost every walk of life, but in the industrial design profession, as in architecture, the situation is reversed: imagination is the rule, and conventional thinking the exception. At school it is frequently the budding designer's originality and irreverence which dictates his or her rejection of economics, science and the other largely 'academic' subjects. The well-rounded design course then takes this creative talent and, through a carefully balanced educational programme, develops it. But the best courses also apply the practical disciplines which the designer will need in industrial employment.

Nor is this the full story. Imagination of the sort described by Levitt may not be the designer's monopoly. But if one includes architects within the definition of 'designer', the crucial companion skill of visualization may well be. The 'mental pictures' in Levitt's definition of imagination are not necessarily visual; like those of many poets, they may be purely verbal, or abstract. In people with the skill to visualize, they conjure up pictures, in living shape and technicolour. But this is not so in everyone.

One of the most illuminating accounts of the power of visualization was given as long ago as 1883, in *Inquiries into Human Faculty*, written by a cousin of Charles Darwin, Francis Galton. A visual image, the Victorian reader was told:

is of importance in every handicraft and profession where design is required. The best workmen are those who visualize the whole of what they propose to do, before they take a tool in their hands...Strategists, artists of all denominations...and in short all who do not follow routine, have need of it.

Galton argued that, just like the village smith and carpenter, engineers needed this skill. The great designer–engineers, men like George Stephenson, the locomotive builder, and Isambard Kingdom Brunel, the civil engineer, did indeed possess it. But Galton was surprised and disappointed to find that most 'men of science' claimed that mental imagery in the literal sense was unknown to them. He concluded that:

Our bookish and wordy education tends to repress this valuable gift of nature. A faculty that is of importance in all technical and artistic occupations, that gives accuracy to our perceptions, and justness to our generalizations, is starved by lazy disuse, instead of being cultivated judiciously in such a way as will on the whole bring the best return.

More than a century later, the education system in most countries remains 'bookish and wordy'. The designer, trained to coordinate words, hands and visual imagery, is still very much the exception.

The skill of visualization is most frequently used by the industrial designer to synthesize other people's ideas and, in particular, to provide concreteness to marketing and engineering concepts. In 1955, Henry Dreyfuss, one of America's most illustrious design consultants, wrote that the designer 'can sit at a table and listen to executives, engineers, production and advertising men throw off suggestions and [can] quickly incorporate them into a sketch that crystallizes their ideas—or shows their impractibility'. But the skill can also be used to pull together the designer's own ideas—if only they are not suppressed in early life by peer group pressure from other functions, and by the corporate hierarchy.

Conclusion

A company does itself a disservice if it sees product design and, with it, the industrial designer's contribution, as merely 'shape and appearance'. Yet that is the rationale which is still often put forward for the renewed interest in design that is developing among businesses across the world. In late 1984 *Business Week* reported that 'in a world where many new products are similar in function, components and even performance, a product's design—its shape, its look, and above all its image—can make all the difference'.

Insofar as the shape and look of a product affect the more obviously 'functional' aspects of its design, this doctrine may very well constitute an argument for starting to involve industrial designers very early in the product development process—as they have been in a handful of European companies since the 1920s. But it is still perilously close to Harley Earl's strategy of skin-deep styling, which held Detroit in its grip until Ford's breakthrough in the 1980s—and is inadequate in the modern world. Except in products where function is of little significance, and emotional make-believe almost all, this approach is unlikely to pass Levitt's test of 'meaningful distinction'.

As the new corporate design converts have learned in recent years, it is in helping to achieve *real* differentiation in strategy, as well as operations, that industrial design can make such a valuable contribution.

References

Clark, K. and Fujimoto, T. (1990) 'The Power of Product Integrity', *Harvard Business Review*, November–December.

'Designing For Product Success—The Triad Design Project' (1989) Boston MA: Design Management Institute.

Dreyfuss, H. (1955) *Designing for People*, New York.

Dumas, A. and Mintzberg, H. (1989) 'Managing Design, Designing Management'. *Design Management Journal*, Fall.

Galton, F. (1883, 2nd ed. 1919) *Inquiries into Human Faculty*, London.

Kotler, P. and Roth, G. A. (1984) 'Design: A Powerful Strategic Tool', *Journal of Business Strategy*, Autumn.

Levitt, T. (1983) 'The Marketing Imagination', New York and London, p. 128.

Lorenz, C. (1986) 'The Design Dimension', Oxford and New York/ Cambridge MA: Blackwell, (Also published in Japanese, French, German, Italian, Portuguese and Swedish.).

Lorenz, C. (1988) 'How Ford Used Intuitive Design', *Financial Times*, September 28.

Lorenz, C. (1989) 'Unleashing the Potential of Design', *Financial Times*, October 27.

Mintzberg, H. (1987) 'Crafting Strategy'. *Harvard Business Review*, July-August.

Peters, T. and Waterman, R. (1982) *In Search of Excellence*, New York: Harper and Row, p. 156.

Porter, M. (1980) 'Competitive Strategy', New York: and (1983) 'Competitive Advantage', New York:

Sanderson, S. W. and Uzumeri, V. (0000) 'Strategies for New Product Development and Renewal: Design Incrementalism', research paper from Center for Science and Technology Policy,

School of Management, Rensselaer Polytechnic Institute, Troy, New York.

'Why Italian Industrial Design is Sweeping the World' (1984), *Business Week*, September 3.

PART TWO   THOUGHTS ON STRATEGIC THINKING

5   Strategic thinking as 'seeing'

Henry Mintzberg

I think it best to begin with what I believe strategic thinking is *not*. It is not simply following an 'industry recipe', not copying a competitor's strategy or continuing to do what was always done—at least not unless those have been carefully considered choices. In other words, strategic thinking is not mindlessness, not imitation, not thoughtless persistence. Nor is it purely cerebral: separating oneself from the subject of one's strategy and working it out ever so cleverly on paper or in a computer, as so much of today's literature urges managers to do.

To me, therefore, strategic thinking differs from ordinary thinking. In fact, because I believe strategic thinkers are appropriately described as 'visionaries', I shall characterize the various ingredients of strategic thinking by 'seeing' rather than 'thinking'. I present below three pairs of ingredients together with a seventh that knits them altogether into a framework of strategic thinking.

Almost everyone would agree that strategic thinking means *seeing ahead* (Figure 5.1). But, in fact, you cannot see ahead unless you can *see behind* (Figure 5.2) because any good vision of the future has to be rooted in an understanding of the past.

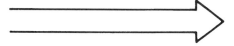

Figs 5.1 Seeing ahead.

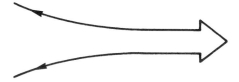

Fig 5.2 Seeing behind.

To paraphrase Kierkegaard, life may be lived forward, but it is understood backward. That is not to say that strategic thinkers extrapolate the past—I have already argued that they do not do this, at least not mindlessly—but simply that one cannot see the future with an ignorance of the past.

Of course, even the best knowledge of the past may not help to see the future. What is key, then, is not to extrapolate trends but to foresee discontinuities. And for that, there are no techniques—you have not much more than informed, creative *intuition*.

Many who comment on strategic thinking in fact believe they should take helicopters. Or, at least, I assume so because they talk so much about being able to distinguish 'the forest from the trees', and the only way I know to do this is to hover well above those trees. To them, therefore, strategic thinking is *seeing above* (Figure 5.3). But I wonder if anyone can get the true 'big picture' by just seeing above. The forest looks like a rug from a helicopter, and anyone who has taken a walk in one knows that forests don't look much like that from the inside. Strategists don't understand much about forests if they stay in helicopters, nor much about organizations if they stay in head offices.

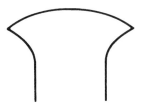

Figure 5.3 Seeing above.

In fact, I prefer another analogy: finding the diamond in the rough. Is that not what strategic thinkers have to do—find the gem of an idea that changes an organization? And that does not come from the big picture at all: it comes from a lot of hard and messy digging. Indeed, there is no big picture (let alone precious gem) readily available to any strategist. Each must construct his or her own, or perhaps I should say paint his or her own, out of the details dug up. Thus, strategic thinking is also inductive thinking: seeing above must be supported by *seeing below* (Figure 5.4).

I believe, however, that you can see ahead by seeing behind, and see above by seeing below, and still not be a strategic thinker. It takes more. For one thing, it requires creativity.

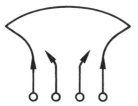

Figure 5.4 Seeing below.

Strategic thinkers see differently from other people; they pick out the precious gems that others miss. They are all, in some sense, innovative entrepreneurs. Strategic thinkers challenge conventional wisdom—the industry recipe, the traditional strategy, the ordinary world perceived by everyone else who wears blinkers—and thereby differentiate their organizations. Since creative thinking has been referred to as lateral thinking. I would like to call this *seeing beside* (Figure 5.5).

Figure 5.5 Seeing beside.

There are many creative ideas in the world, far more than we can handle—just visit any art gallery. And so to think strategically requires more than just thinking beside. Those creative ideas have to be placed into context, to be seen to work in a world that is to unfold. Strategic thinkers, in other words, also have to *see beyond* (Figure 5.6).

Seeing beyond is different from seeing ahead. The latter foresees an expected future by constructing a framework out of the events of the past—it intuitively forecasts discontinuities. The former, in contrast, constructs the future itself—it invents a world that would not otherwise be.

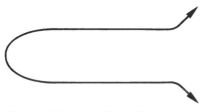

Figure 5.6 Seeing beyond.

But strategic thinking is not finished yet, for there remains one last necessary ingredient. What is the use of doing all this seeing—ahead and behind, above and below, beside and beyond—if nothing gets done? In other words, for a thinker to deserve the label *strategic*, he or she must also *see* it *through* (Figure 5.7).

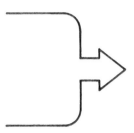

Figure 5.7 Seeing it through.

Put all this together and you get the following: *strategic thinking as seeing*. (Figure 5.8)

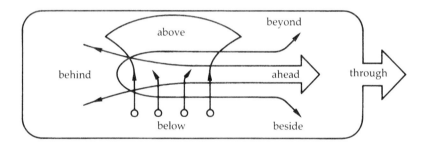

Figure 5.8 Strategic thinking as seeing.

Note

This chapter was amended from a paper of the same title in *Arenas of Strategic Thinking*, J. Nasi (ed.), Foundation for Economic Education, Helsinki, Finland, 1991. Originally, I used the word 'thinking' instead of 'seeing' throughout this chapter, and so this last ingredient became 'thinking through', which means something quite different: the application of analysis to trace the full consequences of a vision. But while creative visions can be assessed, their full consequences can never be understood ahead of time. In other words, to attempt to think them through is necessarily to destroy them. So 'seeing through' really works better than 'thinking through'.

6   Hearing the baby's cry: it's all in the thinking

Colin Sworder

Corporate visions

A chief executive recently expressed to me his dismay at the increasing difficulties he and his board colleagues are having in thinking strategically. He cited the extraordinary unpredictability and speed of change which affects almost every aspect of our lives. These conspire to defeat even the most sophisticated planning techniques and cause businesses to plateau in a whirlwind of tactical decision making and firefighting.

In considering this issue, I pointed out to him that directors have a number of options. These can include giving up, selling out, hiring consultants, indulging in strategic thinking, retiring, self-destruction from heart attack, changing the processes, the systems, the CEO and other directors. There is a more powerful alternative. Discover the underlying causes of the current performance, the reasons for their existence and then address these fundamentals. If the organization acts as if its people are crucial to its success, then every single individual, whatever their role or seniority, is forced to address their response to this policy:

> Ah, we have a vision to guide us through the storm. It has been communicated well through the organization. It is posted on walls, and every employee—and the directors—carries the statement with them at all times, printed on a card. They may not be able to recite it, but it is close to their hearts and at hand for easy reference when desired.

This common assertion is admirable, laudable and probably a significant improvement on the past. For the moment, though, let's ignore the hard question of what difference a vision makes to business performance if it is on a card rather than in the bloodstream. Let's examine the nature, origins and purpose of a vision, and how it relates to strategic thinking and planning.

All too often, vision creation and strategic planning are inextricably linked, being addressed during the same intensive workshop. Is this beneficial? In strategic planning, the big questions concern the method of achieving a goal. Considering long-term, strategic goals and focusing on the 'how to ...' stifles and limits *possibility* thinking. Bold goals meet the pragmatists' challenges such as 'Where and how are we going to obtain the funding? How can we grow that fast, the market is growing at only half that rate? It will never work. No one has ever ...' and so on. In some respects, envisioning and planning require paradoxical *mental activities*, especially given that effective envisioning produces clear end results without the route to achieve them. The value of each is not being questioned here. It is their simultaneous development that is counter-productive and needs to be uncoupled.

Strategic plans are designed precisely to provide the *route* to achieve goals. The annual, or five-year, strategic plan is probably out of date within a month, overtaken by events. So, if the plan is not much more than a short-term guess at a long-term aspiration, what beacon can boards develop to guide them and the organization? And what role does strategic thinking have to play in all this? Surely, if the direction-givers develop strategic plans, these are a function of strategic thinking? This is not necessarily so.

Corporate visions have become the subject of debate in recent years. Many world-class and successful organizations have one. Other organizations eschew them, regarding them as hype or worse. There is some research which affirms that individuals and groups who have clear visions invariably achieve them. There is a basic premise that human beings are drawn towards and become like the dominant images we hold in our minds.

So who needs a 'vision'? What is a vision anyway? Well, every human being has a vision and many of the best 'envisioners' are under ten years old. 'It's easy for them, they don't have to meet performance targets' is a common response. That's true. It also explains why many people over the age of ten can find it quite difficult. What restricts our thinking is the certain knowledge—beliefs—that some things are achievable and others not. This applies to us as individuals, groups, teams and nations. It is these beliefs which can keep us alive, or not, as Icarus discovered too late. We develop our beliefs, in the main, over fairly lengthy periods of time and many factors play a part in their formation. A board can develop common beliefs about the possibilities for their business, their markets, their employees and themselves. Beliefs are powerful—some people will die rather than change them. When leadership harnesses common beliefs in an organization, their organizations are no longer playing roulette with their future, they are playing chess.

The importance of information

Beliefs, or opinions if you prefer, do other things to us. Receiving a surprise can also be a function of a belief. A surprise means that the event was unforeseen. If the opinion, or considered view, of the board is that something is impossible, they will not be alert to the signals of its existence, so how are they going to see it before their competition does? A belief can blind us to information which would alert us to threats and opportunities. We rationalize the situation in some way, by blaming others or claiming we did not have the time or the funds. While that may be true, it is a symptom, rather than a cause, of what is occurring in our mind. Either way, it causes us to decide on taking action or not.

An example of this could be the mother of a young child. She can sleep through the sounds of trucks, airplanes and trains, yet will awaken the instant her baby cries, even in another room. So it is not the decibel level, it is the importance of the information that wakes her. The mother has a sensory blindness to sounds which are insignificant to her. And yet, why does the father remain asleep, lying beside the mother? He knows she will wake. He can give up accountability to her, perhaps like the subordinate does to the boss, and the board to the government or the allegedly 'unfair competition'.

We know we have these 'blind spots', known as scotomas or lacunae. That is not the problem. The problem is that we do not always know *when* we have them. They can be activated by a single thought which shoots up from the subconscious. They can last for a millisecond or a lifetime. Either way, we seldom recognize when they are active—we just think that our view is the truth of the matter. Human beings behave in accordance with the truth, not as it may actually be but as we perceive it. This causes a major blockage in our ability to think strategically.

The importance of beliefs

There is another aspect of our beliefs which influences our thinking. Edward de Bono once said 'logic never changed a belief'. The role of our beliefs is key to what we perceive, literally. If our belief prevents us from seeing the possibility, it will also prevent us from seeing the logic of why we should change our belief. So, if the corporate culture is the sum of the beliefs of the members of the organization, and the board wants to change the culture, they face a major challenge which includes and goes beyond processes and outside the realm of logical persuasion and good communication. This is the quantum world and an arena charged with emotion. As many direction-givers believe that theirs is a world of logic and rationality, they are loath to leave it and enter this other arena.

How do we develop our beliefs? With our present thoughts. So if our present thoughts build our beliefs, we can determine our future. If the present is not what we want, how can we control our present thoughts to bring about the future we do want? What is important to the people in your business? It is not primarily the money or the incentive scheme. These are necessary but not sufficient. What are they talking about in the corridors and informal meetings, in the restaurant, in tea breaks, on training courses; the present, the past, or the way they want the future to be?

Human beings think in words which trigger pictures and emotions. We are also teleological by nature, we are goal seeking. A goal is simply the dominant image in our mind and it will have attached to it a feeling which will either cause us to want to possess it or not. If the feeling is neutral, it cannot be a goal. If individuals and organizations do not have clear goals to which they have consciously attached vivid and clear pictures with the end result benefit—the feeling or emotion they generate—how can they expect to realize them?

To illustrate this point, sometimes I ask the board or management group to write out, individually, their full name, home and office addresses and telephone numbers, and a sketch of the immediate surroundings to their office building and home. About nine separate pieces of information. This is all done automatically, fluently, confidently and with good humour. Easy, isn't it?

The next question asks them to write their top five business and four personal goals. To cover whatever period of time they wish. I do not need to see them. Between 2 and 5 per cent will do this with the same confidence and fluency as they wrote the other items. Most simply cannot, saying they are embarrassed, or can't quite remember the details, and so on. Try this exercise on yourselves. Reflect on, and discuss if you have that level of trust between you, what benefit there would be to you as a board and to your people, if everyone's goals were as clear and deeply embedded as their own names and addresses. It is important to recognize that, like the strategic plan, goals can become invalid for a variety of reasons. Perhaps the most important is because they have already been achieved.

The widespread lack of individual and shared group goals has been identified after exhaustive research around the world. Successful individuals and organizations have clear goals, renewed with regularity so that they are part of automatic thinking. The Peter Principle is well known and can be seen in operation. However, is the rising to a level of personal incompetence the cause of so much direction-giving incompetence or could it be that the individual—or organiz-ation—has run out of goals for the next phase?

What does all this have to do with strategic thinking? Human beings behave in accordance with the truth as we believe it to be and our perception is limited by our beliefs. We are drawn towards the dominant images held in our minds. Seen from this perspective, strategic thinking is quite a challenge. If our strategic thinking is to be effective, we need to break through the scotomas and to do that we often need help. This can come from our colleagues in the boardroom, from the shopfloor—if we let them—and from ourselves. We can do this by priming our filter—remember the baby's cry— to let through information that is significant to us. What is significant? Whatever piece of information, a clue perhaps, which will help us move towards achieving the goals—the dominant images. It is that straightforward. The human brain is actually quite a simple mechanism even though it performs tasks of incredible complexity.

To have any real practical and financial value in providing the beacon there must be a long-term, emotional commitment to its realization. It is the emotional part which ensures the practical, operational commitment, not the other way round. If you do not believe it, how can you see it? If you cannot see it, how can you and your people bring it into reality? If we move towards the dominant image we hold in our mind and the key influencers in a business—shopfloor and boardroom—are talking about the past and all the problems which face them and the organization, is it any wonder that, for these organizations, the future is a repeat of the past?

What is an attitude?

The dramatic change from manager to direction-giver requires, we know, 'a change in attitude and in habits'. What do we mean by this? What is an attitude?

An attitude is a pre-emotional response to a given stimulus. It is neither good nor bad. It is reactive, rather than pre-emptive, thought which either helps us to achieve a goal or hinders us. How do we know we have attitudes? Where do we get our attitudes? Are we born with them? Does an infant have an attitude about mowing the grass or washing the car, or about people of a different background, colour or creed?

If attitudes are reactive—we only know we have one when faced with the triggering event, or possibility of the event—they must be a symptom, a reflection of something else. Their foundation is our belief structure. Managers have a view, opinions—beliefs—about the way they should operate. A direction-giver's *modus operandi* needs to be different. So if the beliefs remain the same, acting like a direction-giver will be unnatural and will lead to a powerful pull to return to behaving 'naturally'. If the managers cannot 'see' themselves in this role, behaving in the appropriate manner will be unlike the real 'me'. Being with others who do behave appropriately may have some effect on the individual over time but can a board afford to speculate with such a potentially valuable asset?

Habits are just the way we think, automatically. They are ingrained thinking patterns, developed over time. They can be reactive and continuous. Try shaking hands using the 'unusual' hand. Try brushing your teeth with the other hand first. Try treating the customer better. Try to see the potential and value in a colleague you have always thought without potential and worthless by listing four good things about him or her before naming one bad aspect.

Like a printed circuit board, our minds have developed their circuitry over time. The 'switches' direct the current in patterns which are determined by the wiring circuits or subconsciously held beliefs.

There is much more to changing our thinking and acting than this. It is not a single element which makes the difference. There are other powerful forces at work in our subconscious minds. These include the level of self-worth, self-esteem and personal accountability. Changing thought patterns developed over a lifetime, or even twenty years in management, are unlikely to occur overnight. They may, but it is important that the changes are sustained. There is information available these days which can help individuals and organizations to develop these elements on a large scale which does not rely on a consulting approach. The real challenge is for direction-givers to realize that the problem exists. It is difficult to see unless you *believe* it exists in the first place. So a common response is 'I am a reasonable individual, just show me. There, you can't show me, can you?'

For managers to 'let go', to change attitudes and habits, and to develop their strategic thinking abilities, fundamental changes to their habitual thinking need to occur first if they are to contribute to the success of the enterprise.

Impacts on strategic thinking

Attitudes, habits, beliefs, scotomas and low self-worth can put the brakes on improving the quality of our thinking, at the operational level, just as much as at the strategic level. When they are favourable, they can have an almost unbelievably beneficial effect on measurable performance indicators. They affect the way the security guard greets your visitors, the quality of the work performed by the delivery driver, the way the shop assistant and bank teller deal with their customers and the quality with which the machinist performs on the shopfloor. They enable, or hinder, the development of trust between individuals and trust is essential if there is to be open communication and effective teamwork. They also affect the relationships we have with our friends and family, our children and colleagues.

Pursuing the question of how boards can assess the quality of their strategic thinking, it is natural (habitual) to grasp external measures of success, such as market share, profitability, sales per employee, and so on. However, there are other, more demanding, measures. Such external measures can hide fundamental questions such as how good are we compared to how good we could be? If we are not as good as we could be, what is preventing us from achieving these levels of performance? How can we know?

For a start, how bold is your vision? Bold enough for you to be comfortable? Do your goals and those of your people challenge you to the limits of your individual and collective credibility? Why? Is it a belief, about yourself and/or colleagues which is causing this? Is it the truth, or just the truth as you have perceived it? How many times in the last two years has the board recognized a scotoma or belief which, when changed, has opened a new horizon of opportunities which were within grasp all the time? How many employee suggestions have been implemented, and what benefits have been generated for the organization? How are people at all levels recognized for their contribution to improving business performance? How many employees at all levels have made a suggestion for improvement during the last two years which has been successfully implemented? How do your customers rate your performance in every aspect relating to service, reliability, value, quality and so on?

It may be that you do decide that you and your people are performing at their optimum and yet the business is still not successful. In this case, perhaps you are in the wrong business. However, before deciding to quit the sector, spend time with your people and find out what their beliefs are. Compare them to your vision. If they are not as passionate as you about it, there may be some fundamental issues which need addressing.

Skilled leaders know how to alter the belief cycle. They do not work on changing the performance, they work on the underlying cause—the belief cycle. They know that, once their people buy into the truth, individually and collectively, they will work to bring about this truth.

Living as we are in this Information Age, directing an organization has become a different challenge from when predictability and stability were the norm. There is so much information bombarding every organization that a small number of board directors cannot cope. This Information Age presents peculiar challenges. Whereas in the era of the product, maintaining the superiority of the product, however measured, was key to success. These days, even though many organizations supply products, customers are more demanding. Aren't we all? When in a restaurant or hotel, aren't our own expectations higher than in the past? Perhaps this is the real economic transformation which is occurring. Every business is a service business. In this environment, the last person with the best idea rewrites the rules. So creating and being aware of the latest best idea is important. With so many 'best ideas' being developed around the world at any one time, how can the board be aware of them? You cannot. However, you can use the minds of your people to be aware, to inform you and to keep generating their best ideas.

Successful leadership also understands how to harness the ingenuity, creativity and initiative of every individual member of the organization. A small number of executives, however smart, cannot hope to be everywhere at once, knowing all that is happening which may affect the livelihood of the business. However good the processes in an organization, can they generate the results of which they are capable, if the people who are needed to make them function do not—for whatever reason—want them to function optimally all day, every day?

If the baby's cry is to be heard by your people ahead of your competitors, it must be significant to them. Successful leadership understands that everyone needs to share the corporate vision, from their own perspective and for their own, personal reasons. That is the real challenge for today's direction-givers.

Strategic thinking is more than a process applied at board level. If direction-givers are serious about competing on a global stage, against the very best in their sector, then improving the quality of thinking at every level and in every aspect of their activities is the foundation upon which they can dare to build a world-class organization.

7 The processes of thinking strategically

Jerry Rhodes

The role you give to thinking

The most strategic action you can take is to choose to think and not to do. Thought is essentially strategic in that it sets the direction of all physical energies. Your mind commands the central ground. Compared with action in the world outside, action in your inner world is fast, economical and very low risk. It is more to do with quality than quantity because it determines what you will *not* do, rejecting many more possibilities than the choice you actually make. And it is clear that the thinking done at the top of any organization will be done at a high level in more ways than one: not only with the power of authority but also at a high conceptual level. This makes writing about strategic thinking somewhat peculiar: you keep switching between strategic thinking (process) and thinking about corporate strategy (content), as shown in Figure 7.1.

There should, indeed, be a flow between this double-loop. If you don't get your strategic processes of thinking right, much of your thinking will be irrelevant, even counter-productive, to the formulation of a sound corporate strategy. If you don't get your corporate strategy right, everything else throughout the organization goes wrong.

All challenging work demands the management of thought. To be effective, people need to learn how to orchestrate their mental energies with one another so as to achieve the results they want. When you are working, either alone or with other people, it is the quality of your thinking that most profoundly impacts the results you get. Thinking is an activity which enables you to avoid doing what would be useless, costly or dangerous. It is 'pretending to do', a rehearsal for action, before putting resources and results at risk. If you fail to use thinking well, you jeopardize the effectiveness of your organization.

Figure 7.1   The strategy and strategic thinking lemniscate

It has been my concern over the past twenty years to produce a practical way forward that enables men and women who manage demanding responsibilities to use their thinking better. Our research with organizations has produced an approach to thinking which is unique in identifying the thought-requirements of management work, at all levels, and the thinking operations of the people concerned, *in the same terms*. This common language of tasks and mind enables people to bring their minds to bear effectively on any task they face. It is this situational matching of task and person that has been so useful, which Figure 7.2 illustrates.

Figure 7.2   The challenging situations and thinking energies lemniscate

Obviously, the applications for improved thinking performance are numerous: it is hard to list any management concern where improved thinking would not be directly relevant. Suffice to say that the value is greatest where the issues are strategic, or where know-how of any kind is a critical competitive advantage. Those who set the strategy of the business had better get the direction right, or else all its efficiency will serve only to get more easily to the wrong place. Wherever quality matters, it is the quality of thinking that makes the difference, just as the production of any product is determined and limited by its design and engineering.

Characteristic thinking style

Everyone has a characteristic thinking style which determines and steers their approach to problems, especially if they are not aware of it. This means that they may deal with a situation demanding creativity in the same way that they would deal with an idea in the process of being evaluated, rejected or adopted. If so, they would be unwittingly divided within themselves. When someone's actions do not bear out their *intention*, their effectiveness suffers. Anyone who consistently ignores certain of his or her mental faculties is obviously vulnerable in situations where those particular faculties are vital. Less obvious is that excessive fondness for any particular mental faculty can make someone quite dangerous.

The funny thing is that people are surprisingly constant and consistent in their approach to quite different management tasks. Some are more aware of their own natural strengths than others, but only a few people can recognize precisely what every task demands from them and deliver just what is needed for it. These few are, by definition, the most effective users of their intelligence.

What are the strategic mental faculties we use in thinking? The model of mind which I have been developing over sixteen years, based on the outcomes of a research project in Philips (Eindhoven) and then with a range of other major corporations in three continents, offers useful data on strategic thinking processes. Twenty-five deep Thinking-Intentions were identified as the inner driving forces of all mental operations. We gave these Thinking-Intentions the collective name of *Thunks*, a new word coined to represent a new concept in the philosophy of thought. We described each of them individually not only with a user-friendly name but also with a symbol that could cross cultural and language barriers (see Figure 7.3). Between them, and in all their combinations, they represent all the mental muscles available for thinking work. Being only few in number, they are, of course, immensely rich, but the simplification is a practical one: it works. The work is described in Jerry Rhodes and Sue Thame (1988) and by Jerry Rhodes (1991).

For our purpose here, it must be enough to say that the 25 *Thunks* formed themselves into three major groupings for which we adopted the metaphor of the three Colours which together produce white light symbolizing wholeness. To Judge what is right was given Blue; to Describe what is true, Red; and to Realize what is new, Green. The fields of these *Thunks* represent the Colours by *shapes* as shown in Figure 7.3. Each of these three massive sectors has a further dimension, which is similar in each Colour and these were given the metaphor Hard and Soft. We chose Hard to represent the drive of the mind to think objectively and Soft to represent the more subjective. Thereby, the entire chemistry of mind could be

Figure 7.3   A general-purpose configuration of the twenty-five Thunks

reproduced strategically in a model which can be used in several configurations of two, three or six elements; one configuration is shown in Figure 7.3.

With these *Thunks*, it is possible to profile the preferred thinking faculties of individuals, of groups and, indeed, even of organizations, thus showing their bias and tendencies which can reveal why and how they act in the ways they do. Just as important, the *Thunks* can be used to profile or *map* any task facing you. We call this *conceptual mapping* but it might also equally be called *strategic mapping*, since the result is to give you a generic, universal guide to *what* to use *when*, in different circumstances. The word 'map' is such a good concept that it is widely used as an illustration for the way thinking works. Buzan's Mind-map and Cognitive Maps based on Kelly's construct theory are modern examples. Our usage sees a conceptual map as a system, containing the essential elements required for a particular generic thinking task. Table 7.1 indicates ten of the most generic thinking tasks people have to deal with. Each of these can be mapped using *Thunks* to show the dynamic thinking tensions inherent within them. Such maps are tools for orchestrating your mind strategically, so that whatever hits you, from any direction, you can turn your attention appropriately to tackle it.

Table 7.1   Strategic process maps

Your concern *If your strategic question is*	The Map *then the Thinking Map to use is*
What is the nature and mission of the organization?	Strategy
Where are we now, in relation to the situation facing us? Which way do we send thinking energy?	Orientation
Which is the best choice? How should we design this? How do the options compare?	Decision
How can what is know inform us on this concern? How should this information be conveyed? How can we work together on this concern?	Information gathering
How can we reach new, unusual ideas?	Creativeness
How can we bring in something new? What bridging is needed between the new idea and its acceptance in its market?	Innovation
What explains or accounts for that happening? Why has this gone differently from expectations?	Find cause
How will we get something done? And what if? Will he or she understand what I want to achieve? Will he or she know what scope they have if it goes badly?	Develop a plan
How will we sell the idea, product, service or method? What can be done if it does not go well?	Selling
What else can be learned from the experience?	Learning

As an example of a Conceptual Map I have chosen to include here, in Figure 7.4, a map of Strategy Formation. This Map shows the seven key *Thunks* that can drive you down the super-highways of strategic thinking for strategy: not *what* to think but *how* to go about thinking about what you should think. By indicating the Colour and the precise *Thunk* involved, you can know what kind of mental energy is being demanded at different stages of the strategy plan as well as the kinds of question that need to be raised. This is vital underpinning for any group trying to work together on strategy. They can organize their diversity of talent so that they can home in on the same mental processes together. At board level, this can be especially important, since directors are usually strong-minded individuals who relish their differences, accentuate their eccentricities and prefer to operate as loners rather than as collaborators.

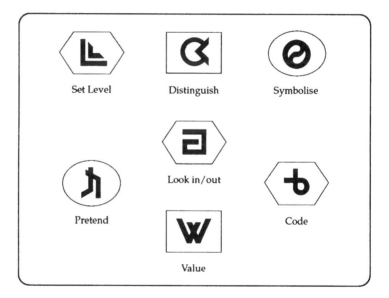

Set Level   Distinguish   Symbolise

Look in/out

Pretend   Code

Value

Figure 7.4   A conceptual map for strategic thinking in Thunks

People regularly rehearse the platitude that what brings strength to a group or a board is the different ways its mem bers think. Yes, if their differences are understood between them, and managed so that the task is actually accomplished and not hijacked by the many directions in which they may all go. The mapping concept allows the flexibility to move from one part of the process to another without a rigid adherence to procedure, so that variety of approach can be embraced, while also ensuring that people can signal to each other how they are applying their thinking energies. 'I'm using my Green Pretend now!'. 'I'm coming at this from Specify.' 'I'm in Blue.' Expect quite different inputs from each! The group can manage itself by saying, 'Let's focus on Set Level'. 'We need to spend some time on Symbolize now.' 'We have neglected Distinguish, so it's time we moved in to Blue.'

A fruitful debate can be held within any boardroom on whether these seven chosen *Thunks* in Figure 7.4 are the most powerfully useful in strategy formation, and whether they are indeed much employed already within board discussion on strategy. Figure 7.5 shows a complete set of *Thunks* applied to strategy. Use it to review your own thinking processes within strategy formulation.

Take any of your own strategy formation agendas and ask yourself, which *Thunks* do we normally use at each step of the Agenda? Perhaps you use a Business Plan for Strategy Formation? See if you can Colour-code each part of it. What other *Thunks* would you see as equally or even more important than those shown in Figure 7.4, and why? How much facility do you have to use the *Thunks* you have chosen? Do you avoid using the ones you find obscure, unappealing or difficult? What about other members of your team or board? These questions may appear simple when placed on the page, but actually raising them live with a real working group leads one into the complexities of *process* and *data* and to refining the group's capacity to think together.

Process and data

When people work together on strategy, as on most tasks, what they usually bring is their values, ideas, experience and knowledge as units of *data* which they feed into the debate to steer and influence the result. The *data* flowing into and around an organization are only as useful as the *processes* that identify the need for them. Thinking adds value to knowledge and experience, i.e. information, by revealing what is needed, by recognizing it when it is there and noticing its absence when it is not, and by processing it in such a way that it does achieve the desired actions. If these thinking *processes* are missing, or if they are inappropriate, then all the values, ideas, knowledge and experience in the world have no useful purpose.

Process therefore determines both the data you consider and how you think about them. In that sense, process is the more strategic. Data die with alarming speed these days,

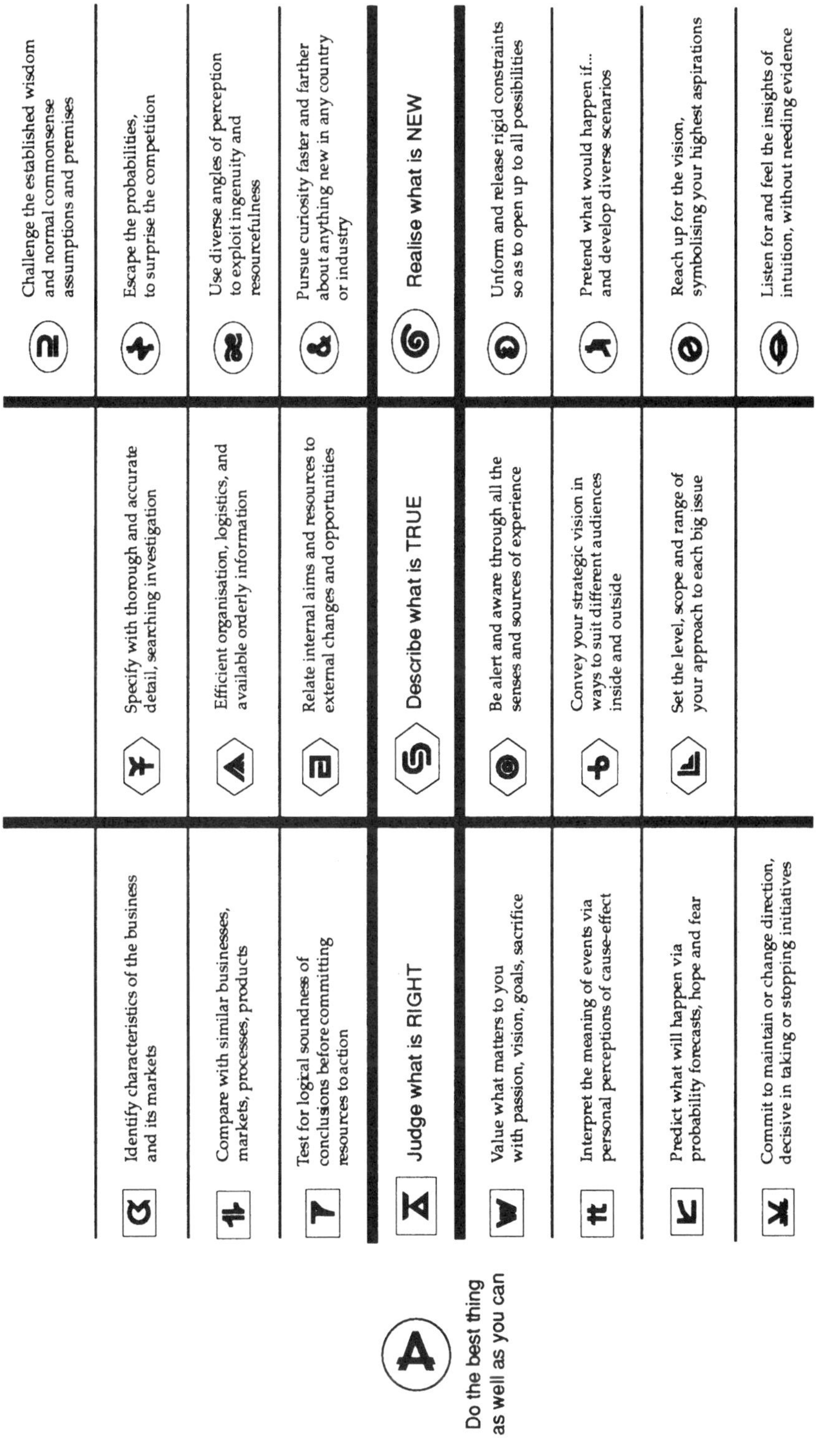

Realise what is NEW

- Challenge the established wisdom and normal commonsense assumptions and premises
- Escape the probabilities, to surprise the competition
- Use diverse angles of perception to exploit ingenuity and resourcefulness
- Pursue curiosity faster and farther about anything new in any country or industry
- Unform and release rigid constraints so as to open up to all possibilities
- Pretend what would happen if... and develop diverse scenarios
- Reach up for the vision, symbolising your highest aspirations
- Listen for and feel the insights of intuition, without needing evidence

Describe what is TRUE

- Specify with thorough and accurate detail, searching investigation
- Efficient organisation, logistics, and available orderly information
- Relate internal aims and resources to external changes and opportunities
- Be alert and aware through all the senses and sources of experience
- Convey your strategic vision in ways to suit different audiences inside and outside
- Set the level, scope and range of your approach to each big issue

Judge what is RIGHT

- Identify characteristics of the business and its markets
- Compare with similar businesses, markets, processes, products
- Test for logical soundness of conclusions before committing resources to action
- Value what matters to you with passion, vision, goals, sacrifice
- Interpret the meaning of events via personal perceptions of cause-effect
- Predict what will happen via probability forecasts, hope and fear
- Commit to maintain or change direction, decisive in taking or stopping initiatives

A

Do the best thing as well as you can

Figure 7.5   Thunks *in strategy*

while process is enhanced the more you *consciously* use it. Using thinking processes consciously and appropriately enables you to ask the questions you need to ask to get at the relevant data for any problem or opportunity you face. The more senior your responsibility, the more you need to be able to employ process. If you continue to stuff your head only with data, you will be interfering with your proper responsibility to become more skilful with process. If you are data-driven, you will also be impinging on the roles of those below you who should properly spend their time knowing more about more data than yourself. Usually, the more junior levels are paid for what they *know* while the more senior levels are paid for what they can *find out* and judge. Figure 7.6 visually demonstrates this.

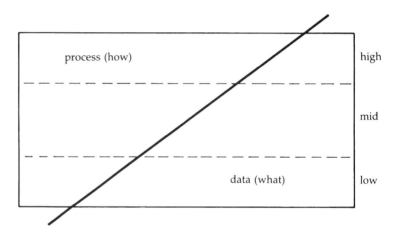

Figure 7.6   The effect of job level on the contribution of data and process

Whatever your organization, and whatever the separation of process and data in the hierarchy, everyone needs to appreciate the value of process for data and vice versa. By altering the rake of the line across Figure 7.6, you can show the different ways organizations proportion process and data up and down their structure.

Using *Thunks* for strategy

Thunks, at a level of simplicity like that shown in Figure 7.5, lay out all the thinking processes open to you and all can be used in formulating corporate strategy. Because they are so few and fundamental, so central and generic, any *Thunk* is essentially strategic. *Thunks* are high-level concepts capable of being used at any point of operation down to the most specific. They are a reference, a source from which to draw and shape the way to handle information (knowledge and experience) in *any* given situation. When it really matters, they are universally useful for determining what process of thinking you want to use. When the task is strategy, turn to the key *Thunks*, shown in Figure 7.4, since we have found that they most fundamentally lift your thoughts into the domain of strategy. They give you the first principles for strategic thinking about strategy. There is no proper order or sequence. On the contrary, my concept of a *map*, as distinct from a *thought-plan*, entails using it as a system rather than a sequence, encouraging spontaneity yet with awareness of where you are and the ground you still need to cover. This gives you control of the strategic thinking process.

The key *Thunks* for strategy

Set Level (Soft Red)

To set the level of thought is to determine its boundaries, its horizon or scope. It might at first seem that strategy has to be, by definition, only at high-level, long-term and thus rather bland. This perhaps explains why its expression in strategy documents is often diffuse and so all-inclusively vague as to have no teeth. From a great height, you can look wider and farther but don't see much on the ground. The power of this *Thunk* is demonstrated when you are able to use your mind as a helicopter which can choose between the wide view and the purposeful dive to specifics which can be essential for the authenticity of high-level ideas. A strategy created through both the abstract and the concrete is stronger by far.

In my work with groups and teams, I have observed that *Set Level* is one of the least understood *Thunks* in people's mental vocabulary and the least well managed. In discussion, one can see how people switch levels oblivious of the hierarchies of thought between themselves, thus confusing the issues and muddling the concepts. The ability to switch levels with conscious control and real awareness is mental gymnastics at its best. Being able to take others with you, showing how you move from the generic to the specific, is a refined art.

Set Level determines what is treated as irrelevant. Great strategists have the faculty of multilayered vision, whereby they change the levels of their thought in order to focus in depth whenever their broader scan alerts them to the need. Management by exception needs also audit in depth. This said, you cannot operate strategically without putting weight on the highest levels. Although it is really the soldiers, not the generals, who win battles, they could not get the chance if the generals chose the wrong field on which to fight. Strategic decisions at the highest level make victory either probable or impossible.

Pretend (Soft Green)   Strategic thought requires us to think beyond what we hold dear and what we know. We must allow ourselves to pretend, to act as if something were so, to imagine *what if* we could do something, even when we have not in the past. At a meta-level, as I mentioned before, to think at all is to *pretend* to do something, a low-risk rehearsal for action: nothing could be more strategic. This *Thunk* entails a temporary suspension of experience and judgement. Using it, we create scenarios, descriptions of solutions that *might* be brought about without having to believe that they actually *are* the solution at that point. These thought-experiments or simulations turn vague possibilities or open spaces in the mind into *virtual realities.*

Operating in a climate of Green (visionary and ingenious) thinking is, for most people, fraught with insecurity and a sense of unsureness. There is no *terra firma* on which to stand. It can be an uncomfortable experience, and one they want to get away from as quickly as possible. Time and again, I watch groups start the process of building scenarios, only to see them shy away once they have one or perhaps two pictures of the future. They have worn themselves out with the effort of looking into the unknown before they had hardly begun; or they have chopped off their pictures of what might be before they could be properly born, with judgements from Blue *Test, Compare* or *Distinguish* far too soon. Being able to relish uncertainty, having a lust for this *Thunk*, is a must for any group trying to formulate strategy. Strategists must build rich pictures of what the future might look like, so that their organization can prepare to face up to it and, better still, take advantage of it.

Look in/out   Any serious attempt at strategy demands we manage the
(Hard Red)   boundary that surrounds us and on which we stand. We must look both ways, inwards and outwards. This is the case whether it is a group of directors or a team at any level in the organization. Organizations may fail because they ignore one and focus twice the effort on the other. Some leaders are captivated by the attractions of opportunities out there in the

wide world. Others experience the strength of their people and the physical assets of their business as the driving energy for their direction. Both perspectives are needed so as to compare the one with the other. Scanning the surrounding world for changes, threats and opportunities is, of course, essential but not adequate. Penetrating analysis of your own assets and capabilities is just as important, so as to exploit fully what you are and to be aware of what you lack.

In fact, this *Thunk* recognizes the tensions and dependencies between all aspects of any system: and, when forming a strategy, your internal system needs balance against the system of environmental forces outside. Government has to manage its domestic and its foreign policy, both. Every person must operate in the context of their group, and every organization in the light of its own stakeholders.

It is a phenomenon that few groups do look both ways, inwards and outwards. If they do, the big mistake I see them making is their tendency to see-saw between the two, when they really need to look at the inner *through* an understanding of the outer and vice versa. Looking outwards enables you to view your own internal culture, values, systems, services and products from perspectives you seldom consider. Looking inwards enables you to measure the outside world in your own terms, marking its foibles and how you cope with them, or otherwise.

Since *Look in/out* is central to strategy formulation, because you should look at everything in terms of *Look in/out*, it is disturbing to discover that, for many people, it is a mental operation but poorly understood. *Look in/out* embodies the concept of *gestalt*, figure and ground, and of turning inwards and outwards in conceptual space. The funny thing is there is no word in the English dictionary for it. In our culture, *Look in/out* is understood by the business executive as systems thinking and the person in the street knows it as ecology. Both are, relatively speaking, new concepts in our society. It is not so surprising, then, that many folk find it a difficult *Thunk* to grapple with.

Distinguish (Hard Blue)

Whether some strategic vision should become a mission is largely determined by this *Thunk*. *Distinguish* is the powerfully rational counterpart to *Symbolize* and, indeed, they can act as rivals and competitors. Using this faculty, you characterize what is special about your organization, as distinct from comparable firms, and in contrast to things that do not sit well with you. Any future vision is submitted to similar scrutiny to determine the kind of match or fit. Thus, unrealistic strategy is rejected. Equally, when some new strategy strongly resonates with your strengths or your values, this mental operation will help to assess how great is the stride required to reach it, and what kinds of gap between present reality and the future vision need to be bridged. *Distinguish* either rejects a favourite idea or begins the process of forming a practical strategy.

How is it abused and misused? *Distinguish* is logically ruthless, uncompromisingly objective, so that human warmth and tentative ideas can be destroyed. The biggest task any group faces with *Distinguish* is to know how to govern it so that it operates to advantage rather than to destruction. If this *Thunk* is lodged in the mental powerhouse of the most vociferous or most extrovert member of the group, then goodbye to all Soft Green and farewell to an imaginative strategy. Conversely, if the group has an awareness of this *Thunk's* destructive forces, they may step so warily around it that they may actually fail to employ it to good effect. Knowing when to bring in *Distinguish* will ensure its happy residence in the strategy debate. Here you can see the particular value of having a conceptual map to help you all agree when to use *Distinguish*.

Symbolize (Soft Green)	As directors, we invoke this *Thunk* when reaching for an entirely unusual perception of the nature and positioning of our organization. We need new ideas, whether about the future or about what is already within our experience. Thinking symbolically instead of literally opens up the chance of making connections either across high boundary walls or between things normally remote from one another. Anyone can put together things that are closely similar and therefore normal and obvious. Breakthrough insights, by contrast, are usually the result of a huge mental surge which provides the power to unite concepts that no one would normally associate with each other. This is why this *Thunk* is seen as a flash of inspiration, a kind of magic, a vision.

Yet the further out the idea, the more it will bewilder those who are operating within the bounds of normal perceptions and of logic. Great ideas arouse the greatest opposition. If your colleagues cannot swoop the conceptual distances with you, you will be lonely, out on a limb, with small chance to bring the idea into the ring for serious consideration. This *Thunk* requires responsible use and responsible handling within the boardroom. A clear process for recognizing quantum ideas, developing the information they require and coming to judgement for or against, is needed.

Most organizations cannot handle this well. Usually, men and women with 'ideas' have to found their own businesses to succeed with it, or seek one of the few imaginative companies that can run with the unusual. 'Never be the first with a new idea' might be the motto of bureaucracies and dinosaurs all over the world. They die. A board without imagination does not offer safe hands: it simply turns aside from the leadership which could secure the future by getting there first.

Value (Soft Blue)

Value reflects what really matters to those forming strategy. It is the means whereby they align themselves with the organization, as a living entity, to determine the motive force which will govern what is ultimately done. It accounts for preferences, desires and aversions, and the reasons for making sacrifices to attain the organization's goals. *Value* enshrines the will to make things happen. It is the powerhouse of action. In exercising this *Thunk*, you set goals or objectives; adopt some criteria and not others when influencing the amount of risk you will undertake. On your values you stand. They represent much of what you believe in, discriminate between hope and fear, and draw the line as to what you will certainly *not* do. *Value* informs your code of ethics, and even whether you bother with such a thing. And no vision is worth tuppence unless it is attuned to the deep passion that makes you want to reach it, embrace it and live it.

Value is a matter of the heart as well as of the head. The strategies of many organizations are viewed with some cynicism because the integrity of those who form them are not seen to be embodied in them. Strategy cannot satisfactorily be created by people who are not involved in nor caring about the outcome. When a board forms its strategy, each director needs to ask, 'Do I stand by this with my head and my heart?'

Code (Soft Red)

To encode the message can be as important as the message itself. This is especially true of anything new and unfamiliar. Strategy is hard to formulate, harder still to convey to all concerned, even when they have been to some extent involved. *Code* is vital when it comes to getting a strategy understood and accepted so that it can actually work. A good strategy that fails to reach the heart means that it will not influence what everyone does day to day. *Code* is the communication *Thunk*, embodying the art of transmitting the message to all the different people involved so that its truth is authentically conveyed. It is not about deception, overlarding the cake or papering over the cracks. It should not overly depend on editing, and omissions made to bias reality on purpose. It does require genuine empathy with the 'audience' and this is hard to reach from the Olympian heights where strategy is made. The will to *Code* and the skills to do it have been the hallmark of many outstanding leaders. This is why it is chosen here as a special *Thunk* for the strategist.

To reach out beyond the group that forms the strategy is a task in itself that flows alongside the work within the group. However, as perhaps this short tour around the seven key *Thunks* implies, the ways in which the group itself manages to communicate within are just as important. A common language of understanding, of managing process and data, and of building trust, such that it is possible for members to disclose their values and tread the uncertainties of *Pretend* and *Symbolize*, is vital. I find, though, that few boards ever take the time to examine their ways of working together. They usually view their time as too precious to be spent on finding out how they could actually address the serious matter of forming strategy better.

Conscious awareness

These seven *Thunks* could drive you down the super-highways of strategic thinking. If you choose others, then it would have a profound effect on the results you achieve. But whichever *Thunks* you adopt as drivers, it's absurd to feel that any handful would be enough for any major issue: they simply provide a focus. Often discussions become stuck, blood pressure rises, frustration debilitates, or we just go round in circles. Then, by selecting a different *Thunk*, you can lead off into a fresh initiative, a new angle and with new life. This is a proven way to maintain the high energy and purpose required for complex tasks such as strategy making.

Another approach is to identify in advance the kind of support that each driving *Thunk* in the Map may require. You might care to try to plan ahead the sequence of your thinking-steps, especially useful if you are leading the discussion. It prepares your mind for the ground you want to cover. In practice, few powerful discussions hold to any such idealized sequence because in reality what is said (data) will change the process which is supposed to be driving it. This still holds true even if pauses are made to take stock and review progress, and also even when the board makes use of a skilled facilitator of their process. So be it. Spontaneity is rewarding and too much self-discipline inhibits potential. The most practical solution seems to be that all concerned adopt a Map, the same map, and agree to move around it more or less together. Any individual who needs to speak from a different part of the Map just signals his or her intention, to avoid taking the others by surprise or arousing needless opposition. For example, if the group as a whole is centred on its values (Blue), anyone speaking from Green imagination might get a hot reception if he or she does not declare his or her position on the Map.

Many of the things done in and by an organization are either ineffective or wrong because they are counter to its strategy. This is why there is so much concern today about strategy. It is vital for organizations to create the most useful vision for the way forward, to express it clearly so that it is understood and agreed, and to translate the strategy into objectives and processes at various levels. Likewise, for individual persons, when they are disappointed with their own actions and results, it so often turns out that they were not clear about their own corporate strategies. Being unsure of your goal makes sure you miss it. Most of the things we get wrong are through poor thinking and, quite often, the thoughts and conclusions we reach do not actually carry out our real intentions. We have shot ourselves in the foot.

Awareness of one's own thinking intentions can be a big stride towards control over one's own thought. Those people who have almost achieved this have gained a real maturity. It is to be hoped that those who govern a significant organization, of whatever size, will be developing and using compatible thinking strategies when establishing and steering its corporate strategy.

References

Rhodes, J. (1991) *Conceptual Toolmaking*, Oxford: Blackwell.
Rhodes, J. and Thame, S. (1988) *The Colours of Your Mind*, London: HarperCollins.

PART THREE

THE DEVELOPMENTAL PROCESSES FOR STRATEGIC THINKING

8 Strategic dilemmas occasioned by using alternative scenarios of the future

Charles Hampden-Turner

Is strategy a viable concept?

The theme of this chapter is that the best-laid plans of strategic thinkers go awry if the future turns out differently from the way strategists expect. Indeed, many of the conflicts within management teams charged with making strategy are not differences in goals or even personalities, but differences in assumption and beliefs about probable futures. You face many difficulties in devising strategy if you are unsure about the future state of the environment which that strategy will engage.

In a world economy of growing turbulence and uncertainty, does it make much sense to have a strategy at all? Strategy is, in its origins, a military term. But the job of a general, however personally hazardous, is at least capable of clear definition—aiming to engage and defeat the enemy. But business strategy has never been entirely sure who the 'enemies' are, whether they exist at all and, if they do exist, whether we should beat them or join them.

The problem lies in the fact that business competition is really mock combat. The idea is less to defeat or kill and more to move available resources to the best-managed companies and put the less well-managed under pressure to improve or, if they cannot, to do something else! The purpose of the whole exercise is to *learn* how to conduct business with greater and greater skill and effectiveness.

This raises the issue of what 'victory' or 'defeat' means. Is it in the interests of Japan or Germany to 'beat' us? What would they then sell to us or buy from us? The strategy-as-war school of thinking needs to ask itself what 'winning' entails. Is the idea to reduce the number of contestants in a given market by knocking out one or more? If so, this process will lead to oligopoly and eventually to monopoly and we shall probably be worse off! Victory for the company becomes defeat for the economy. How does one develop the intellectual attitudes and skills to resolve such dilemmas? A powerful approach is to construct scenarios of alternative futures from which strategies can be derived.

Visions of the future of capitalism

You cannot really decide on a good strategy unless you have a clear idea about the nature of capitalism. Until recently, capitalism was easy to define. It was what the moral leaders of the Western nations—Ronald Reagan and Margaret Thatcher—said it was. Capitalism was the antithesis of Communism. It was individualist, not collectivist; competitive, not cooperative; private, not public; free in the sense of *laissez-faire* and not state-managed. If some capitalist countries were not *quite* like that—Germany and Japan, for example—at least they kept a low profile, as befits the losers in the Second World War.

Now, however, these sharply polarized certainties have all but disappeared. Those parts of the world growing fastest—China, Malaysia, Singapore, Hong Kong, South Korea, the Argentine—are, at best, soft authoritarian, if that is not a description too generous to China! Most are collectivist and cooperative in spirit, if not still Communist, and all try to manage their economies. Moreover, the growth rates of these economies are unprecedented. The UK and the United States, even in the heydays of their industrial revolutions, did not grow as fast. Are they 'just' catching up or might their momentum, like that of Japan, take them past us? How can we use scenarios to help us resolve the dilemmas arising from our strategic thinking?

Scenarios describing the dominance of three different capitalisms

It is the year 2003. The world economic scene has changed dramatically. I will present three scenarios of how we got to 2003. Each will be written in the style of a contemporary historian with all the advantages of hindsight. Each scenario will be as logical, coherent, persuasive and self-contained as I can make it. Each is based on our research into the different strategic calculus of a major economic bloc. I shall argue for the economic dominance, by 2003, of North America, Greater Europe and East Asia respectively. We need scenarios because we do not know, as of now, which of the strategic calculi, utilized by each bloc, will prove the strongest and most effective.

However, the different strategies of the three blocs are connectable. Nay more, each is reconcilable with the other in a meta-model of world economic development. It follows that the most robust strategy for a multinational or global corporation is one that connects all three worlds, rather than isolates them, so that we can switch strategies as the scene shifts. This chapter will:

- describe three future worlds
- express their logics as a strategic calculus
- connect all three logics into a learning loop
- recommend a master-strategy for accelerated learning which could render all three of these futures survivable and profitable
- describe the dilemmas which will have to be recognized and fine-tuned in order for organizations to perform effectively
- show how these dilemmas are fine-tuned.

This chapter highlights the thirteen elements of the dilemmas constantly facing strategists and direction-givers in corporations and governments. Each needs resolutions at any one time *and* the mental flexibility to scan the changing external environment continuously to allow further evolution of each dilemma through the use of scenario construction.

Three reminders

There are three important principles underlying the rationale for scenario construction which are, in my experience, too often misunderstood:

1. Executives can rarely recognize meaningful patterns in the world unless they generate *models* of these patterns.
2. By definition, most scenarios will be wrong. The reason for having three sets of conjectures is that *only* then can we notice their refutations. Information is 'news of difference'. Without models of expectations, there are no differences.
3. It follows that we should not stake our company's future on any *one* preferred outcome. The point of scenarios is to survive and prosper across all potential futures, however foreign these might be. As we shall see, at least two of our three scenarios are very foreign.

Finally, all the facts underlying this chapter are taken from a book *The Seven Cultures of Capitalism*, written by the author and Fons Trompenaars. This chapter builds from the data within it.

The three scenarios are as follows:

I   The Triumph of Creativity: NAFTA Leads the North American Renaissance

II   Greater Europe Rebounds: The Rise of the Cooperative Era

III   Japan Rides the Chinese Tiger: How the Logic of Whole Systems Prevailed.

Describe three future worlds

I   The Triumph of Creativity: NAFTA Leads the North American Renaissance

It was inevitable, with hindsight, that the much-trumpeted decline of American and English-speaking economic power would prove alarmist. As Mark Twain is supposed to have said, 'the report of my death was an exaggeration'. What saved the United States was that the country turned its individualism into creativity and away from self-indulgence and voracious consumption. Rival economies in Europe and East Asia had been adept at catching up but, when they hit the front, there was no one left to emulate. They showed themselves incapable of leadership.

Indeed, the whole logic of catch-up capitalism as opposed to pioneer capitalism involves managers, the government, unions, academicians and industrial associations *agreeing* to create technologies and industries, *known* to work in Britain or the United States. With an assured outcome, cooperation develops along predictable parameters. But it all comes off the rails when there are no rails, i.e. no extant technology or industry to copy. When catch-up capitalism faces the unknown and unknowable, its alliances came unstuck. There is no transcendent aim or purpose. You cannot *invent* the future and know that every interest group will be taken care of, no matter how the cookie crumbles. Consensus needs fixed aims. Yet, by 2003, these had all been washed away. North America, used to wide-open frontiers and trackless wastes, was happy. Europe and East Asia clutched at imaginary certainties and found themselves clinging instead to wreckage in the flood.

Memories from the Second World War remained stubbornly enduring and it was North America and Britain that had emerged from the first half of the twentieth century with moral authority, further enhanced by the collapse of Communism in the late 1980s. As it turned out, neither

Germany nor Japan could succeed in creating a world order in which neighbouring nations had much confidence. China bitterly distrusted Japan and preferred to trade with the West. Germany was unable, because of its past, to play any major role in settling conflicts in the Balkans, the Middle East or the Russian Federation. East Asians in general, and Japan in particular, lacked any interest in or conception of a new world order to which nations might voluntarily adhere. Japan's skills of empathic communications and 'belly talk' was found to work only in the Japanese cultural context. Policy was made over the telephone to Tokyo at night. Luckless Western executives would arrive at their desks in the morning to find that all decisions had been made. They were outside the *ringi*.

But what finally ensured American hegemony was its native creativity, ingenuity and innovation. You can socialize risks, like the Japanese and Germans attempted to do, but only if those risks are calculable. You can go with the flow if you can find it. Only North Americans, aided by a rapidly industrializing Mexico and Latin America could create the fountain itself and genuinely originate. For example, who but the Americans could develop virtual reality until surgeons could work within a computerized replica of the human stomach as large as a closet? Three technologies which virtually guaranteed American dominance were superconductivity, biotechnology and nanotechnology, the engine of creation itself as Eric Drexler argued.

But it was in aerospace and communications that America's political power and high-tech creativity was best exemplified as an unbeatable combination. By 1998, Motorola had perfected its IRIDIUM system of low-flying satellites and mobile, battery-operated phones, able to communicate from any point on earth, person to person, person to thing, thing to thing. The first satellites were launched by The Great Wall of China Company using the Short March Rocket, the satirically named successor of the Great Leap Upwards. In creating the IRIDIUM Consortium, American political power had forged for itself an impregnable competitive position in telecommunications. This new world communications infrastructure went far beyond the scope of antitrust legislation. It was the age of world consortia and the only remaining superpower was not slow in ensuring its own leverage. Because of the cost and waste of duplicating satellites, no alternative system could compete.

Yet American corporations knew better than to imitate the Great Trusts of the late nineteenth century. Because the unit cost of communications fell with ever-wider use of the extra-terrestrial phone and, because as late as 1990, half the world's population still lived two hours from a terrestrial phone, the technology became a liberator. Anyone could talk to anyone untapped. The world's surviving dictatorships ran out of secret police. There was simply too much talk to intercept. Moreover, communications became a crucial thread in the tapestries of economic development. Few complained of the facilitation necessary to their own development. A 'Law of Accelerating Returns', first identified by the Santa Fé Institute, became the driving force behind this technology-of-takeoff. America had always led the world in business scholarship. While early attempts to generalize about business administration had sometimes proved untrue and unbeautiful, business studies came into their own when Americans began seriously to study different cultures of competitive advantage and chose the best from each nation. For example, the early Japanese advantage in quality, in manufacturing processes, in getting faster to market, in mass customization, in setting higher standards and empowering work teams were carefully studied and then exceeded. Americans were the world's prime codifiers. They could develop any advantage into a training programme, ere the bat squeaked thrice.

In the 1970s and 1980s, American corporations had suffered from innovating only at the level of products, not process. But once process innovation took hold, there was no stopping it. When, in 1999, President Gore unveiled the manufacturing Hall of Fame, the whole nation learned to extol its tiny minority of superskilled manufacturing workers who had won the world leagues, a more appropriate title than had once been reserved for the 'university' of baseball. Americans had only to define manufacturing as a game and fiercely competitive feats of excellence followed.

The Americans' traditional weakness had occurred when their products reached maturity and customers wanted hundreds of particular variations on a theme. Other nations, using American-licensed technologies and strong norms of reciprocity within communitarian cultures, produced re-engineered versions of American-originated products and appealed to nascent nationalism. Yet, as the century drew to a close, it appeared that America had learned. Easy licensing had given way to a fierce worldwide campaign for intellectual property rights. American lawyers were employable, after all. The world learned to pay its dues to entrepreneurialism. It had been the American century after all.

But it was the inclusion of women into the higher ranks of executives that contributed most to the mellowing of

American management and its new-found concern with the durability of relationships. When Japanese women began to volunteer in droves to work for US corporations, the success was complete.

Perhaps more than anything else, it had been the triumph of the market. No quicker signalling system, no automatic regulator of the tiniest detail, no commitment to a super-ordinate goal could prevail against market forces. Those with moral reservations about its workings simply slowed down their own adaption and suffered thereby. Those who embraced reality prospered.

One by one, the sandcastles crumbled before the incoming tide. Japanese rice was an early casualty, Japanese retailing and German coal mining casualties of the late 1990s. Even British believers in the power of speech could not talk the pound sterling into anything more than a blip on computer screens.

Speaking of the British, they were thankful to have stuck with the American capitalism and spurned the siren songs of Rhenish capitalism, wafting across the Channel from Europe. The really important memberships for Britain turned out to be those in the English-speaking world.

I hope that my first scenario has cheered the reader's sense of optimism and patriotism. I fear that my second and third scenarios will *not* do so. On the other hand, learning to meet these threats will be a greater challenge.

II   Greater Europe Rebounds: The Rise of the Cooperative Era

It was inevitable, with hindsight, that Greater Europe would at last come into its own. Had Germany not overtaken Britain by 1912, again by 1937 and a third time by 1953? Only wars of devastating destructiveness held the country back.

Early in this century, the great American psychologist, William James, had written that the world must now find its moral equivalent of war, something with the excitements and ideals of war, but without its destructiveness. Not surprisingly, this 'moral equivalence' has been seized upon much earlier by those who lost these wars rather than by those who won them. Both Germany and Japan have discovered that economic developments beat fighting. It is not clear that Britain and America have yet made that discovery. Beaten nations are allowed no other outlets for their energies. Winning nations have their time cut out assuming postures on the world stage—some of which they can't afford. No wonder, then, that the losers have developed economically faster than the winners. When the Germans hold up three fingers to Americans, they are not being triply obscene, they are reminding us that it now take three dollars or more to buy a Deutschmark, up from one dollar to the Deutschmark in 1948.

By 2003, Germany had planted Rhenish capitalism at the heart of Europe. Because those who lose wars do not talk as much or as loudly as those who win them, the whole idea of alternative capitalism did not emerge until the mid-1990s. In the case of Japan, the country had not simply lost a war but had strict rules against confrontation. It followed that, even as Germany and Japan prospered, Britain and America talked...and talked. To her dying day, Baroness Thatcher believed that the Iron Curtain had trembled and crashed at the sound of her voice. The truth was more mundane. West German affluence had relentlessly belied all Communist protestations of improvement. As those who personally fought in the Second World War had died off, the military victories were eclipsed by the economic defeats.

Greater Europe's chief claim to economic development arose from its institution building. The EEC had been built, brick by brick, into a social market that eventually embraced 292 million people, the largest market of properly educated and developed people on earth. In contrast, Japan was despised by the Chinese, the Koreans, the Malaysians, the Indonesians and the Taiwanese and, by 2003, had yet to apologize fully for its atrocities in China and the Pacific from 1935 to 1945. Its attempt to monopolize high-tech and cut every forest save its own caused bitter accusations of a new imperialism. East Asia preferred to trade with Europe rather than its ancient enemy. Unlike Europe, Japan had built no conflict-resolving institutions beyond its own shores.

The Social Charter, which Britain refused to sign until 1997, was the symbol and outrider of Rhenish capitalism. It was based on the conviction that disputes about wealth *distribution* had to cease in the interests of consensual wealth *creation*. A nation could not develop economically by taking from its workers or from its entrepreneurs. Once the issue of cheaper labour was laid to rest and removed from the political agenda, the signatories to the Social Charter could concentrate on the mass upgrading of employee skills, a process Germany had historically pioneered, through its meso-economic institutions, the economies of industry associations and clusters. If you couldn't make labour cheaper, you could make it more skilful and adept. In this way, the entire workforce marched as one to greater affluence. Work councils, co-determination and life-long training were simply the same pattern of European cooperatism at the level of the factory and the plant, as pertained at the level of the nation state and the European Parliament.

The success of Greater Europe coincided with what Robert Axelrod had once called 'The Evolution of Cooperation'. Once, wealth had been created largely by competing individuals. By the mid-twentieth century, the role of the corporation had been widely accepted (albeit with protest, see *The Organization Man*). By the late 1980s, Michael Porter was arguing that wealth was created by industry *clusters* with governments (perish the thought!) sometimes facilitating, as in the Swedish cluster of business serving the handicapped.

Now Germans had used clusters since 1871, when Bismark 'married' iron to rye and brought food to the new metal industries. In 1998, Europe, at Germany's instigation, copied an old practice of the German chemical industry. Cash prizes funded by the whole industry were given to inventors in lieu of patents. In return for sponsored creativity, innovations were disseminated after one or two years, as opposed to five to ten. The whole system of invention, dissemination and new invention was speeded up. The pause imposed by profit making via a temporary monopoly was greatly reduced.

Germany's intense social ways of conducting business were imitated throughout Europe, especially by the old Eastern bloc, who had found American capitalism too fierce and unsettling. American and Asian corporations now faced industry structures as dense and labyrinthine as the German forests, which Nietzsche had once compared to the German soul, with its secret hiding places and baffling complexities. Germans can be prickly people and difficult to know intimately but, once inside their reserve, you are a friend for life and relationships forged at some cost are not lightly abandoned.

What happened when American companies came calling was that they had to knock on the back doors of Siemens, Bosch and Daimler-Benz to offer their improved products, their faster times to markets and their lower defects per million. What they found was Nixdorf or other European rivals in the front room, discussing a partnership, joint venture and/or a bosom friendship that was already five years old, and ripening. Corporations weren't competing head to head like players in American football, they were connecting themselves semi-permanently to each other.

If Intel, AMD or Analog Devices proved that their products were better, that did not necessarily win the order. It simply raised the standards partners demanded of each other. Bosch would give Nixdorf several weeks to meet Intel's standards, yet the relationship would be preserved if possible. Americans who believed that the door should always be open and new deals never foreclosed found that doors were at least half-closed. A world of reciprocity was replacing a world of dealing.

Most especially, this was a long-term reaction to complexity which Germans and the French relish but which the English-speaking world distrusts as too 'deep' and 'intellectual'. The more complex products become, the more executives need to rely upon close relationships to process this complexity. For many years, Germany had been deliberately complexifying its products using EU standards committees to fix community industrial standards at a level Germany had just reached. Over 60 per cent of the EU's industrial standards committees were chaired by German engineers from 1990 on. Not surprisingly, community-wide standards for safety, the environment and quality in general get fixed at the standards which German had recently achieved, a process that cuts out several competitive offers but ensures a continuous upgrading.

Rhenish capitalism developed a bias in favour of engineering, manufacturing and production and a bias against large money markets and dominance by financial institutions. In Sweden, Holland, Germany, Belgium, France and Italy, the status of the engineer remained close to that of the *ingénieur*— the ingenious one—while America and Britain continued to worship the quick buck, money made in the shortest time possible by keyboard entrepreneurs and market makers. In contrast, Germany taught Europe to despise easy money. Haunted by its past inflations, Germany put its faith in education, machinery and lifetime partnerships whose value endured. While American personal consumption reached 70 per cent of GNP by 1997, Germany's remained below 50 per cent. Unlike America and Britain, both consumers were not devouring the industrial infrastructure by trying to earn as much as possible for the smallest contribution.

But it was European education which proved to be the coiled spring for its twenty-first-century triumph, well grounded in maths, science and modern languages. The level of learning in Eastern Europe was far ahead of its capacity for wealth creation. When wealth creation finally caught up, it did so with a vengeance. The cradle of civilization turned its mind to some of the finest products ever known.

In one sense, the Anglo-American apostles for market forces, the new Calvinist deity, with His impersonal face, were right. Markets ruled the world but in one fatal respect they were mistaken. While world market benchmarks had to be met and exceeded, this was *not* best achieved by those human behaviours most closely associated with marketplaces. Human relations in markets are fleeting. The information is typically abstract and 'this'. The ideal is the commodity. The winning edge is information *not* shared.

But successful industrial behaviours are precisely opposite. Human relations endure. Information is increasingly concrete, personal, 'thick' with descriptiveness and complex. The ideal is not the commodity but the uniquely valuable product, incomparable with others. The winning edge is information quickly volunteered and shared.

When Lloyd's of London appealed to the House of Lords against a billion-pound judgement handed down in 1997, the whole problem was symbolized by its plea. It argued that, while it had long called itself a society, it was really a market. As such, it owed no duty of care and attention to its 'names'. The cracked Lutine bell was tolling for the death of Anglo-American 'predatory' capitalism. In the same week, the national Education Association announced that 26 per cent of Americans were functionally illiterate, a huge growing underclass of losers were clinging to the immobilized legs of the American economy. The tourist industry had collapsed the year before, a victim of uncontrollable crime.

III   Japan Rides the Chinese Tiger: How the Logic of Whole Systems Prevailed

It was inevitable, with hindsight, that Japan overcame its temporary troubles of the early 1990s. The immediate cause was the breakneck speed of Chinese economic development, as the world's economic centre of gravity shifted massively to East Asia. A population of 1.2 billion people growing at 10-12 per cent per annum had changed everything by 2003. Japan had been strategizing to make China dependent upon it since the early 1960s. Second-hand Japanese cars shipped to China as they aged made the latter chronically dependent on spare parts. The pattern was repeated in technology after technology. The Japanese may not have been popular but they were necessary.

Japan's real competitive advantage came from the way the country thought, so different from the West but familiar to most of South-East Asia and to China from whom Japan had borrowed culturally. Japan thought in wholes, not in parts, hence its strategic thinking was inclusive, multidimensional, mutualist and aimed at elevating whole clusters of economic actors.

The difference began with the decision on what to make. Japan targeted all the meta-technologies (that is, the tools that make the tools), sometimes called horizontal technologies because hundreds of vertical technologies benefit from them. For example, Japan targeted numerically controlled machine tools on the grounds that these tooled whole factories. Industrial robots were targeted because they could change all manufacturing decisively. Japan targeted microchips, which they called 'the rice of industry', because these are the tiny brains of any original equipment that includes them. Metal ceramics were targeted and, behold, Japan's energy import bill had been halved by 1999, and solar glass and engines became major exports.

Mired in neo-classical economic theory, the Anglo-Saxons were still insisting that a million dollars' worth of microchips were no more valuable than a million dollars' worth of potato chips, thereby illustrating Oscar Wilde's adage that we know the price of everything and the value of nothing.

Unbelievably, mutterings about 'level playing fields' and 'picking winners' were still being heard in conferences on economics as late as 1997. When it finally dawned on the Anglo-Saxons that Japan and Europe had been picking *teachers*, technologies that taught industry how to upgrade itself, it was too late. Most advanced technology had slipped into the hands of competitors. The Japanese had calculated that the nation which makes the best semiconductors is almost bound to make the best original equipment containing semiconductors, leading to at least a thousand production lines. Moreover, those designing, manufacturing, distributing and consuming microprocessors, not to mention equipment guided by the chips, would be permanently educated by this experience. Potato chips, on the other hand, might ruin only your complexion.

The problem with economics is not so much that it is wrong but that it is self-fulfilling. By 2003, America was still selling Coke, fast food, under-arm deodorants and chewing gum. Japan was selling nearly all the world's fax machines, compact interactive disc players and home entertainment systems. The international balance of payments testified to the consequence of these choices.

Of course, Japan could simply win any technology it wanted by rendering the contest unprofitable. In 1985, RCA had sold its consumer electronics division to Philips because it could not make 15 per cent ROI. In 1995, Philips sold the same division to Toshiba because it could not make 7 per cent ROI. The idea that *each industrial unit* has to make a profit is

Western to the core. The Japanese believe that, if necessary, a supplier of semiconductors can *lose* money, provided the supplier of original equipment containing those chips *makes* money as a consequence.

Since the Japanese corporations are typically organized into *keiretsu* (consortia), who 'makes' money and who 'loses' money may be of academic interest only, provided the whole consortium prospers. It became impossible for even American lawyers, who outnumbered the Japanese profession fifty to one, to discover how much a particular Japanese corporation was making or losing. Mazda, for example, could show that it was making 15 per cent ROI but this was because other members of the Sumitomo *keiretsu* were supplying it at ludicrously low prices. When the Supreme Court ruled, in 1998, that internal *keiretsu* arrangements were irrelevant, by which they meant it was impossible to discover what they were up to, 500 suits against 'dumpers' had to be dropped. Now the Japanese could underprice with impunity and cross-subsidize aggressively. They took every meta-technology they wanted.

In fact, the four little tigers, plus China, Indonesia and Malaysia, had been running down goods of low knowledge intensity and targeting goods of higher knowledge from the early 1970s onwards. The more knowledge within goods, the higher the prices they would tend to fetch in a world market where knowledge was scarce. Moreover, a nation could only afford strong educational institutions if that education found its way into products. Countries where business had a cultural reputation for philistinism, i.e. Britain and America, found themselves disadvantaged.

Japanese corporations tended to win competitive contests for another reason having to do with holism. They fought less for profits than for market share. It followed from this that they would persevere with low prices, while the profit-seeking nations backed off. Market share measures what you put into a relationship. Profit measures what you take out. Those who put most in, stayed in. British, Americans and European countries began to retreat to small, profitable niche products but they had surrendered the strategic volume markets and could be picked off whenever the Japanese chose to do so. For, as in cars, the Japanese would eventually move upmarket, cross-subsidizing their expensive products with volume ones.

If Americans had thought German relationships were difficult to penetrate, that was because they had not fully encountered the reciprocities of East Asia, especially Japan. While Westerners calculate their profits, Japanese suppliers often threaten to make losses unless their partners rescue them from their own excesses of generosity. In a very real sense, it is the *relationship* that makes money in Japan, the partners joined rather than separated. It is not uncommon to serve someone at such high cost to yourself that, unless he or she doubles or trebles the order, you will be out of pocket. And, very frequently, the customer does double or treble it and so reciprocates the favour shown. This is not so much 'enlightened self-interest' as 'strategic benevolence'.

However, the effect was to keep Americans out of the more sophisticated Asian markets while Asians easily penetrated American ones. Americans faced Japanese partnerships in which each had 'saved' the other from loss at least a dozen times as reciprocal indulgence accelerated on each side. This induced an almost unbreakable trust which the Japanese showed to each other, but not to outsiders. You 'own' the identity of those you have saved.

As if this were not enough, the Japanese had developed (as early as 1980) the technique of Latent Need Analysis, which effectively binds them to suppliers and customers, long term, in a learning alliance. The customers were told about what the technology being supplied could accomplish, say, eight years from that day. Did the customers have a 'latent need' for this development? They usually did. So the Japanese locked their customers in, long term, using 'pull' strategies to get all promised resources to the future *rendezvous* where, for example, Proton, the Malaysian car maker, would launch the world's first ceramic engine, running at 300 miles to the gallon. The year was 2001 but, from 1993 onwards, only Japanese metals fabricators could get near Proton.

While much of the developing world went ape over cybernetic learning systems, even here the Japanese differed. While Americans were forever trying to correct 'defects', as if the word had been defined by John Calvin himself with the aid of Holy Writ, the Japanese would pounce on any deviation that satisfied the customer better than before. They went for deviance-amplifying feedback, not just deviance-correcting. Indeed, their marketing was like a speeded-up model of evolution. Hundreds of deviations were thrown against a tough environment and those who survived were followed up speedily, while the rest perished. They thus discovered what people wanted in half the time by making *more*, rather than fewer, mistakes.

In the meantime, neo-classical economics stuck grimly to its orthodoxies, looking for declining marginal utilities even while the information economy offered accelerating ones, reducing selling costs even as the Japanese gambled on reciprocity. By 1994, it was official. World economic development was inversely proportionate to the number of economists employed. There had to be something wrong with a discipline which had awarded nineteen of the last twenty-two Nobel Prizes, not simply to Americans but to the University of Chicago. In 1992 it had been pointed out that the rate of economic development correlated positively with the number of engineers but negatively with the number of MBAs (scant comfort for this author, who has a DBA as well).

But the final blow to Western aspirations came from the discovery that the Japanese were creating new products in record numbers, a skill they were supposed to lack. As early as 1985, they had twice America's annual number of recorded patents, yet Japanese creativity derived from a totally different mindset. It was planned for, not spontaneous. What they did was deliberately to cross-fertilize streams of knowledge where creative breakthroughs were most probable.

By 1995, there were over a thousand Institutes of Mechatronics in Japan. These were dedicated to the proposition that a large number of future processes in manufacturing and in final products would fuse electrical (or electronic) engineering with mechanical engineering. The Japanese approach to the bullet train was to push locomotive and aeronautical engineers into the same room to solve problems of high-speed vibration. The Seiko resonant quartz circuit was similarly created by jewellery: watch and quartz experts assembled in the same room, long term. Ironically, America did this in Operation Manhattan, which developed the atom bomb. Outside of defence emergencies, however, it is considered somehow indecent to force rapid development in this way. American creators sported themselves in bucolic surroundings and waited for inspiration to strike.

By analysing the customer's latent needs, Japanese companies could also cross-fertilize the developing knowledge of the customer with the developing knowledge of its own technologies. Breakthroughs were not the work of lone Western geniuses but co-created as a 'value-star' between company and client, with the value residing in the relationship itself which would be abandoned only in dire circumstances. America faced a world of closed circles of creativity which were loath to admit that country while the standards it set would be met, but by insiders.

Far too late, the Western economies finally went for industrial policy but, even then, they misunderstood. The sight of a British prime minister, Tony Blair, riding to the rescue of the Northampton boot and shoe industry was comical. We were now backing losers because they hurt. It was the old, old argument reborn. The boot and shoe makers should have been retrained a generation earlier to make more complex products.

Let us now take each scenario and apply our intellect to it.

Express their logics as a strategic calculus

We are now in a position to summarize our three scenarios according to the *strategic logics* which underlie these. Let us take these in turn.

I The Triumph of Creativity: NAFTA Leads the North American Renaissance

The strategy can be distilled as follows. By means of brilliant *innovation* and *designed strategy*, America used its *political leadership* to create an unassailable *competitive position*, while systematically raising *standards of quality* and *benchmarking*. By the careful *correction of defects*, it put all its faith into the *sovereignty of markets* or the customers' responses.

II Greater Europe Rebounds: The Rise of the Cooperative Era

This strategy starts two-thirds of the way through the American strategy before continuing into unfamiliar territory. By *systematically raising standards of quality* through European-wide committees and carefully *correcting defects*, Greater Europe creates an ever-wider social *market*, encourages *strategies to emerge* from worker and employee co-determination while idealizing a kind of *economic nationalism*, or Europeanism, to replace ancient enmities. In doing so, it builds European-wide *clusters of cooperating partners* to compete in skills, but not in lowered wages.

III Japan Rides the Chinese Tiger: How the Logic of Whole Systems Prevailed

The Japanese strategy starts about halfway through the German one but proceeds with further steps. By encouraging the *emergence of strategy* for middle managers and workers and setting out to substitute *economic nationalism* for war, the Japanese obligate each other by mutual dependence to form tight *clusters of cooperating partners*, whose *latent needs* they explore, pouncing on any *positive deviance* in products and *amplifying* this while plotting *converging paths* with their customers towards a *future rendezvous*, which shuts out rivals yet generates creative *innovation* by deliberately cross-fertilizing promising streams of knowledge.

We should note at this point that all the thirteen strategic elements are stressed by well-known writers and business academics.

1. The idea that *strategy is designed* at the top of the corporation has been the standard Harvard Business School position since the 1960s as propounded by Kenneth Andrews (1980) in *The Concept of Corporate Strategy*).
2. The motion of strategy as an act of *political* leadership is identified with writers such as Andrew Pettigrew (1985) and Andrew Kakabadse, *et al.* (1988).
3. The concept of building a *competitive position* is from books by Michael Porter (1980).
4. The relentless escalation of *standards* is as old as Frederick Winslow Taylor (1947) with *quality* components coming from W. Edwards Deming (1982) and Joseph Juran (1974) and *benchmarking* from Michael Hammer (1993).
5. *Error correction* is also at the heart of Deming's approach and has more recently been popularized by Peter Senge (1980) and the System Dynamics Group.
6. The idea of *sovereign markets* as the *sole* arbiter's value is as old as Adam Smith with the torch now carried by Milton Friedman (1981) and many others.
7. That strategy *emerges* from spontaneous attempts by the grassroots of the company to cope with customers' demands is the position of Henry Mintzberg (1990).
8. The role played by *economic nationalism*, especially in Japan, is described by Akio Morita (1986), Chalmers Johnson (1982), Ezra Vogel (1985) and, in Germany, Janice McCormick (1988).
9. The *clusters of cooperating partners* are described by Michael Porter (1990), James Abegglen and George Stalk (1985) and Clyde V. Prestowitz (1989).
10. The *mutual indulgence of latent needs* is described by Takeo Doi (1976) and Robert M. March (1988).
11. *Amplifying positive deviances* in Japanese-style management is explained by Magorah Maruyama (1994).
12. The 'pulling' of converging strategies towards a future *rendezvous* is described by Fons Trompenaars (1993) and by Charles Hampden-Turner and Trompenaars (1994).
13. The *co-created value star* is from the work of Richard Normann and Ray Ramirez (1993).

The fact that many of these academics attack each other rather than trying to reconcile their positions is a good description of the problem of economic growth in English-speaking democracies.

Connect all three logics into a learning loop   Is it possible to connect these three logics? I believe it is. Figures 8.1 and 8.2 are strategy cycles or learning loops, with twelve elements and one in the middle to mediate.

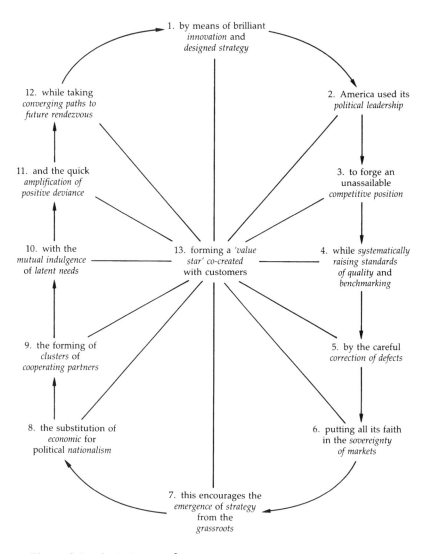

1. by means of brilliant *innovation* and *designed strategy*

12. while taking *converging paths to future rendezvous*

2. America used its *political leadership*

11. and the quick *amplification of positive deviance*

3. to forge an unassailable *competitive position*

10. with the *mutual indulgence* of *latent needs*

13. forming a *'value star'* co-created with customers

4. while *systematically raising standards of quality* and *benchmarking*

9. the forming of *clusters* of *cooperating partners*

5. by the careful *correction of defects*

8. the substitution of *economic* for political *nationalism*

6. putting all its faith in the *sovereignty of markets*

7. this encourages the *emergence* of strategy from the *grassroots*

Figure 8.1   A strategy cycle

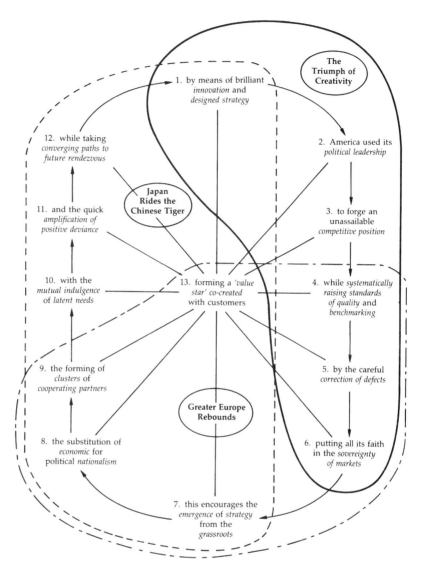

Figure 8.2 A strategy cycle

The American Triumph of Creativity emphasizes elements of the circle 1 to 6. The Greater Europe Rebounds strategy emphasizes elements 4 to 9. Japan Rides the Chinese Tiger emphasizes elements 7 to 12, 1 and 13. All are linked together in the larger strategy cycle.

The origins of these various emphases are the *national cultures* of the blocs involved. As Hampden-Turner and Trompenaars show in *The Seven Cultures of Capitalism*, Americans and English speakers generally like to:

- Use codified and universalized approaches, i.e. spell out strategy
- Analyse in preference to synthesize, i.e. go for specific numerical targets
- Be individualistic rather than communitarian, i.e. conceive of the corporation as a competing unit
- Be inner-directed rather than outer-directed, i.e. pay more attention to one's own strategic calculations than to environmental demands and shifts
- Have a sequential attitude to time, i.e. do things as quickly as possible
- Achieve rather than attribute status to people, projects, etc., i.e. go with 'success' and not question its inherent value.

Our discovery that the United States scored very high on these six characteristics led us to attribute the first six elements of the strategic cycle to the United States, the UK, Canada, Australia, etc. German holism, communitarianism and rigorous adherence to standards led us to attribute elements 4 to 9 to a German-dominated Europe while Japanese particularism, holism, communitarianism, outer-directed and synchronous attitudes to time led us to attribute elements 7 to 13 to Japanese-dominated East Asia.

Recommend a master strategy for accelerated learning which could render all these futures survivable and profitable

A robust strategy capable of meeting the challenges of NAFTA, Greater Europe and Japan-rampant-upon-China is indicated by the *whole* strategic cycle, most especially the *value star* in the centre, *co-created* between economic partners. All elements must be held in a vital balance. Only then will the learning cycle revolve swiftly, developing each of its elements in the process.

The faster this circle revolves, the more accelerated is the learning of the corporation. It is not a question of strengthening one's competitive position *or* cooperating within clusters but of cooperating so effectively *that* one's competitive position is enhanced, while competing so well that would-be allies seek to cluster around you. It is not a question of correcting defects or amplifying deviances but of asking yourself every time a deviation occurs, 'Is this "mistake" fortunate or unfortunate for my customer? Should I repeat it, or eliminate it?'

Indeed, it could help us to regard this strategic cycle as a *helix* which 'spirals upward' with more cleverly designed strategies created from more emergent initiatives at the grassroots, more political power which is increasingly sensitive to the levers of national economic power, and so on. In the words of Arie de Geus (1988), we should plan or strategize *in order to learn* or, as Don Michael (1973) put it over twenty years ago, we should 'learn to plan and plan to learn' in an endlessly iterative process.

Describe the dilemmas which will have to be reconciled in order for your organization to perform effectively

All elements *opposite* to each other on the strategic cycle may be regarded as dilemmas so there is very real tension between.

1. *Innovation* and *designed* versus 7. *Emergent strategy* from
   strategy (top-down)   the *grassroots*
                                            (bottom-up)
2. *Political leadership* and versus 8. Emphasis on *economic*
   nationalism   *nationalism*
3. Forging an unassailable versus 9. Forming *clusters of*
   competitive position   *cooperating partners*
4. *Systematically raising* versus 10. *Mutual indulgence* of
   quality standards and   *latent needs*
   benchmarks
5. *Correcting defects* from versus 11. *Amplifying* positive
   our expectations   *deviations* and *useful*
                                            exceptions
6 Celebrating the   versus 12. *Converging* towards
   sovereignty of *markets*   *future rendezvous*
   (short term)   (long term)

We will consider the visuo-spatial structure of *all* our dilemmas before continuing to consider each one. Instead of a dilemma having two 'horns', we will represent this as twin axes of a dual-axis diagram as in Figure 8.3. For each of the six dilemmas.

- The vertical axis may dominate and prove top-heavy, 9/1
- The horizontal axis may dominate and prove lop-sided, 1/9
- There may be a stand-off, 5/5
- There may be a vicious circle between the two principles (adversary)
- Or there may be synergy or a virtuous circle, 9/9.

There is no automatic progress towards synergy. New concepts, metaphors or creations must be devised in order to achieve reconciliation. Learning is not simply *vertical* thinking, as when 1, 2, 3, 4 and 5 on the circle follow upon each other, but also *lateral* thinking, as when 1 and 7, 2 and 8, 3 and 9, etc.

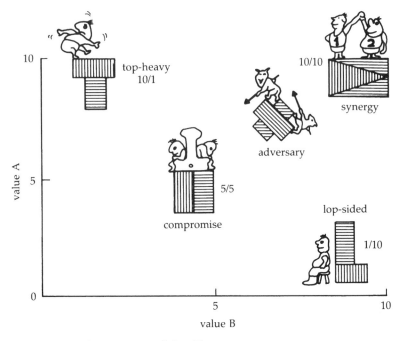

Figure 8.3   The structure of the dilemmas

achieve better resolutions. Lateral thinking is a response to vexing issues and stubborn dilemmas (see Edward De Bono, 1992).

Show how these dilemmas are fine-tuned

Dilemma 1-7

Innovation and *designed* versus *Emergent* strategy from the *strategy* (top-down)   *grassroots* (bottom-up)

The problems of designing strategy at the top of the organization and then hoping 'they' will implement it are notorious. The strategy so created, however abstractedly clever or artful, may not fit the culture of the corporation, may not be acceptable to customers, may be seen as representing an imposition from above and so attack the scope for discretion which working managers previously enjoyed, and may create an invidious distinction between those who think and those who do, which is unflattering to the latter group.

In an environment changing so quickly, the notion of a strategy set by one level of management but implemented by another, months or years after, could prove slow and cumbersome.

I have called the belief that top management can 'know' what strategy is right, the dogma of immaculate perception. Equally perilous, however, is the belief that *only* those eyeball to eyeball with customers know what it's all about. I call this 'strategy-on-the-hoof' (Figure 8.4(a)).

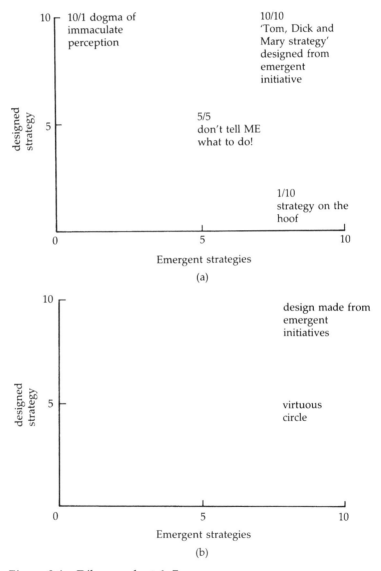

Figure 8.4   Dilemma chart 1–7

The stand-off and adversary position entails 'Don't tell ME what to do!' at levels of smouldering anger (5/5) or inflammatory (8/8), but the synergistic resolution (10/10) is more complex. Here strategy is designed by top management *out of* the emergent achievements and strategies of the grassroots. The Tom, Dick and Mary strategy is so called because those three persons already achieved it and top management has elevated their achievements to the status of a general policy for others to follow. Instead of designing with ideas read about in the *Harvard Business Review*, top managers design with the extant initiatives of their own subordinates, distinguishing between the one-off success that has no relevance for others and the indicative successes which hold lessons for everyone. The virtuous circle starts at the bottom with the emerging achievements and then feeds around:

Top managers reward and embody these
into an overall *strategic design*
which facilitates . . .

The viable *strategies* which *emerge* from
the grassroots as successful ways
of coping . . .

Note that top management neither tells the grassroots nor drops the reins of governance but manages *the process by which* information on successful initiatives is discovered, circulated and organized into meaningful patterns. The process appears as in Figure 8.4(b).

Dilemma 2-8	*Political leadership and* nationalism	versus	*Emphasis on economic nationalism*

Of the two forms of nationalism—political and economic—both are prone to excess. The American view appears to be that the government can interface only if the goal is sufficiently noble and elevated. 'Atoms for Peace', space exploration (*literally* out of this world) and defending against Communism are all goals *so* superordinate as to justify government initiatives. These initiatives are *not* primarily aimed at the economy yet have historically impacted on it via defence and space expenditure and nuclear power programmes. Yet the drain on the economy of making weapons whose ostensible 'purpose' is that they not be used is increasingly unaffordable. With the end of the cold war, we are fresh out of excuses to support high-tech.

If, on the other hand, you seek cultural self-expression through *economic* nationalism, the preferred route of Japan, France and Germany, you are in danger of ending up with the command economies which failed so disastrously in Eastern Europe, or a neo-mercantilism harking back to Colbertism. Nuclear, defence and aerospace spending in Western democracies have included all the notorious political misjudgements we associate with the public sector.

One reason the dilemma between political and economic nationalisms *must* be resolved is that relative rates of economic development are now the only remaining way that nations can legitimately rise or fall in global influence. One reason for the wide unpopularity of politicians is that they seem quite incapable of understanding, much less delivering, economic growth. The dilemma for the corporation operating in the modern environment appears as in Figure 8.5(a). Here we see that government as defender and referee of free enterprise gives too little attention to the economy and leaves politicians helpless to sustain economic development. Reducing regulation leaves them with even less influence. Yet worse effects arise from governments taking charge and giving us the full benefits of their inexperience. Modern economies are now *so* complex that attempts to 'command' them are absurd and catastrophic.

The resolution borrows from the same dynamic described in Figure 8.4(b). The government's key role is not to *impose* a national strategy but to elicit these from various key industries, listen and learn from these industries, remove obstacles from their path, coach, symbolize and celebrate their enhanced performance and generally preside over the 'developmental state' which has economic development in *chosen* fields as its main focus. Choosing is not commanding but choosing, from *among* viable strategies, those most conducive to the health, wealth and welfare of the nation. Once again, the virtuous circle reads from the bottom up:

Its skill at political leadership
of wealth creation is greatly enhanced

Because the government listens,
coaches and facilitates the
national economy

The reason governments must do this is that there is no one else who represents the economy as a whole, who is in a position to consider the synergy arising from two or more

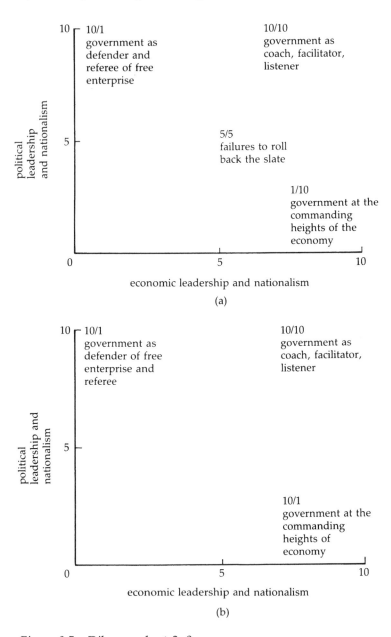

Figure 8.5　Dilemma chart 2–8

industrial initiatives which reinforce each other. Government does not *know* better, but sets out to *learn*, through a helical process (Figure 8.5(b)). For the distinction between the government as coach and as referee, I am indebted to Bruce Scott (1985).

Dilemma 3-9   Forging an unassailable   versus   Forming *clusters* of
                       competitive position   *cooperating partners*

Should a corporation go flat out to enhance its competitive position, as Michael Porter (1980) suggests? This includes enhancing its power over retailers or suppliers, gaining a large market share and attacking those trying to enter, achieving a superior technological edge and/or privileged access to scarce resources. According to this view, the corporation has an adversarial stance *vis-à-vis* most other economic actors. To cooperate extensively with other economic units will lead inexorably to *collusion*, that is, to companies ganging up on some third party, typically the consumer. The only route to ever higher quality and ever lowered costs is competitiveness and *more* competitiveness. This is the emphatic position of Anglo-American-type capitalism in which serving the consumer is essentially the by-product of competitive rivalry in which self-interest is the key.

The other side of the dilemma argues that it is the cooperative aspects of the European Union, of the Japanese *keiretsu*, or consortium of companies, that is the real key to economic strength. Moreover, it is the *cluster* of companies in an industry, not single competitors, which are the genuine sources of economic advantage at the industry level. A group of companies playing as a team, feeding resources to whomsoever confronts foreign competition, is bound to get the better of solo players. The problem with too many competitive and adversarial relationships is high transaction costs involved in opportunistic behaviours, exploitative manipulations and hidden or distorted information. Consumers are *supposed* to be your allies but all too often they are treated as adversaries, too, to be bombarded with blandishments. 'You can fool some of the people some of the time ...' .

The dilemma appears in Figure 8.6(a). Caught between pressures to compete more ferociously and find a business with more profit for less work, many industries opt for the compromise 'limited competition' (5/5), or 'all for a quiet life'. No plots are required. The agreement is tacit. 'I'll take it easy if you will.' In fact, the whole system is inherently unstable. If you compete hard enough to put rivals out of business, limiting competition and colluding with the remaining players becomes that much easier! Upset by price wars, whole industries seek more comfortable arrangements and performance suffers.

Is it possible to reconcile these conflicts and create a synergy of 'cooperative competing'? It is possible but you need to be

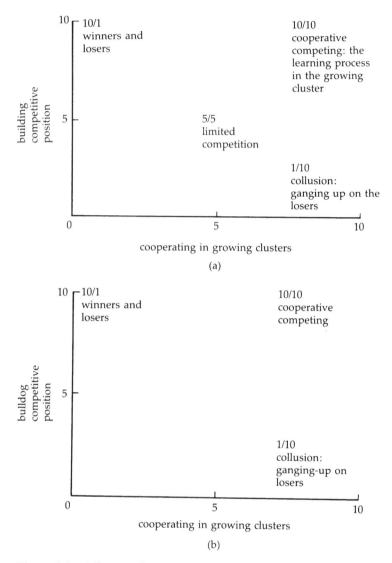

Figure 8.6   Dilemma chart 3–9

absolutely clear as to what you are aiming for and how these values can be fine-tuned and what the learning process which combines these values looks like.

When we compete, we *differentiate* products, people and performances. We see them in contrast with each other, the better and the worse, sometimes on several dimensions. When we cooperate, we communicate and transfer these contrasts, so that others learn what is best as 'winners', teach 'losers' how they won but, of course, the fortunes of the 'losers' are thereby transformed. All life and learning requires differentiation and integration. When we compete, we differentiate ourselves. When we cooperate, we re-integrate ourselves.

When we have a competitor 'on the ropes' we might be wise to stop and 'not break another man's rice bowl' as Akio Morita (1986) has put it. If we stop, we *maintain* fourteen competitive organizations in the Japanese forklift truck industry. If we insist on 'winning', there will soon be an oligopoly with all its attendant problems. You compete more by cooperating more, *not* by pushing competitiveness to its logical conclusion. Again, we have a virtuous circle, starting at the top:

> Fierce competition between numerous
> rivals creates vitally
> important contrasts
>
> which, communicated cooperatively,
> benefit the whole industry
> cluster by . . .

While cooperating and competing need 'fine-tuning', we should be clear where the major deficit lies. Japanese and German industry are far more cooperative than Anglo-American industry with, in the case of Germany, powerful meso-economic industry associations that train workers, raise skills and transfer technology. The process is helical as before (Figure 8.6(b)).

Dilemma 4	*Systematically raising* versus *Mutual indulgence* of *quality standards* and *latent needs* *benchmarking*	

With the advent of Taylorism as a serious movement in the 1920s and the founding of the Harvard Business School, the American economy embarked upon a sustained effort to define standards, if possible numerically, and raise them systematically. Instead of competing with other companies who may be comparatively slow in their ways of working, it became possible to race against the clock or against ideals. Faster was better than slower, fewer defects were better than more and surpassing standards was better than falling below them. It remained only to make rewards and incentives, commensurate with benchmarks achieved. The company with the highest standards would win in any contest of comparative excellence. It was as simple as that.

But, of course, it never *is* that simple. The customer is not in a perpetual state of non-affiliation, choosing who will supply him or her on rational criteria. The customer has *particular* needs, not standard needs, and has *latent* needs for products and services still in the stage of development, but likely to be crucially important, one to ten years from now. As we saw in our scenarios, it is difficult to make a sales pitch based on higher standards to a customer *already* 'in bed' with a rival and having mutual needs indulged. All that is likely to happen is that your sales target turns to his or her regular supplier and demands the same quality and prices as you are offering. The customer will not risk breaking up a close partnership.

My reference to 'indulgence' is not ribald and not intended as an erotic metaphor. The Japanese term *amae* roughly translates as 'indulgent love' or caring that is above and beyond contractual obligations. The idea is to do 'too much' for your customer, who then indulges you in return. This entails the *actual risk of making losses* unless the indulgence is returned by, say, increasing the size of the order. Trust is engendered by 'the anatomy of dependence' as Takeo Doi (1976) has called it. A depends on B to rescue him from 'excessive' generosity. B then depends on A to do the same and a spiral of escalating mutuality results. So close and intense do such relationships become that an outsider with 'higher' standards is likely to be rebuffed and only his or her performance, not the product, accepted.

Of course, close relationships that *ignore* steadily rising standards are going to prove disastrous, a *folie à deux* but, in practice, partners who rely upon each other have the right to ask and to receive service equal or better than the best available on the open market. There is a risk of 'getting too cosy' but no reason to suppose that closeness is fatal. The dilemma appears as in Figure 8.7(a).

It may be of no use to have 'ever-improving numbers' if you have to knock on the back door while your competitor is deeply engaged with your would-be customer in the front parlour. It may be no use indulging close friendships and mutual needs if the wider market and its ever-rising standards are passing you by. Nor is it any use sacrificing friends to standards or standards to friends in some wretched compromise.

The synergy of our two principles of strategy involves *starting* with latent needs, that is, several years before the product is even developed and subsequently basing your standards, not on some pseudo-universal but *on the level of performance that the customer requires*, so that needs grow *into* standards over time. This is a social market rather than the marketplace enshrined in neo-classical economics, because

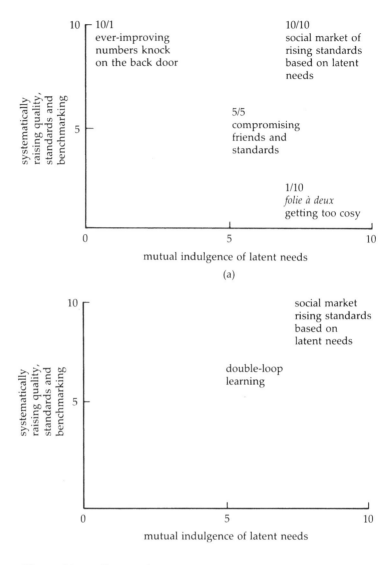

Figure 8.7 Dilemma chart 4–10

intimate relationships are attempting to outperform marketplace behaviours, which they will usually succeed in doing because close and trusting relationships can better handle complexity, as we argued earlier.

The process of eliciting the customer's latent needs, holding the customer close to you in a relationship of several years' duration, and systematically raising the standards of your service on mutually agreed criteria, forms a virtuous circle, starting at the bottom:

becomes the basis of ever-rising
standards that equal or beat
the marketplace, so that...

by eliciting the latent needs of
the customer, the product is developed in
secret mutuality and...

In a world where customers are becoming more and more diverse, particular and unique, the idea of 'the highest standards' as an abstraction of universal meaningfulness may now be questionable. Standards depend upon what the customer wants and he or she might want something different from 'the standard' as the supplier conceives it. When Chris Argyris and Donald Schon call for double-loop learning, they are saying, in effect, that fallible human needs must learn from standards, but *fallible human standards must also learn from newly emerging needs*. We can illustrate this in Figure 8.7(b).

Dilemma 5-11   *Correcting defects*   versus   *Amplifying positive deviations*
                          from our expectations   and useful *exceptions*

In his famous essay, 'The effect of conscious purpose on human adaptation', Gregory Bateson (1975) argues that one of the major problems in life is that our 'willpower' fulfils itself but then the consequences are catastrophic for us, ecologically and psychologically. Most Western cybernetics are based on the 'helmsman' (Kubernetes) having his way. He steers to starboard, the wind blows him slightly off course. He corrects. Unquestioned is the belief that *he or we should have our way*. Hovering like a shadow behind our helmsman is the 'scientific' idea that prediction and control is the basis of sound knowledge. But *is* it?

Does not the customer have a 'strategy' and a 'conscious purpose' and why do we feel that our own strategy needs to prevail? If it is *learning* we seek to increase, then two sides of a dilemma need to be entertained simultaneously. There is a 'defect' that needs 'correcting', i.e. something we did not expect. And there is a 'deviance' that needs 'amplifying' because *what we did not expect was superior in the customer's eye to what we intended*. It was Churchill who remarked, 'we keep stumbling up and hurrying along as if nothing had happened'. If learning is our aim, then being *surprised* rather than being confirmed in our original purposes is the greater teacher. The dilemma appears as in Figure 8.8(a).

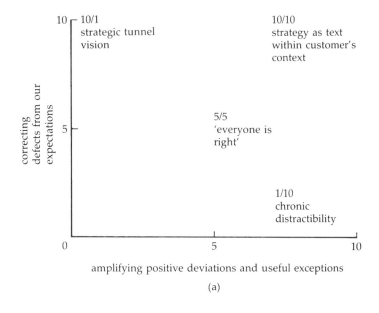

(a)

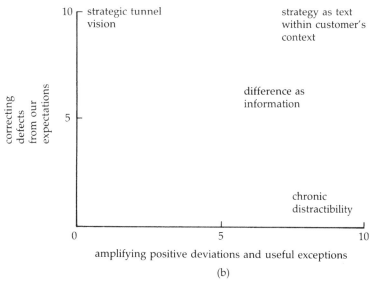

(b)

Figure 8.8 Dilemma chart 5–11

Of course, both values can be pushed too far. If every difference from what we expected is an 'error', we suffer strategic tunnel vision but, if every customer request is allowed to interrupt our concentration, we suffer chronic distractibility. We try to please everyone and satisfy no one and dilute our core competence. Yet there is no doubt in which direction the English-speaking economies tend to err. We are preponderantly inner-directed, wanting *our* strategy to prevail and insisting that strategy is singular, a formula that deals with allcomers and which serves customers in general.

The Japanese and Germans do not speak much of strategy as a winning formula because, for them, the *customer provides the context into which the strategic text must fit*. If you are making dough-kneading machines for large bakeries, then that bakery is the strategic context. You either advance the strategy of *that customer* or you fail. You can, of course, have a strategy of your own but this can never be more than the text within the context, the means to a larger end. It is not just you who must 'get his way', but the customer and 'your way' is a derivative of his, part of a larger whole. The virtuous circle below is entered from the bottom:

> ...*corrected*, depending upon the customer's larger context

> Any deviance from our expectations should be *amplified* or ...

The importance to Japanese culture of unforeseen deviance amplification is stressed by Magorah Maruyama (1982) who called it 'the second cybernetic revolution'. Because of the influence of Shinto religion, it comes naturally to Japanese executives to see themselves as only a part of more powerful natural forces in the universe. To be swept up in the customer's larger context is a matter of virtue and of piety. The Japanese and most East Asians are outer-directed and proud of it.

If we seek to learn fast, we need to correct our errors *and* re-conceive our entire strategy in the light of the customer's orientation. The process is helical (Figure 8.8(b)).

The important point to remember is that *information is news of differences*. We should not evaluate differences as positive or negative until we have thoroughly appreciated the customer's context of operations.

Dilemma 6-12	Celebrating the *sovereignty of markets* (short term)	versus	*Converging* towards *future rendezvous* (long term)

There are two views about how the business environment should be engaged. These are oriented respectively to the short term and the long term. Those who celebrate the *sovereignty of markets* believe the market to be a machine—the market mechanism—that automatically signals prices, which are the intersections of supply and demand curves. Ideally, no one controls the amount supplied or demanded. These are mass aggregates and, as such, impartial, impersonal, objective and arguably 'democratic' in the sense of being the sum of many inputs.

It follows that, the faster a corporation responds to the market, the more it gets its costs down. The more respectful it is towards 'market forces', the better its chance of survival and prosperity.

You cannot 'beat the market' in the sense of fixing prices and restraining trade. Those who try will simply fall behind sheltered by protectionist measures from the full rigours of having to compete or go under. Protect steel, for example, and slap a tariff on imports and *everything made from steel* will carry that surcharge. Control rents, and rental housing disappears. It is not worth the owner's time to make it available. Markets have almost god-like properties to many of their proponents and behave like Moby Dick, the Great White Whale in Melville's story. They do no one harm until you try to fight them! Then convulsions and the thrashing begin and whole enterprises are ruined.

But the notion that you cannot 'interfere' with markets is more superstition than fact. Markets are not given but made by our own offerings. Those who only 'respond' to a force already there may be doing too little, too late. Equally suspect is the Anglo-American idea of the market as a machine. The danger here is of idolatry, an image stripped of human endowments:

> Mouths they have but speak not.
> Eyes have they that see not . . .

There is also a whole host of interventions *consistent with the way markets operate*, ways of going with the market, not *against* it.

Among such 'market-augmenting' activities are plans to cross-fertilize two converging lines of products to create a future synthesis and rendezvous over the long term. In no sense does this go against market. Rather, it anticipates some of their known dynamics.

We know, for example, that higher prices are paid for premium products and that, if these are filled with rare knowledge, then the number of companies that can compete with us are fewer because that knowledge is scarce. We also know that the price a component fetches on the market is not its sole value. It may make a second, third, fourth and nth product more valuable still. Hence an industrial robot has a value to the manufacturer who pays for it but it also adds value to everything it is subsequently used to manufacture. A semiconductor has a market value but this value is more than the price paid by the original equipment manufacturer, who may rely on this product to make a whole variety of original equipment more useful and valuable to customers. A break-through in microprocessor technology may make possible products not previously practicable. Value then is *not* simply a price statistic but *an element capable of new creative combinations*.

Now, laying long-term plans to have two streams of knowledge or technology converge at some future time is not risk-free. A completely different solution to the same problem, using different knowledge streams, may beat you to it. Your relationship to your partner could turn out to be a blind alley, not the breakthrough path which you both hoped for. The dilemma appears as in Figure 8.9(a).

To enter into a partnership *may* be motivated by a wish to limit competition in your industry, i.e. to weaken the market mechanism. A company with which you are hatching schemes is less likely to take you on but this only succeeds in compromising both values or sides of the dilemma.

How, then, do we get to synergy between the short-term need to respond to markets and the long-term necessity to cross-fertilize our competencies with those of partners? How do we reach the goal of creating combinational value? Consider a specific example. A car manufacturer joins forces with a supplier of auto-electronic components with the aim of giving a diesel engine the same performance as a petrol engine, together with the near-certainty of not bursting into flames on impact, partly because diesel oil is less combustible and partly because firefighting foam automatically smothers all ignitable elements in the event of a collision.

Now, both the engine and the electronic components sell on the open market in the short term at reasonable prices. They are able to cope with market forces as separate products but their *combinational value*—a fireproof, high-performing diesel engine car—is worth *much* more than the two products in isolation. This is especially true when the government decides to put a lower tax on diesel and when insurers lower the premium for diesel cars. But the combinational value does not occur by chance. Two partners develop their engines and electronics over five years to make it happen, perhaps encouraged by government and the insurance industry.

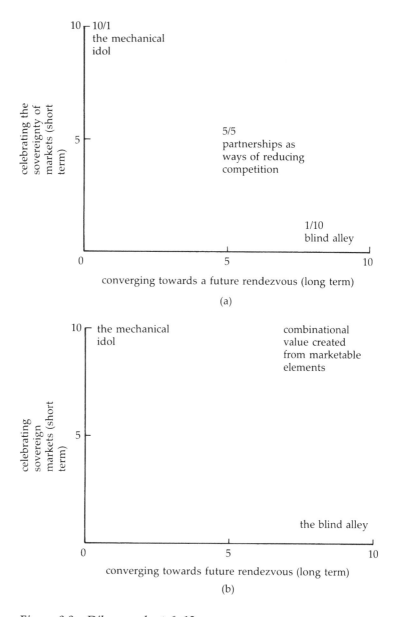

Figure 8.9   Dilemma chart 6–12

What is it worth to a nation *not* to have 3000 people horribly burned per annum? Everyone who stands to gain by this should be prepared to contribute to a values combination. The virtuous circle reads as follows, starting from the bottom:

> ...as well as ensuring their short-term
> marketplace prices as separate elements

By having two viable products converge at
a future rendezvous, you get their
combination long-term value.

This virtuous circle goes a long way in explaining the fierce
competitive momentum building in East Asia, starting with
Japan and now evidenced among the overseas Chinese in
Hong Kong, Singapore and Taiwan, in South Korea, Malaysia
and much of Indonesia. Almost without exception, these
countries think synchronously or convergently about time and
most target products with multiple uses and combinations.

For while the long term *includes* the short term, since new
combinations consist of products and components with their
own immediate markets, the short term too often *excludes* the
long term as we react but do not build. The dilemma is
reconciled by a helical process (Figure 8.9(b)).

Towards a new creativity

Going for combinational value is a lower-risk strategy than
inventing or creating from scratch, since the elements you are
trying to combine have value in themselves and are saleable
even if their combination does not work. You are taking two
known market values and attempting to create a third
unknown but, potentially, greater value, which if realized
would increase demand for the separate components as well!

Moreover, the shared excitement of this co-creativity shuts
you away from competitors trying to sell to your partner.
They are unlikely to have anything which engages your
partner so deeply and in which he or she has invested as much
time and energy. This raises the issue as to whether the
Japanese may not have developed a 'creativity equivalent' by
their capacity to spot promising convergences between
different streams of knowledge. Is it not predictable that
industrial robots will cross-fertilize with manufacturing
processes, that electronics will monitor and improve mechanical engineering, that photovoltaic cells will augment consumer electronics, that metal ceramics will conserve heat and
revolutionize engine efficiency? They appear to be deliberately
bringing these technologies together in purpose-made, cross-
disciplinary institutes. For the Japanese, creativity is the
deliberate fusion of social, technological and informational
forces. It may be insufficient to win Nobel Prizes but it could
keep them ahead in business innovation.

Towards the value star

We come finally to element 13 in the centre of our circular strategy cycle (see Figures 8.1 and 8.2). Richard Normann and Ray Ramirez speak of the need to co-create a value star with customers. We have seen that all our six dilemmas have had to be negotiated, the strategy designed from emergent initiatives, the government coaching key industries, the process of cooperative competing, the social market of rising standards based on latent needs, the text within the context, the combinational value formed from marketable elements. All are the products of dialogue, the fruits of protracted negotiation, the potential points of a 'star' that includes them all and is *more* valuable than the separated parts. For the ultimate container of what we have to learn is not simply our individual minds but our shared culture, relationships, memories, understandings and networks. Not just organizations, but the interstices between them, carry our learnings and pass this on.

This is the challenge for our direction-givers, both governmental and corporate, to take up so that we can create the virtuous circles of learning in the twenty-first century.

References

Abegglen, J. and Stalk, G. (1985) *Kaistia: The Japanese Corporation*, New York: Basic books.

Andrews, K. (1980) *The Concept of Corporate Strategy*, Homewood, IL: R. D. Irwin.

Bateson, G. (1975) 'The effect of conscious purpose on human adaptation' in *Steps to an Ecology of Mind*, New York: Ballantine.

De Bono, E. (1982) *Water Logic*, London: Penguin.

De Geus, A. (1988) 'Planning as learning', *Harvard Business Review*, March-April.

Deming, E. W. (1982) *Quality, Production and Competitive Position*, Cambridge MA: MIT Press.

Doi, T. (1976) *The Anatomy of Dependence*, New York: Kondamshi/ Harper.

Friedman, M. and Friedman, R. (1981) *Free to Choose*, New York: Avon.

Hammer, M (1993) 'Re-engineering work — don't automate, obliterate' in *The information Infrastructure, Harvard Business Review*.

Hampden-Turner, C. and Trompenaars, F. (1994) *The Seven Cultures of Capitalism*, London: Piatkus.

Johnson, C. (1982) *MITI and the Japanese Miracle*, Stanford University Press.

Juran, J., *et al.* (1974) *Quality Control Handbook*, New York: McGraw-Hill.

Kakabadse, A., *et al.* (1988) *Working in Organizations*, London: Penguin.

March, R. M. (1988) *The Japanese Negotiator*, Tokyo/New York: Kondamski.

Maruyama, M. (1994) *Mindscapes of Management*.

McCormick, J. (1988) 'Ideological divisions and global reality' in Lodge, G. C. and Vogel, E. F. (eds) *Ideology and National Competitiveness*, Boston, MA: Harvard Business School Press.

Michael, D. (1973) *On Learning to Plan and Planning to Learn*, San Francisco, CA: Jossey-Bass.

Mintzberg, H. and Quinn, J. B. (eds) (1990) *The Strategy Process: Concepts, Context, Cases*, London: Prentice-Hall International.

Muruyama, M. (1982) 'The second cybernetics: deviation amplifying mutual causal processes', *American Scientist*, **51**, 67–79.

Pettigrew, A. (1985) *The Awakening Giant*, Oxford: Blackwell.

Porter, M. (1980) *Competitive Strategy*, New York: Free Press.

Porter, M. (1980) *The Competitive Advantage of Nations*, New York: Free Press.

Prestowitz, C. V. (1989) *Trading Places*, New York: Basic Books.

Scott, B. (1985) *American Competitiveness*, Boston, MA: Harvard Business School Press.

Senge, P. (1980) *The Fifth Discipline* Doubleday.

Taylor, F. W. (1947) *The Principles of Scientific Management*, New York: W. W. Norton.

Trompenaars, F. (1993) *Riding the Waves of Culture*, London: Economist Books.

Vogel, E. (1985) *Japan as No. 1*, New York: HarperCollins.

9 The use of scenario thinking: can a scenario a day keep the business doctor away?

Bill Weinstein

The management studies subject which professional schools of management find the toughest to teach is implementation of action plans. Until now, although efforts are made, it has been recognized that the principal means of learning about implementation is by acting and seeing what happens or fails to happen. Case studies and simulations try to get close to replicating real action situations but, thus far, the Holy Grail of teaching 'implementation' has proved elusive. Teaching situations and materials emphasize naturally diagnostic and analytical tools, such as models and concepts. These, however problem-solving in their orientation, are often felt to be at least one step removed from the real life of implementation—not merely the taking of strategic decisions but that of making things happen. No doubt progress will be made as more organizations demand less theory and more practical value from courses.

At the other end of the management subject range is 'thinking'—analysis only—about how to define visions, missions, strategic goals and objectives, and to develop strategic plans. Here there is a history of development over several decades, many specific company and industry sector studies and, in consequence, a surplus of competing and complementary tools and methods. It has been recognized that *strategic planning* can serve a variety of purposes in one and the same organization, such as stimulating debate, bringing issues to the surface, setting criteria for resource allocation, learning about issues, serving as a process for winning people's commitment to agreed plans, anticipating the need for a change of direction and defining measurements of performance. However, such strategic planning has tended to concentrate more on planning and prediction than on the more intellectually searching process of thinking about the possible futures which the direction-givers must consider.

So far, *scenario thinking* plays a surprisingly modest or even non-existent part. Few organizations practise it regularly, if at all, and there are serious misapplications and distortions or misunderstandings. For example, one company defined only a *single* 'scenario' for its future. Although not discredited as an approach to corporate planning, scenario thinking is thought to be so strange and to require so much long and arduous research behind it that only very large and well-heeled organizations can engage in it.

The chief objective of this chapter is to outline its *demonstrated*—not merely potential—utility for management. Its distinctive domain will be marked out as well as its limitations in practice. The form in which scenario thinking can be accessible and rapidly used by managers at many different levels of organization, private or public, will be described such that its use can become regular and familiar. It will be advanced as a means of building and sustaining organizational health, although it cannot quite aspire to the status of a quick fix—the apple a day which will keep the business doctor away. Learning how to use scenario thinking will be likened to success in learning how to ride a bicycle— practise is essential. Once you have it, you can pick it up quickly even after periods of under-use.

Scenarios: what and why

Short-term predictions

The key challenge to the direction of an organization which scenario thinking helps to meet is how to anticipate changes in the external environment which will impact positively or adversely on both the organization's goals and the means of achieving them. This challenge would be easy to meet if only we could predict the future with a high degree—80-90 per cent—of accuracy. We know from experience that, for any one-year operating plan in an organization, predictions— whether eventually valid or not—*must* be made. We must gear a production and purchasing system to predictions of sales which, in turn, depend on predictions of effective demand in the market and how customers will choose between our offering and that predicted of existing and possible (predicted) competitors; or we must predict the quantity and qualitative type of human resource required to support a predicted volume of service requirement; or we must calculate ahead the cost of working capital based on a predicted rate of interest. These are all relatively short-term predictions, and yet we all know how fallible they can be, especially given the unreliability of government or other forecasters' predictions of economic growth affecting demand and interest rates. Without short-term predictions, however, there cannot be any basis for operating plans. There is no escaping the need to predict. A key issue is when we should *not* respond to that need. The frequency with which such annual plans need major or minor adjustment, due to external factors beyond not only our power to affect but even our capacity to foresee them, is testimony to the fallibility of predictions. One important quality of directors and managers is their ability to adapt rapidly to mistaken short-term predictions.

Long-term possibilities: the essence of scenario thinking

How much more uncertain must be the validity of longer-term predictions? Those made for three to ten or more years ahead when, say, committing to a long-term research project or a giant project involving vast sums of fixed capital which, when productive, may be operating in an environment—political, economic, social or technological—quite different from that envisaged when the commitment had first been made, will be very uncertain indeed. The problem starts by our recognizing that, in betting on a particular view of the future, we are not betting with a 50:50 chance that it will be either A or B, but rather that it will be either A (what we have assumed) or any number of possible alternatives to A, which means not only B but also C, D, E and F. It is the *variety* of possible future long-term outcomes which itself lowers the chances of successful prediction and increases the utility of scenario thinking.

It is even more doubtful that predictions can carry validity as a basis for single-track thinking about the future. One needs only to consider how the macro-factors in our world— political, economic and cultural changes—have been so exceptionally accurately forecast: wars, booms, recessions, major religious or value changes. Moreover, although *someone* somewhere may be the author of this or that accurate prediction, the problem remains (before the event or fully evolved trend has emerged) which source is to be heeded and which of the conflicting sources rejected? Also, although a few forecasters have a much better track record than others on a restricted range of predictions (e.g. bond markets, currency movements) overall the depiction of the relevant factors for the future of an organization involves a large array of mixed inputs for which virtually no one can claim a privileged position in forecasting, least of all long term. Let us therefore make one leading and one subordinate assumption.

The first is that, although the struggle to achieve accurate predictions must continue, there is little or nothing to demonstrate that the art of predicting has substantially improved in recent years. The second is that, whenever it is practically possible, do not predict: make predictions only when we feel we must. By deliberately restricting the range of prediction making, the mental space is opened for an alternative approach—different possible futures.

If organizations have been so fallible in their ability to forecast, then how come so many survive? The first response is sceptical: is it 'so many' after all? How many companies of forty years ago still exist? The *Fortune 500* list of companies suggests that US corporations have an average life of 45 years. In any case, is sheer survival to be our criterion of success? In recent decades the years of leadership by a company have been decreasing in many sectors. The question in the second place is which types of organization survive? Some may be anchored against many vicissitudes by virtue of their support from the wider community, e.g. certain government and public service or religious organizations. Others, including many in the market, have actually failed in one sense or another. These often include the failure to take key profit or growth opportunities, due to a misreading of the future environment. Still others have demonstrated outstanding ability to manoeuvre rapidly in response to unexpected changes—thereby demonstrating that even deficiencies in the ability to foresee the future can sometimes be compensated by highly energetic, flexible people. Still another answer is that some external environmental developments, even when not predicted, are slow-moving enough to be recognized well before reaching their full power to impact on an organization and therefore there may still be time to make an adjustment.

Scenario thinking is a response to the weakness of prediction making. It represents an attempt to side-step or circumvent the hazards of predicting and, in the process, to reap certain mental and practical gains which are commonly sacrificed in single-track predicting. It is therefore both an alternative and a supplement to predictions. It is a response, itself limited and imperfect, to an important phenomenon. The steering of organizations requires both an accurate predictive compass and navigational charts into the future—but there is a persistent gap between this need and the means of satisfying it. It is one principal case in which the human need itself cannot generate anything like an adequate means of satisfying it. Where predictions represent an imperfectly achievable human aspiration to know the future, scenario thinking is a direct and humble response to the severe limitations upon our ability to know the future.

Scenarios as a mental development process

Scenario thinking involves mental preparation for more than one future. It enters this by describing several different possible future environments in which an organization may find itself. Each scenario depicts, within what someone believes to fall within the bounds of the 'reasonably possible', an environment whose factors are beyond the control of the organization. Individual and group opinions will differ over what is 'reasonably possible' in the future, but those differences will be useful grist for a scenario mill. An important feature of scenario thinking is that it opens our minds to different possible futures which can impact in different ways on our organization. Also, far from inducing mental and practical paralysis, scenario thinking is compatible with the strong determination of an organization, or its leadership, to steer its own consistent course into the future. The emphasis in scenario thinking on the external environment does not rule out an organization's ability to make changes within its environment that would support its own goals or methods, e.g. to change consumers' standards or preferences, or to replace one technology with another.

What kind of thinking is involved? The difference between scenario thinking and predicting is highlighted by the fact that the former starts from the phrase 'What if...?' Scenarios raise questions, within whatever we take at a given moment to be the bounds of credibility, as to what could or might happen in the future. Individually, each scenario—a description of conditions some years ahead which could affect the organization—expresses a hypothetical idea. Collectively, whatever range of scenarios we come up with expresses our uncertainty about the future—they might favour or make intolerable our expected costs, or they might render our current products sustainable or obsolete, or they might provide a boost or a blind alley for our territorial spread of risks, etc. One immediate function of such thinking is to stimulate greater awareness of the *assumptions* of the direction-givers about the external environment which even our relatively short-term strategy depends upon.

For example, if our current business is centuries'-old conventional book publishing, it would be reasonable to construct more than one scenario for five or ten years ahead.

One scenario may be very close to current conditions, another may suggest that the spread of certain types of interactive electronic communications involving computers, telephony, television combined with databases, data network management and software productions could radically undermine book publishing as presently understood. Yet another scenario would suggest scope for specialized segments in such publishing with, however, some expansion of the medium beyond the printed paper page. The scenarios taken together express our real uncertainty as to the future. Each scenario on its own is depicted as coherently and plausibly as possible, so that it will be taken seriously—not as a prediction but as a 'reasonably possible' pathway into the future.

The purpose of scenario thinking is not to terminate the overall uncertainty. On the contrary, it is to *express* our uncertainty in a structured and credible form. By this means, we can seriously ask 'If the environment were X and not Y, what would be the impact on our organization?' Asking this question exposes the possibility that what is now a relevant strength in virtue of the current environment might not be one in one or more future environments (e.g. being the lowest-cost book producer or the publisher with the best retail distributors) and what is now a strength could even be a weakness in the future, e.g. remaining with the current technology or market segment. It is also possible to expose the possibility that what is now seen as a weakness would not be so, or such a weighty weakness, in some other future environment. Overall, we start to get a feel as to how the organization might have to be repositioned in several ways if the environment were to change.

As another example: what if a national health service had to cater for an ageing population which *either* had large personal and family caring resources at its disposal (due to high earnings and lifetime savings, long-term steady employment, late retirement, strong obligations of children to care for parents) *or* experienced early retirement on low savings (due to poor economic growth and periodic unemployment, with low family-based caring availability)? Without here delving into the background data collection and interpretation that these points would involve, the key value of such scenarios would be to raise the first, but not final, question: how different would the service have to be in each case to carry out its statutory mission? Would the mission become impossible in one scenario unless certain policies and resources were changed radically? At least to become aware that, in these specific respects, the future could be different from the present is a step forward. An even larger step could be taken by going further and determining what would be the distinctive strategic problem or challenge or issue that would attach to each scenario.

An important feature of scenario thinking is that it is not designed to resolve uncertainty, nor does it tell us what we should do. Attention is focused instead on working out the relationships between a particular goal, its critical success factors which management can influence, and features of a future external environment which could impact on those factors and, in consequence, the feasibility of the goal. What is critically important is that those participating in this process should be able to take seriously the question 'But what if the future really did happen this way?' In other words, if the materials for thinking about a future scenario were constructed merely pro forma, and did not reflect some hard thinking by the directors, then much of its impact would be lost.

Scenarios contrasted with contingency planning

By stating the focus of scenario thinking in this fashion, one naturally invites the question, 'But is this not the same as contingency planning?' An important distinction is needed here. Consider a battle plan: if the best tank regiment is to get to Hill 386 by 0600 hours, it must be asked 'But what would we do with the infantry if the tanks didn't make it?' Consider a marketing plan: if our £1 million advertising campaign doesn't yield a 15 per cent increase in sales, what then would we do? This kind of questioning leads to contingency planning—the provision of an alternative, Plan B, if something goes wrong with Plan A. If Plan B is taken seriously, given the risk analysis of Plan A, then we invest in advance in Plan B. Contingency planning starts from the question 'What could go wrong with our preferred plan?'

Scenario thinking has an apparent similarity. When two different scenarios are posed, A and B, it is natural to anticipate that a current strategy which assumes A might be wrong if the environment turns out in a few years to be like B, not A. So B helps us to anticipate how assuming A could be wrong. However, scenarios characteristically precede a strategic decision or commitment. It is not as if we had a plan and are asking 'What could go wrong?' It is more like still being in a state of uncertainty as to what plan to have— because we haven't yet worked out which *goal* would be feasible in which external conditions. Even if we have a goal, we are not only testing its conditions of achievability in scenario thinking—we are considering which goal among several would be more or less achievable in which types of external environment.

Murphy's Law says that, if something can go wrong, it will. That expresses the motivation for contingency planning. When the *Koran* says that whoever tries to prophesy the long-term future is a 'liar', it is expressing the motivation for scenario thinking—to capture a range of large-scale futures, any one of which (including those we haven't yet conceived) might turn out to be aligned with reality.

We can now position properly the role of scenario thinking. It is *thinking before planning*. Strategic thinking specifies a goal on the basis of which resources and organization are to be structured. Scenario thinking is pre-strategic planning thinking. It is about the features of possible future environments relative to each of which a certain organizational profile, starting with a goal, is determined to be able to flourish, or could flourish, provided certain specified challenges were met. The pay-off of scenario thinking is therefore the identification of the *challenges*—different for different scenarios—which an organization would confront. In one growth scenario, for example, it would be a 'How would we achieve critical mass in resources to take opportunities?' type challenge; in a different scenario, it would be a 'How to shrink to a viable base?' type challenge. The mentality is less 'What do we want to achieve and how can we achieve it?' and more 'What problem will future history set before us?' Scenario thinking limbers up the direction-givers' mental muscles prior to planning. It increases their sensitivity to that external environment.

The first eligible candidate for a question about planning that attaches to scenario thinking is: 'If we conceive of two or three different possible futures, could we at least consider what kind of organization would be *robust* against, or in, each of these futures?' In other words, if we cannot yet know which of these futures will be actual, instead of responding by dissolving our uncertainty and betting on one such future from now on, should we plan to build strengths and remedy weaknesses that would be valuable moves in two or more possible futures? Or, at least, even if we bet on one future, could we plan for that in such a way that we could also balance and mix characteristics that would give us resilience just in case the other future we now take seriously were to happen? Here is where an element of contingency planning is starting; but only *after* we have seriously considered alternative scenarios and without the explicit purpose of settling on a strategy that would deliberately seek to build strengths and remedy weaknesses where the concern would be with factors common to two or more scenarios. When we build scenarios, we cannot even know in advance whether they will allow us to find strengths and concerns about weaknesses which are common to two or more scenarios. Indeed, it may turn out that, when we inspect our most relevant scenarios, there would be no practicable way of taking out an insurance policy which can cover several different futures.

Decision-making and scenarios

It is widely believed among the managers with whom I have done scenario exercises that, after scenarios have been constructed and their respective strategic issues or challenges have been identified, then the superficial preliminaries can be dispensed with and we can now get down to the serious business we are all here for—to declare which scenario is the most probable and discard the others. No doubt there must come a time—today or tomorrow or perhaps it ought to have been yesterday—when we must dispose of the uncertainties which scenarios can structure but not resolve. We must decide which horse to back. Once, however, we move into this mode, when decisions one way or the other must be taken, the utility distinctive to scenario thinking must be ended and predictions, right or wrong, must be made.

Nevertheless, it is important to recognize that scenarios retain their value so long as we can keep them in play mentally. Making predictions tends to push the alternative views to the peripheries or wastebaskets of our minds. We become planning and action-orientated and thus single-minded, tightly focused, however complex the prediction may be. There is no incompatibility between engagement in scenario thinking and decisiveness. Two different mental operations are involved. By refusing to rate the probabilities among scenarios which have survived serious, open-minded analysis, we continue to think about the different strategic challenges which each scenario can pose; we keep alive the questioning about the validity of the assumptions of any current strategic plan; we retain that much more mental flexibility. For the sake of determining a definite strategy and its supporting plans, we must make predictions on the imperfect evidence available. Once we do so, we dissolve the role of scenario thinking temporarily but the role of scenario thinking is not invalidated.

That role is to enable us to have sufficiently varied mental maps to allow us to consider what we should be decisive *about*—that is, to know what we will ultimately have to choose among alternative pathways for the future. Being decisive is a behavioural disposition. Quite different is the direction-giving activity of exploring the options about which we can then be decisive when we think we must. 'Paralysis by analysis' is a *canard* against scenario thinking, merely because it organizes uncertainty, having admitted uncertainty as a reality, and because it implies that useful learning about possible futures can be achieved by not rushing into a resolution of uncertainty.

How scenarios are made and what is to be done with them

Many of the assertions made above will be clarified and supported by considering how scenarios are best made and what can be done with them. Imagine a large bulk chemicals business, concentrated heavily in Western Europe for production and sales, which is broadly uncertain about how much to depend on bulk chemicals, as distinct from speciality chemicals, new biochemicals and pharmaceuticals. On a straight-line view of the future, its leaders may determine that there will be an upturn from the downturn of 1991-4, that plants and jobs must be cut, investments made in cost-efficiencies and quality improvements, and further productivity improvements, to improve margins eventually, can all be made by increasing the scale economies of plants—which would be helped if smaller or less efficient competitors were soon to withdraw. On this basis—with a tightening of cost controls and speeding up of response times to customers—the company will get through. The emphasis is on doing everything better and faster and cheaper: effectiveness in implementation is crucial for future success. Scenario reasoning will now raise the question: implement for what kind of longer-term future?

Suppose they were to conjure with scenarios and thereby stretch their timescales of thinking by several years? They would then try to think about their business, say, seven years ahead, *as if the future had already happened*. What kind of business would they have if the world went one way or in another way—conceived in terms of either sharply contrasting opposites or just two different worlds with different factors predominating in the environment? Into the mental melting pot would pour the raw material for at least two different views of that future. The material would include: positive and negative (best or worst case) assumptions about bulk chemicals' product maturity; energy, transport and labour costs; environmental regulation; market demand related to the general rate of economic growth; changes in the size or behaviour of different market segments; the scale and efficiency of direct competitors; and the possibilities of substitutes arising from technological innovations, of competitors from newly developed regions pouring cheaper, just-as-good product into Western Europe, of local customers disappearing and their markets being supplied in final-product form by foreign sources using bulk chemicals made in their own territories (e.g. imported cars), of attempts at differentiation to overcome price competition, etc.

At the first pass at this material, suppose three scenarios were sketched (see Figure 9.1).

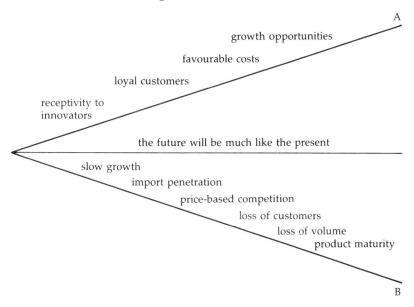

Figure 9.1   Three scenarios for bulk chemicals

Assume that the middle scenario would be a future in which the key features of the current environment would more or less persist. Then try a thought experiment in which many of the worst features could occur. In scenario B, they are 'worst' relative to the consensus in the company as to what the company should be aiming at now for the long-term future—improved profitability based on lowest cost to produce, a robust range of high-volume customers, and ability to differentiate from competitors in spite of product maturity and the threat of commoditization. What would that environment look like—in virtue of external factors that are beyond the control of the company? It would be one marked by new imports of both bulk chemicals and finished products, consequential loss of volume, technology changes hastening product maturity and shrinking applications, and high costs of production. In scenario B, the current preferred policies would run into serious difficulties.

For the sake of economy of exposition here, assume that a best-case scenario, A, would simply be the converse of the worst case although this would be only one possibility. What then would be learned?

1. A detailed look at impacts of various environmental factors, such as those mentioned above and possibly with varying degrees of intensity to achieve a feel for heavy or light impacts upon what the company's managers have deemed to be the handful of top-priority critical success factors needed for achievement of the long-term goal, specified in profit terms. To structure this for the sake of initial simplicity, array all the positive impacts into one best-case set of impacts and the negative impacts into one worst-case. (A necessary second pass would experiment with complicated mixed impact cases, and with examination in further detail of single-factor scenarios, i.e. sub-scenarios looking at one factor at a time such as exchange rates, labour costs, etc., which may change the earlier impact assessment done for the large-scale scenario work.) From these two extreme sets, artificially arrayed, would be viewed two types of scenario—one full of threats, B, and the other opportunities, A—the latter informing managers more fully that this is the kind of world that would have to happen if their best hopes were to be achievable and the former the converse.

2. Having observed the impacts (with simplified initial assessments, noting and keeping for future scenario work the elements of assessment that have been deleted), an overall judgement is then made about the challenges—problems, questions, issues, threats or opportunities—that would confront this business in the future. For example, in one future environment it would be virtually impossible to achieve larger-scale economies, to avoid price wars and to count on customer loyalty. The challenge (subject to a variety of formulations and disagreements) would be at least that many of their current strategies, designed to cope with the 1991-4 down-swing of the business cycle, could not cope with the larger-scale structural changes. One issue

that could emerge from this is: should we consider moving a significant part of the supply source for Western Europe to a lower-cost region of the world? Another is that, if markets elsewhere are growing faster, should we try to locate production in those markets and use them to increase supply to Western Europe? For a company with large fixed assets in Western Europe, these are uncomfortable questions. They also demonstrate that the initial range of environmental scanning was somewhat narrow and must be broadened to include other regions and the global economy (a point about the scope of scenarios to which we return below).

3. The same general impression is formulated for the best- or better-case scenario, A—which will be shown to generate a different set of challenges, such as how to achieve balance sheet strength or technological innovations to take advantage of such favourable external conditions. Put crudely, one difference between scenarios is that, in the former the question of cost reduction becomes a mortal one, whereas in the latter, though cost control remains important, it is not as high a priority.

4. It will now be coming to the surface that the achievability of the company's goal requires possibly significant changes of position in one scenario rather than the other. The management mind has been broadened simply through the expansionary pressure of scenario thinking.

5. It will now be clearer that only one group of assumptions about the external world have been made in endorsing and acting upon the current strategy. In consequence, the strengths being striven for at present may not be altogether relevant for at least one of the possible alternative long-term futures. By the same token, what is now not perceived as a real weakness may emerge as such if one scenario were to become reality.

6. There will almost inevitably proceed a search for a strategy which tries to achieve company robustness against more than one scenario—to find the commonalities across scenarios so far as company strengths and weakness are concerned. Of course, the full design of such a strategy should be compared with the currently preferred strategy and the points of difference will be marked. It does not follow logically that the scenario-sensitive strategy would or should be preferred to the single-line strategy. But reflection on the sharply contrasting impacts of different scenarios might lead to a revision, large or small, of the initially preferred strategy.

7. Consideration of alternative scenarios, each of which is uncertain, will give managers a more sensitive radarscope for picking up and interpreting the signals of change from now on. What this means is of considerable importance for scenario construction, and requires separate discussion. This point and other points about the utility and limitations of scenario reasoning will occupy the concluding part of this chapter.

Benefits and complications of scenario thinking

The need for 'story building'

The sketch of scenario creation and its application provided above omitted one vital element. For the sake of brevity, we focused on scenario material constructed out of 'end points', i.e. what the environment in this or that respect would look like seven years from now. We emphasized the importance of creating different photographs of possible future environments. All that we had to think about were key occurrences. We made no effort to explain how these occurrences would, in fact, occur. To fill that gap, we have to write a story—a kind of film or theatre script—which explains by what series of events or by virtue of what course of development the external environment moves from where we are now to where we could find ourselves in several years' time. Although this is the toughest part of scenario construction and is, in fact, the part that often needs expert help, its creation has a twofold benefit. The first is internal to scenario thinking: the process of 'story building' gives us a basis for *critically evaluating* the photographs of outcomes or endpoints which we initially judged possible, and perhaps revising or rejecting them. This process lends greater credibility to the content of scenario thinking. It also helps to sharpen scepticism about the use of the most recent events as a basis for long-term projections. The second is an external benefit, a spin-off from familiarity with the contents of scenarios: once we know what the stories look like, we can then *compare* them with what subsequently occurs in the intervening period, including the possibility that real-world events start to strengthen the evidence in favour of a particular scenario and directly or by implication may weaken the credibility of another scenario. Altogether, the story contents provide managers with a rapid reference point for judging events and trends as they emerge over time—there are several frames of reference in fact in which what emerges may be interpreted at speed.

The need for revisions   Sharpening the appreciation of the key challenges that could confront an organization under different future conditions is a major benefit of scenario thinking. Fresh thinking about the feasibility of organizational goals is one important consequence. A further consequence is that managers are stimulated to think more deeply about the dynamics of their organization and the requisites for future success. It puts discontinuities about the external environment on the agenda—therefore it puts organizational change and flexibility on the agenda as well. However, there is no guarantee that any scenario we construct will be 'right'. The fact that we may be less taken by surprise if equipped with several mental pathways into the long-term future, compared with a single-line prediction (even when it predicts a big change from the present), could be illusory. For none of what will emerge in the future may correspond with any of the scenarios which we build—they may be no better in their durability than sandcastles built by children on the beach. It has to be true that, if we see key developments diverging from each and every scenario we have constructed, then we must consider rejecting at least one of them and creating a new one in its place, or even starting again with a new set of scenarios. Organizations which have experienced this upset have responded in this way: they start again! At least having the scenarios in the first instance gives us a head-start in recognizing the need to change our mental furniture. Furthermore, it is commonly accepted among the most devout practitioners of scenario thinking that, even without such divergences from reality—e.g. when no 1980s scenario depicted the collapse of the former Soviet Union—not only must their content be monitored regularly but it is also an advantage to go through the process every few years of reconstructing the earlier scenarios. Each reconstruction process not only updates our (imperfect) thinking about how the external environment will be moving in future, it also gives a fresh impetus to the organization to rethink its prevailing assumptions, to conduct a mental health check on its directions and priorities. Scenario reasoning is, we have conceded, subject to the fallibility of the human mind to predict the long-term future but, at the same time, it provides a partial remedy.

The scope of scenarios   Another feature of the example of the bulk chemicals business was the use of external environment factors which were relatively immediate or close-up to the business. Immediate input costs, customers (direct and indirect), industry-specific environmental regulation, direct competitors and the like were prominently featured. What, however, did not appear were large-scale global economic–political etc. scenarios—only against that 'macro' or broader background would the more close-up factors make sense. The thinking about the external environment was too restricted, for much of the variability of the uncertain external factors mentioned in the example would depend on a larger, wider range of factors—national, regional and global—which should constitute the material for scenarios of great scope.

There must be a two-sided response to this point. First, it is a valid point and, therefore, full-blooded scenario thinking must engage large-scale impressions of how the world could be moving. The more immediate external environment factors for a particular organization or sector of activity would be more intelligible, even more credible, when positioned within such 'macro' scenarios. This, of course, takes time, money and skill, and many different opinions, internally and outside an organization, should be canvassed. For most organizations, such an expansive project, executed with sufficient depth, would be beyond their means or willpower.

Second, there is, however, a practical advantage in reducing the scope of scenario thinking to relatively more proximate external factors. For the vast majority of executives and professionals it is not merely the case that the 'macro' scenarios are difficult to grasp, as they assume considerable background knowledge across a wide range of subject disciplines even when they are reduced to two overall, but not diametrically opposed, scenarios, as is the longstanding practice in Shell's global scenarios. It is the more positive point, gleaned from my own experience, that.

- The majority of executives find that their own participation in scenario construction and the extraction of the key challenges has an immediacy and relevance of considerable interest and mental impact when the scope of scenario stories is made relatively close-up to their own organization, and
- Many are quite capable, without benefit of professional expertise, to link immediate points about their organization's future environments to some knowledge of the broader 'macro' factors to which they relate.

The involvement and development of managers

The question last considered, about the scope of scenario content, whether 'micro' or 'macro', provides an appropriate platform for a concluding observation. Drawing upon my extensive experience of working on scenarios with managers of many different levels and disciplines in a wide variety of organizations, as well as with corporate planners, my chief claim is that scenario reasoning need not be the special preserve of professional planners. The process of assessing the viability of current or potential organizational goals, resources and practices against different possible futures is available readily to almost all executives.

That process is made all the more valid for such participants by their engagement in linking external factors, in the form of alternative scenarios, to their current views of the critical success factors for their organization's future. Most of them are not used to such an exercise, but it is well within their reach when properly structured. The results are often revelatory and broadening: they also derive from a disciplined means of matching up external factors with their impacts on various key aspects of the organization. This observation is reinforced by three further considerations.

1. It is frequently experienced by those who produce grand-scale 'macro' scenarios that, when these are presented to practising executives and professionals in the organization, a mental struggle then ensues to relate the 'macro' scenarios to the more concrete concerns of people in the organization. It can be a frustrating task because of its sheer methodological complexity, and can turn people off. There is often a problem about making connections between the 'macro' economic, political, technological scenarios to the 'micro' scenarios which are expected of the receivers. What then must be produced are more 'focused' scenarios which pertain to a particular area of activity or the organization as a whole. It is often more constructive to show people the method and let them get on providing the raw material for scenarios even if that material is highly immediate rather than global in scope.

2. Even global or similar grand-scale, long-term scenarios have to be compressed into two or three simplified alternatives. Rich though the background material may be, scenarios are not normally usable unless a simplified version is brought to bear on the specifics of an organization. Multidimensional mental chess is not most people's strength—not when trying to combine many

different yet overlapping strands of analysis. This argues strongly for engaging a diversity of executives in scenario-creating exercises themselves, even when their capacity to envisage different scenarios is strongly influenced by their relatively immediate concerns.

3. The key value of scenario thinking is that, because it is based on relatively close-up factors in the external environment, albeit projected into the distant future, and demonstrates that different futures can create different challenges, for the majority of managers it can be a distinctive contribution to their mental preparation for more than one future. If compromising the breadth of scope of scenarios is the price one pays for adding range and flexibility to the minds of many managers, then it is a price worth paying. They will develop both their individual and the organization's mental capabilities of shaping the future. As the toppling of business giants by smaller competitors has shown in recent years, becoming a leader in learning can be a greater asset than money or market share.

10 Developing director and executive competencies in strategic thinking

Phil Hanford

Some comments on strategic thinking

To put this chapter in a broader context, I will start by briefly discussing the purposes and basic nature of strategic thinking. You will undervalue developing your competencies in it if you don't fully appreciate what it can do for you.

The purposes of strategic thinking

'Strategic thinking' in essence amounts to a richer and more creative way of thinking about and managing *key* issues and opportunities facing your organization. I maintain that an 'effective strategy' blends a range of external environment factors, business objectives, human resource and organization culture issues. That's easier to say than to achieve. Yet what a powerful basis for running your organization it can create! Strategic thinking underscores both the formulation and implementation of your organization's effective strategy (see Table 10.1).

Additional insights into the purposes of strategic thinking are provided by Roger Kaufman (1991). Like myself, he believes in thinking holistically about your organization and engaging both 'insiders' and 'outsiders' in planning its future:

> Thinking strategically is learning, as the members of the organization, to identify and deal, on an on-going basis, with opportunities and threats, issues of the future and of survival. Strategic thinking is characterized by a switch from seeing the organization as a splintered conglomerate of disassociated parts competing for resources, to seeing and dealing with the corporation as a holistic system that integrates each part in relationship to the whole. Strategic thinking is based on agreed-upon, mutually rewarding, visions and payoffs. It's a shift from means-oriented tactics to a future-oriented and holistic frame of reference in which means are selected on the basis of mutually rewarding ends. Strategic thinking is practical and ethical.

Table 10.1   Purposes of strategic thinking

In direction setting	'Locating, attracting, and holding customers is the purpose of strategic thinking' (Hickman and Silva, 1984)
In establishing 'the change agenda'	'Most organizations are effective in many of the things they do and deliver. Strategic thinking is about identifying what to change, modify, add, delete or acquire' (Kaufman, 1991)
In resource allocation	'Strategic thinking is about making the best use of what will always be a limited amount and quality of resources' (Hanford, 1983)

Strategic thinking contrasted with operational thinking

If you are like 99 per cent of directors and executives, you have a thorough understanding of and skills in 'operational thinking'. You may also have a distinct bias toward operational thinking, intentionally or just out of habit. That's understandable since operational thinking is more familiar to you and you've been rewarded for it over a long period of time. However, as one executive put it:

> I know I have to think more strategically, and I want to. But I have a lot to learn. I've been an operational person all my working life.

Strategic and operational thinking represent very different, albeit complementary, orientations and skills (Table 10.2). Indeed, sustainable organizational success requires competencies in *both* strategic and operational thinking. Unfortunately, far less has been done to develop strategic thinking skills. Fortunately, that's now changing.

The short term versus the longer term

Although this is only one aspect of the contrasts between strategic thinking and operational thinking, it gets a lot of attention, and for good reason. Your organization has to, and always will have to, react to short-term, even immediate, problems. But if all you do is to react to today's problems, that's all you'll ever do. Your organization will be an eternal prisoner of the 'tyranny of short-termism'. At best, you'll be embroiled in 'problem-driven management'. Worse than that,

Table 10.2   Distinguishing strategic and operational thinking

Strategic thinking	Operational thinking
• Longer term	• Immediate term
• Conceptual	• Concrete
• Reflective/learning	• Action/doing
• Identification of key issues/ opportunities	• Resolution of existing performance problems
• Breaking new ground	• Routine/on-going
• Effectiveness	• Efficiency
• 'Hands-off' approach	• 'Hands-on' approach
• 'Helicopter' perspective	• 'On-the-ground' perspective

you'll end up trapped in 'crisis management', going down the gurgler fast! That happens for two basic reasons. First, your organization becomes increasingly vulnerable to competition and other external threats through lack of foresight and preparation. Second, you miss out on identifying and capitalizing on key opportunities that would lead to sustainable success. The most amazing thing, however, is that most directors and executives would agree 100 per cent with everything I just said...and then go about acting out the 'tyranny of short-termism'!

The answer to this paradox lies in one's values, beliefs and assumptions. For many people, the short term drives out the longer term because, deep down, that's seen as vital to success. An alternative value is to have the longer term driving the short term because, deep down, that's seen as the road to success. (Incidentally, anyone holding this value will put the short term first whenever a *genuine* crisis exists.)

I firmly believe that successful organizations in the 1990s and beyond will be those whose leaders are firmly committed to 'proactive futuring'—the act of deciding what you want to happen and then setting out to make it happen (Pfeiffer *et al.*, 1989). This concept rests on recognizing both the short- and the longer-term demands for what they really are—inevitabilities. Short-term needs and demands will always be confronting you, and the longer term cannot be ignored forever. When it wants to be heard, it cannot be silenced! Mismanaging either the short or the longer term will bring your organization unstuck. Consequently, proactive futuring involves the following attitudes and actions:

• Shifting from 'a fixation to short-term reactions' to valuing 'the longer term driving the short term'.

- Putting time, effort and resources into opportunity identification as well as problem minimization or, better still, problem avoidance.
- Responding to short-term problems with purposeful reactions, i.e. reacting in ways that move your organization closer to its longer-term objectives rather than merely solving immediate problems.
- Continually working at getting the right 'mix' of longer term and short term for your circumstances which, of course, continually change.

I don't believe it would be overstating the case to propose that the number one strategic challenge confronting most directors and executives is to find, for your situation, the correct balance between the short and the longer term. That balance is best determined by first clarifying what short term-longer term relationship your organization will adopt as a matter of policy.

Developing your strategic thinking competencies

Some facts about competencies in strategic thinking

In my experience, there are recurring misconceptions about competencies in strategic thinking that should be cleared up at the outset.

- Being competent in strategic thinking does *not* mean being a 'mental giant' possessing an Einstein-like genius level of intellectual ability.
- In fact, the vast majority of people can become competent in strategic thinking, regardless of their work or educational background.
- Moreover, we can all add to our competence in strategic thinking. A person doesn't achieve some accredited level of proficiency and get awarded a degree in strategic thinking. Instead, you just get better and better at it with continual learning and practice.
- All that's required by you is an average intelligence and willingness, i.e.:
  — The motivation to think more strategically
  — An openness to learning about strategic thinking as it applies to you and your situation

— A commitment of your time, no different from what you'd do to become competent at driving a car or playing a musical instrument.
• The pay-offs from your investment can be enormous. A relatively small increase in your strategic thinking competencies will lead to an even larger increase in organizational success and personal effectiveness.

Why developing director and executive competencies in strategic thinking is now so crucial to organizational success

In 1992, an international Strategic Management Conference was held in London. The conference was entitled, 'Strategic Renaissance', the point being that the change in the global economy and in organizations today is comparable to the medieval renaissance; that we're living through a period of great economic and social discontinuity no less significant than the Industrial Revolution or the Renaissance; and that the purpose, scope and shape of organizations is changing in very fundamental ways...and will continue to do so.[1]

On the one hand, 'Few large corporations live even half as long as a person. In 1983 a Royal Dutch/Shell survey found that one third of the firms in the *Fortune 500* in 1970 had vanished' (de Geus, 1988). On the other hand, the 1990s and beyond present a very large number and variety of opportunities for businesses to capitalize on—both large and not-so-large companies. Public sector organizations are also heavily involved in major change. In response to societal issues and economic pressures, we're witnessing the slow-but-sure 'death of bureaucracy' as more and more public sector organizations transform themselves, are replaced by new organizations, or have their functions transferred to the private sector. The once-clear boundaries between public sector and private sector are rapidly blurring.

Marvin Weisbord (1991), himself a corporate director and executive and now a renowned international consultant, talks in terms of 'third wave managing and consulting':

> Any reader of the business press knows that a sea tide is surging through the work world different from anything that has gone before. Futurist Alvin Toffler calls it 'the third wave', to differentiate it from the agricultural and industrial revolutions of bygone eras. We are changing our workplaces from physical to knowledge work, mechanical to process technologies, manufacturing to service economies, central to local control. I have borrowed Toffler's term to describe the new conditions we face.

Between 1985 and 1990, the Massachusetts Institute of Technology teamed up with ten major American companies,

British Petroleum and International Computers to research the critical business issues for the 1990s. This study, entitled 'Management in the 1990s', examined the impact on businesses of increased competition, economic turbulence, the enabling role of information technology and new organizational patterns. A key conclusion was that 'strategic management—which includes not only creating a company's strategy but also flexibly implementing it—is the discipline of the 1990s'.[2] In turn, strategic thinking is at the very heart of strategic management.

I am convinced that competency in strategic thinking, at all levels of your organization, but starting at the director and executive level, is now a business imperative and a leading source of competitive advantage. I would not be at all surprised if it became *the* main competitive advantage before the turn of the century. Indeed, 'the thinking revolution' is upon us!

The case for developing director and executive strategic thinking competencies is summarized very well by Beckhard and Pritchard (1992) when they say:

> A paradox of today's world is the increasing need for leadership to become involved with creating an organization that is actively moving towards its potential while, at the same time, solving today's crisis or emergency. Since often the 'urgent drives out the important', the organization's 'becoming' is forced to wait its turn. It is our contention that organizations wishing to be top competitors in the years ahead must move the effort 'to become' to the head of the line.

Competence in strategic thinking underscores your organization's 'becoming'.

'But I'm already competent at thinking strategically'

This is a view held by many directors and executives and for good reason, because it seems true. But it's also not true.

It concerns me that a lot of leaders are giving themselves a mixed message. On the one hand, they want continued success for their organization. On the other, they are blind to and/or resistant to the very things that are required for continued success.

In an environment of rapid change, often jolting change, increased complexity and much tougher competition, yester-year's ways of directing and managing organizations are simply inadequate. Increasingly, they are breaking down altogether. New approaches are clearly required. In talking about the top job, the renowned former ICI boss, Sir John

Harvey-Jones, said: 'It is only when you become aware of the range, scope, and incredible responsibility of the [top] job that you realize that there is an almost limitless opportunity to be ineffective, *unless you are totally clear about how you are going to set about it*' [italics added].[3] Adding to your competencies in strategic thinking, alongside other directors and executives doing the same thing, both clarifies your leadership role and provides you with increased capacity to perform your role well.

Many years ago, perhaps you learned to ride a bicycle and, if so, you mastered it for life. Likewise, in years gone by, you learned your functional speciality—your trade—and were then able to competently and confidently apply it. But what have any of us formally learned about thinking? Edward De Bono (1985) makes what I believe to be a very significant observation when he says:

> Thinking is the ultimate human resource. Yet most people are convinced they are competent at thinking and thus make little, if any, effort to improve their thinking competencies.

As you well know, the number and complexity of challenges confronting today's directors and executives have increased significantly, and will continue to do so. Obviously, it makes sense to first benchmark and then increase your capacity to handle these challenges. That's where strategic thinking competencies come in. De Bono (1988) illustrates this by considering one element of strategic thinking, namely, conceptual thinking:

> Efficient management and problem solving can be a road to disaster . . . . .[Before] efficient management and problem solving were enough. But no more. The efficient management of a tired idea is a waste of efficiency. We have to add a third essential leg to the management tripod, namely, conceptual thinking. Every leader has to enhance his or her conceptual thinking skills to improve existing concepts and develop new concepts.

My own version of this idea is that efficiency management is all about keeping the cart on the road. Problem solving is all about getting the cart back on the road whenever it falls off, as inevitably it will. In contrast, conceptual thinking is about questioning—do we have to have a cart in the first place? Why? For whom? If we do require a cart, does it have to run on a road? What are the alternatives?

If it's so obvious that increasing competencies in strategic thinking is now a necessity for director or executive effectiveness, why do I encounter so much blindness and/or resistance to this need? I've found two main reasons for this.

First, people misjudge the relevance of their background to the contemporary business environment. Competence in strategic thinking *cannot* be assumed, no matter how impressive one's CV of past experience and accomplishments. Often though, directors and executives, due to their long years of experience and their lofty position in the organization's hierarchy, hold the belief that they are above developing their competencies any further in something as basic to the top job as strategic thinking. This belief is not necessarily egotistical or a defensive reaction. In many cases it is a genuinely felt opinion. Unfortunately, it is frequently unfounded and, whenever that's the case, it is very damaging to the organization's survival and thrival.

Second, leaders can get tangled up in others' expectations of them. To be effective in the 1990s and beyond, directors and executives have two key tasks:

1. Set directions for the organization—where are we headed, why, for whom, and broadly how will we get there? And interlinked with this . . .
2. Ensure that necessary organizational changes are fairly and productively implemented—i.e. changes required to make the organization valuable both to its external environment and to itself, leading, in turn, to sustainable organizational success.

Other people, both insiders and outsiders, expect that the organization's leaders will perform their direction-setting and change management tasks well. Those in top jobs usually accept others' expectations of them. But here's the rub. Since strategic thinking underscores both these tasks, others just automatically assume that the organization's leaders are competent at 'thinking strategically' (though not necessarily using that label). Many leaders, however, are not so convinced. Bob Garratt, a company director and also a renowned international consultant, has consulted to some 1500 top-level people around the world over the past 12 years—300 of them in-depth and for at least one year. Many of these directors and executives have confided in Bob that they don't feel sufficiently confident and competent to meet the expectations placed upon them. In particular, their career backgrounds and lack of induction into the top job has not prepared them to think strategically as well as they should (Garratt, 1990).

To make matters worse, a director or executive may fear that, if he or she participates in a development programme designed to increase strategic thinking competencies, others will lose confidence in their ability to lead. In such circumstances, the leader gets lured into avoiding their own development with all sorts of plausible reasons (read 'rationalizations'). Instead, the director or executive plods on, pretending to feel confident and competent at thinking strategically while, in fact, feeling increasingly uncomfortable. Eventually, all this may well lead to stress-related illnesses. Even if that doesn't happen, surely there must be a better way?

If the above scenario applies to you—and you certainly aren't alone if it does—the following initiatives are a way out (though not necessarily in these words):

- Educate others that the external environment has changed so much that fundamental changes are required inside the organization.
- In turn, that means a lot of unlearning old ways and learning new ones.
- And that you and the top team are going to lead by example by going off-line to sharpen your competencies in strategic thinking to, in turn, equip you to lead better.

I often advise my clients to adopt this level of openness about the situation and themselves and to 'lead by example'. They find the above approach goes a long way in winning the hearts and minds of those whose commitment they require to do their job of directing and managing. Additionally, they feel a lot more relaxed within themselves because they've taken the time and made the effort to increase their capacity to meet the increased challenges they face.

So we've come full circle back to you doing your job well. The difference is that the above approach results in you getting fully on top of your job rather than being a prisoner of others' expectations and your own self-doubts.

Time to think strategically versus time urgency

Another major block to directors and executives developing their competencies in strategic thinking is 'time urgency'. Some leaders are 'wed to the rush'. That spills over into a negative attitude about thinking more strategically—the famous 'I haven't got time for it' syndrome. An opposite view is well expressed in the immortal question posed by the

American philosopher, Henry David Thoreau: 'Why should we be in such a desperate haste to succeed?'

At an operational level it makes perfectly good sense to push for time urgency in producing goods/delivering services quicker. Speed can be a powerful source of competitive advantage. At a strategic level, however, speed can be the surest way of not being strategic, e.g. scheduling time slots that are ridiculously short for thinking through a key issue or opportunity; or for learning something new; or to change and clarify key organizational roles. All these strategic challenges take time. Time urgency here would be counter-productive (without, of course, going to the other extreme and needlessly dragging things out).

The ancient Chinese concept of balance, Yin-Yang, is useful in summarizing the time issue with relative to thinking versus acting.

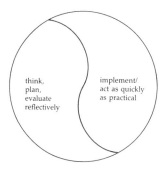

In this 'Age of Redefinition', as Hugh Mackay (1993) labels it, I reckon we're all learners. Let's stop any pretence that we're masters at strategic thinking and/or don't have the time to improve in it and get on with some serious learning and development of our competencies in strategic thinking.

'Tools for Thinking Strategically' programme

A programme for developing your strategic thinking competencies

The *'Tools for Thinking Strategically' (TTS)* is an intensive learning programme designed specifically for directors and executives interested in developing their and their colleagues' competencies in strategic thinking. The TTS programme is run both in-company and as an open programme across organizations.

Key prerequisites for developing your strategic thinking competencies are space, time and stimulation. These may well be in short supply in your situation. The TTS programme provides space and time by getting away to a different setting for several days with a clear focus in mind. Stimulation is provided through learning powerful new ideas and techniques, developing practical skills, gaining a better understanding of yourself, and hearing the experiences and thoughts of fellow directors and executives. Further stimulation comes from the programme leaders/coaches as they guide you through a comprehensive and in-depth learning experience, sharing their insights and suggestions along the way.

The value of the TTS programme stems from three interlinked elements:

- the usefulness of the content to today's changing, complex and competitive environment and your unique situation
- the interactions amongst participants about their real-life issues and opportunities, and their willingness to explore and experiment with the programme's content in relation to these issues and opportunities
- the quality of the programme leaders/coaches—i.e. experienced people who know what they're doing, are both conceptually strong and practical, and have a good grasp of both the contemporary business and human aspects of organizations.

What developing your strategic thinking competencies involves

The TTS programme is designed to achieve the following learning goals:

1. Understanding more fully what strategic thinking is, where it fits into directing and managing, and its importance in the 1990s and beyond.
2. Redefining, or confirming, your director/executive role as 'setting direction' by 'looking outward, upward and forward' and implementing major organizational changes/improvements.
3. Becoming more skilled at directing the formulation and successful implementation of effective policies and strategies for your organization's survival and thrival.
4. Getting more comfortable with radically different behaviours—e.g. 'hands-off' purposeful reflection rather than the more common 'hands-on' action fixation.
5. Being more adept at mentally integrating the strategic and operational cycles of your organization by:

- knowing when to 'be in your helicopter' and when to 'be on the ground', and
- becoming more skilled at making the switch.
6. Being more personally effective—e.g. making better use of your time and other personal resources to 'tackle the important'; pinpointing key elements of issues/opportunities and being more creative about alternative courses of action; adding more value to your organization by focusing more on key results and less on activities; presenting a stronger case for things you want as a result of stronger thinking skills; seeing 'the big picture' more clearly, thereby spotting opportunities better; being more innovative about capitalizing on opportunities.
7. Gaining more confidence in thinking strategically, both about 'the big issues' confronting you and everyday matters—thinking better simply increases one's self-confidence.
8. Achieving constancy in strategic thinking as a direct result of increased competence and confidence.

Blockages to strategic thinking: it takes time to develop competencies

For example, the TTS programme comprises a residential workshop of four or five days (depending on learning needs versus time constraints). This is followed by two one-day recall sessions, usually within a few months of the workshop. These sessions reinforce the workshop learning and provide valuable peer support.

The workshop is intensive with no fat. A residential format is used to further increase time efficiency via concentrated learning. A residential also allows time to break some bad thinking habits while also doing some 'purposeful reflection' —a strategic thinking skill worth mastering.

Any negative reactions to the programme's duration seem to be of two varieties. Some people object to the duration in principle, saying that it's too long; that surely the material could be covered in less time. In reply, I freely admit that six or seven days in total *is* a lot of time. But let's look at this more closely.

- First, certain tasks just take a certain amount of time and cannot be 'squeezed for time' and still achieve worthwhile results. You don't become a competent engineer, or doctor, or electrician, or artist after only six months of study. Becoming competent in strategic thinking is no different. It takes a certain minimum amount of time.

- Second, developing your competencies in strategic thinking is *not* some extra task added to your job. Increasing your strategic thinking competencies *is* your job. A solid learning programme is the 'kick-start.'
- Third, don't underestimate the power of bad thinking habits. It takes time to break them, starting with a concentrated burst of new learning and reinforcement. It's very similar to trying to give up smoking. The 'quit smoking' programmes that actually 'break the habit' take time.
- Finally, if, for example, the TTS programme were condensed to, say, a one-day seminar, it would only be superficial awareness raising. A substantive impact would not be made. You'd leave the seminar feeling better and perhaps a small bit wiser. But even this very limited gain would quickly vanish.

A second objection to the programme's duration is tied up in personal priorities—the 'I haven't got time for it' syndrome mentioned earlier. This concern reminds me of the story of the busy executive with a bad toothache. The dentist examined the problem and found the solution. The executive asked the dentist, 'How long will it take?' The dentist said 'Two hours'. At that point, the busy executive said, 'Oh, I'm too busy for that. I can only spend thirty minutes'. The dentist simply replied, 'What's more important to you, your time or getting healthy?'

A framework for thinking more strategically

Development of director and executive competencies in strategic thinking is based upon a simple but very powerful premise:

**Managing more strategically begins
with thinking more strategically.**

This premise comes alive by developing your understanding of and abilities in four types of 'strategic thinking tools'—i.e. processes/how to's—as they apply to the context and content of your unique situation. By taking this action-learning approach, the TTS programme progresses strategic issues and opportunities facing your organization while also enhancing your own personal competence and confidence in thinking more strategically.

In designing a TTS programme the framework shown in Figure 10.1 is used. The TTS programme is *not* a 'stock standard design'. Instead, the specific content for a given programme is selected from the range of available tools in response to particular members' particular needs and backgrounds. The programme design will, however, always include a mix of skills, concepts, styles and techniques in the belief that developing strategic thinking competencies has to be a balanced proposition.

The remainder of this chapter describes the range of strategic thinking tools that are available. This will put some flesh on the bones of Figure 10.1. It is beyond the scope of this chapter to give any more than a 'snapshot' of these tools.

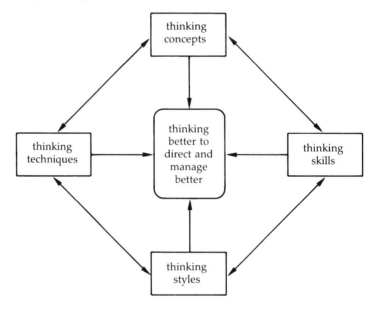

Figure 10.1   Tools for thinking strategically

The range of strategic thinking tools and skills

Reframing

I first came across this tool while on a consulting assignment with an alcohol dependence agency. I was fascinated with the approach the therapists took. In essence, they would encourage an alcoholic client to shift their attention away from drinking too much (the act) to getting rid of their pain/

hurt/etc. (the reason). Shifting the focus to the reason resulted in clients seeing their life situation more clearly. In turn, this led to discovering alternative ways to lessen their pain and, in turn, to breaking their dependence on alcohol. The success rate of this agency was quite impressive. The therapists were teaching their clients the 'reframing' skill—deliberately looking at a situation from more than one vantage point.

A common example at work is managers engaging in lots of activities but with little or even no lasting or meaningful results. Sound familiar? By shifting your focus to the results and not the activities, you reframe the situation in your mind to become really clear about what you're trying to achieve, for whom and why. In turn, only those activities that are truly warranted in the light of desired results get attention. Furthermore, those activities get planned and managed from a results vantage point rather than from an activities perspective.

Reframing is the skill involved in directors and executives taking a 'helicopter' view of their organization's key issues and opportunities. Reframing is all about expanding choices in generating creative responses to serious challenges instead of falling victim to the syndrome of 'there's only one way to go'. There is always more than one way to go. They begin to surface when you reframe an issue.

Six thinking hats

This is a brilliant piece of work from De Bono (1985)—in my opinion, his most useful tool. It's based on two key observations. For one, most management thinking is coping or reactive in content. That's necessary but not sufficient for success. A more strategic approach is what De Bono calls 'map-making'—i.e. deliberate thinking aimed at mapping an issue as fully as possible and only then identifying and deciding what to do about it. Second, he observes that most management interactions are competitive, even adversarial, in which people exchange their predetermined views on an issue and then argue the logic of their predetermined solution. Each person, or group, is aiming to have their solution prevail over the rest. Sound familiar?

The pressures of business are leading to more collaborative ways of interacting. These are easier on people and relationships and lead to better-quality solutions. As a result, there is a higher level of commitment to making the solutions work. *Six Thinking Hats* pulls together the notions of map-making thinking and collaborative interactions. In essence, at a meeting everyone present pitches in a variety of information to 'map' the issue at hand. When the issue is more fully understood, everyone again pitches in ideas on what to do about it. The 'six thinking hats' provide a structure to both the content and the process of the meeting.

- *White hat*　is neutral and objective; provides facts and figures
- *Red hat*　is how people feel; surfaces emotional responses to things
- *Yellow hat*　is positive and constructive; sees the benefits in ideas
- *Black hat*　is negative (but not negativity); gives a critical assessment
- *Green hat*　is creative; provides alternatives and new angles to issues
- *Blue hat*　acts as the 'chair'; controls the flow, ensures that all hats are used.

Searching questions to explore

As a director or executive, you'll find this skill especially useful in relation to 'the big issues' confronting your organization. A broad example: is the world a fair place? Obviously not. Should it be a fair place? Obviously yes, but that's asking too much. Could the world be a fairer place? Yes, of course. In what specific ways could it be made fairer? How can these things happen? In this example, we went from 'what is?' to 'what should be?' in order to get to 'what could be?' all as a catalyst for asking some promising questions with real potential.

The aim of searching questions is to open up possibilities that would probably otherwise go unnoticed. Asking searching questions is a skill for stimulating 'what ifs?' and 'why nots?' as a means of getting to a course of action that is both creative and practical. It's all about asking the right questions, allowing other questions to surface, and not rushing for answers. As a consequence, you are freed up to explore, to challenge conventional wisdom, to discover. Although this comes naturally to some people, for many it's difficult to let go of the urge to get answers long enough to ask questions. That urge can be extremely wasteful!

Effective questions to empower

Increasingly, the work of directors and executives includes 'empowering' others. This brings out their creativity, increases their commitment to organizational goals, and maximizes their contribution and work satisfaction. Questions, if they are effective, are part of the empowering process. Great questions make people eager to answer them. Asking poor questions is 'telling in disguise' and intimidates people. 'Managing by fear' is quite unproductive and outdated.

What makes an effective question is its essence. Therefore, learning the skill of asking effective questions to empower others is all about becoming more aware of where you are 'coming from' rather than learning a set of prescriptions. The fundamentals of effective questions are things like being open-ended, being forward-oriented, asking 'what's?' and 'how's?' rather than 'why's?' (read 'blaming'), focusing on the other person's views, concerns, etc. and helping them to learn.

Strategic thinking concepts

Three core concepts, or 'thinking templates'

1 Holistic thinking model—breadth of your thinking

There are several insights attached to this model—e.g. 'everything has a context and the context determines everything'. Directors and executives have found the holistic thinking model very useful in at least three significant ways:

1. It helps them to more fully understand key issues or opportunities.
2. Once learned by a group (which is fairly easy), it establishes a sound and convenient way to conceptualize and discuss issues/opportunities.
3. It greatly facilitates effective planning and implementation of plans for successfully addressing key issues/opportunities.

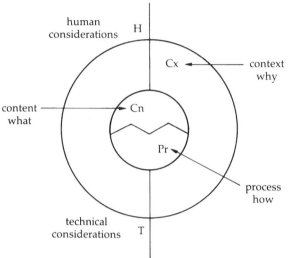

Figure 10.2   *The holistic thinking model*

2   (RAVBA) Results, actions, values, beliefs, assumptions

Results are dependent upon actions being appropriate, adequately resourced and properly implemented. However, when actions fail to get desired results, often the true cause will be found in your values, beliefs or assumptions. Your values, beliefs or assumptions also heavily influence your choice of desired results (Figure 10.3).

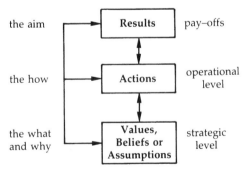

Figure 10.3   *RAVBA—the depth of your thinking*

Paradigms are your core beliefs and assumptions. 'The world is flat' is a good example of a paradigm. From this model/ framework/'rules of the game', you would hold certain values, take certain actions, and prize certain results. If your paradigm was 'the world is round', you would hold quite different values, take quite different actions, and want quite different results. Changing your model from 'the world is flat' to 'the world is round' is a paradigm shift. Paradigms are extremely powerful and, in these times, paradigm shifts are frequently essential for success. Many of the challenges that tax the energy and imagination of directors and executives are tied up in paradigms—what are our current paradigms? What are their consequences? What alternative paradigms could we/should we hold? How can we effect a paradigm shift? Indeed, returning to my example, a pressing need for organizational survival and thrival in the 1990s and beyond is to shift 'flat-earth thinkers' into 'global thinkers'.

3   Types of thinking

A lot of director and executive thinking is what is referred to as 'either/or thinking'—it's either X or it's Y; we'll do either X or Y, and so on. To be sure, there is a place for 'either/or thinking'—e.g. balance sheets either balance or they don't and, in turn, we all count on balance sheets balancing. But 'either/or thinking' is incredibly limited, especially when applied to contemporary challenges and changes that your organization has to address. Two alternatives are available: 'more/less thinking' and 'both/and thinking' (Figure 10.4).

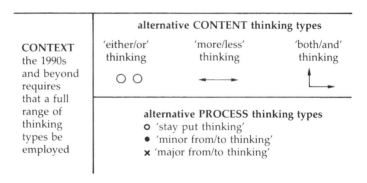

Figure 10.4   Types of thinking

At the process-of-thinking level, there are also alternatives. Inspired by Chris Argyris's (1993) work on 'single- and double-loop learning' there is what I've called 'stay put thinking'. This is fine for straightforward issues in stable circumstances, where your approach is essentially sound and just requires some fine-tuning or, when things go wrong, some routine adjustments. In short, what you're doing is working so 'stay put' with it. Like the saying goes: 'If it ain't broken, don't fix it.'

Increasingly, however, leaders and people at all levels are having to engage in what I've called 'from/to thinking', of which there are two basic types: 'minor from/to thinking' (transitions) and 'major from/to thinking' (transformations). Either way, 'from/to thinking' is mentally and emotionally difficult because it calls for increasing both the breadth and depth of your thinking—i.e. thinking more and questioning your values, beliefs and assumptions. Despite the inherent difficulties, 'from/to thinking' is here to stay and has to be fully understood.

*Two core directing/
leading concepts*

a) Planning perspective—outward, upward and forward

My favourite contemporary management quote is from Russell Ackoff (1981): 'Surviving in a world demanding more responsiveness from its institutions.' This succinctly captures the crux of the 1990s way of doing business. It explains things like the strong push for increased director accountability, the constant and growing pressures to be 'green and clean', customers voting with their feet when they don't get quality products/services delivered in a quality way. Continued success nowadays for many organizations requires some radical changes to their 'planning perspective'. Roger Kaufman's model is useful in understanding this (Figure 10.5).

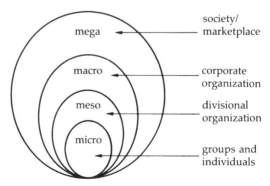

Figure 10.5   A nest of plans and actions

Chances are the big issues you're wrestling with are at the mega level. Yet much of managerial theory and practice has been at the micro, meso and macro levels. Strategic planning to date has been macro based—what does your organization want to achieve (read 'win', or even 'take', from its environment)? This is called 'inside-out' planning. It's based on internal needs with the external world being seen (albeit often in 'nice' ways) as an arena for satisfying those needs.

In contrast, 'outside-in' planning begins with a clear, participative identification of key external needs. Your organization then works out how it can best *serve* these needs. Benefits accrue to you by putting outside needs first. This is mega-based planning. It involves an 'upward' perspective in striving for higher ideals and adopting a win–win approach to doing business. It's also 'forward' in proactively identifying key external needs and then delivering on them as far as you can. These features are what Ackoff means by responsiveness. For the changed conditions of the 1990s, they are the ingredients in truly strategic strategic planning.

b) Prerequisites to change

The strategy for your organization's continued success will in all likelihood call for organization members to change their behaviour in some way—e.g. providing customer-friendly service, empowering workers, using new information systems, etc. For behaviour to change, it is essential that directors and executives:

- understand more fully what's involved in people changing their behaviour
- have a carefully thought-out plan for implementing behaviour changes
- take an active role in the change process.

The 'prerequisites to change' model is very useful in coming to grips with your 'change agent' role. The simple premise is that three things—all three—have to be present for people to change their behaviour:

- clear directions (understanding what's expected of me/us)
- ability (being able to do what's expected of me/us—both personally and organizationally, and

- willingness (being committed to doing what's expected of me/us).

There's more to this model, but the important thing is to fully recognize that whenever it's necessary for organization members to change their behaviour, you and your colleagues at the top have a definite role to play in actually implementing the changes, not just identifying them.

Strategic thinking techniques

Both/and thinking

I'll use myself to illustrate this tool. I regard myself, and am regarded by my clients, as an 'integrity consultant'—i.e. a consultancy isn't 'just a job'. I actually want the project to make a positive and worthy contribution to the client system. Frequently, this involves a dilemma as shown in Figure 10.6. In this not-so-hypothetical example, what is currently being done goes a fair way towards what the client wants but is far short of what I professionally judge as being required. If I'm too purist in pushing for what's required, I may alienate the client. Yet if I don't confront the client about what's required, I risk not making much of a contribution. Avoiding the dilemma means that both the client and I miss out on the benefits of its resolution. The 'both/and thinking' technique helps to map the dilemma and then generate some ways out of it.

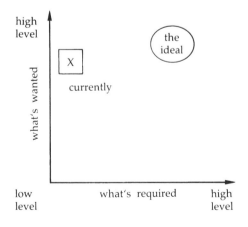

Figure 10.6   Both/and thinking

Mind mapping your strategic challenge

Your organization's 'strategic challenge' is the essence of what your organization has to actually do to fulfil its mission (purpose) and achieve its vision (overall goal). A recent client example is: expand our client base and the services we offer while we also broaden, protect and even strengthen our technical excellence and good reputation in programme management. (Incidentally, you can state your own personal strategic challenge by asking what must you do overall to fulfil your role (purpose) and achieve your personal vision for your role.)

'Mind mapping', as developed by Tony Buzan, is a thinking technique used for a variety of tasks. In a strategic thinking context, mind mapping could be used to identify the essential elements in achieving a strategic challenge and the inter-relationships involved. These insights would then be used in planning how exactly to meet the challenge.

SLIM priority–setting technique

'SLIM' is an acronym for 'Strategic Leading Issues Matrix'. (To refer to issues as both strategic and leading is tautological but I wanted to use the word 'slim'.) An executive client once said to me: 'Phil, before we began this [strategic management] process, I spent 90 per cent of my time doing 90 things. Now [a year later], I'm spending 90 per cent of my time doing nine things.' He had 'slimmed' down in what he took on and instead concentrated his efforts on the really important issues.

There's two parts to this client's increase in effectiveness. First, he adopted a new paradigm; namely, 'when you take on too much, you don't achieve much'. Second, he used the SLIM technique for setting the priorities for his executive role. As wise as it is to set priorities, this unfortunately is often done in a very unwise way. The problem is the word 'important'— what does it really mean? A colleague and I identified that important items have four elements:

Urgency	meaning:	critical that the item be dealt with now
Relevance	meaning:	essential item to achieving higher-order goals
Growth	meaning:	item will have a longer-term positive effect
Ease	meaning:	item can be achieved in the short term

The SLIM technique takes account of these multiple elements in arriving at a more strategic and realistic set of priorities for your organization, or for yourself.

Choices and consequences thinking

Once some aspect of your organization's functioning has been selected as a key area for action, the choices and consequences technique is useful for identifying alternative courses of action and determining their relative merit. Deciding what action to take is often a classic abuse of 'either/or thinking'—we'll do either this or we'll do that. In contrast, the choices and consequences technique is based on 'more/less thinking'. In the first phase, a special continuum is used to surface a richer and wider range of choices for action than would otherwise be the case. In the second phase, each promising choice is evaluated by considering both positive and negative likely consequences in both the short and the longer term.

Thinking styles

Thinking intentions profile (TIP)

The TIP self-questionnaire is extremely useful for you as a director or executive in performing your complex and challenging role. TIP gives you unique insights into your 'thinking style'—i.e. *how* you go about thinking. Your thinking style directly influences your thoughts—the conclusions you reach—about situations and, in turn, the actions you take and results you achieve.

The key to your thinking style lies in your intentions. They act like objectives. The style you choose will reflect what you want to achieve from your thinking. There are three generic objectives that your thinking can seek to satisfy:

- Realize some new idea
- Describe what is true
- Judge what is right

When you focus on one of these intentions, you exclude the other two because they are irrelevant to your aims. All three have their value but can also be overused at the expense of other objectives. In all likelihood, your thinking will currently place emphasis on one of the generic objectives. Additionally, there are two main biases in your thinking: 'hard', which is likened to objective 'science', and 'soft', which is likened to subjective 'art'. Both of these are essential to your personal as well as organizational success. However, the chances are that you favour one over the other. TIP identifies your current thinking style and shows you how you can develop an enriched and more balanced style appropriate to your leadership role (Figure 10.7).

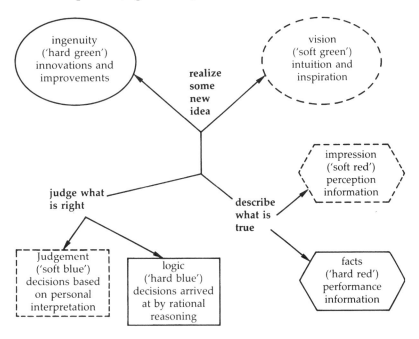

Figure 10.7   Thinking intentions as 'colours of your mind'
© *Jerry Rhodes and Sue Thame 1988*

Kinds of thinkers (i$_n$Q)

The 'i$_n$Q' is another self-questionnaire to give you insights into how you think. It is different from but complementary to the TIP questionnaire. Whereas TIP helps you to understand how you typically think about situations in your director or executive role, the 'i$_n$Q' sheds valuable light on the kind of thinker you are.

- *The synthesist*   sees likenesses in apparent unlikes, seeks synthesis, interested in change.
- *The idealist*   welcomes a broad range of views, seeks ideal solutions, interested in values.

- *The pragmatist*   supports 'whatever works', seeks shortest route to pay-off, interested in innovation.
- *The analyst*   uses formal logic and deduction, seeks 'the one best way', interested in 'scientific' solutions.
- *The realist*   relies on 'facts' and expert opinions, seeks solutions that meet current needs, interested in concrete results.

Whether you are aware of it or not, you employ a set of specific strategies for thinking through problems or decisions. These strategies reflect the kind of thinker you are. Most people use only one and perhaps two kinds of thinking. This limits the thinking strategies you use, thereby limiting the quality of your thinking. The 'i_nQ' assists you to expand your range of thinking strategies.

Learning styles questionnaire (LSQ)

In conditions of increased change, complexity and competition, it is essential that your organization continually improves both what it does and how it does it.

Continual improvement is based on continual learning. By 'learning', I mean detecting and closing gaps between what's intended or required and what actually happens. Creating a 'culture of continual learning' starts with you and your colleagues at the top. *How* you learn (the process) is as critical as *what* you learn (the content). Very few people, however, know their 'learning style'. The LSQ is a self-questionnaire providing you with insights into your current approach to learning, its pluses and minuses, and what is involved in strengthening your learning style and/or developing other styles currently under-utilized. In short, the LSQ helps you to learn more and learn it better.

Conclusion

This chapter has, I hope, given you some ideas on thinking worth thinking about. In the context of your role as a director or executive in today's tough business environment, I put it to you that a very strategic use of your time would be to take time out to increase your strategic thinking competencies.

Time spent thinking about thinking and learning how to think better is time well spent!

Details of the 'Tools for Thinking Strategically' Development Programme can be obtained from Phil Hanford, PO Box 170, Randwick, New South Wales 2031, Australia. Fax: (02) 314 6687.

Notes

1. Interview with Doug Stace about the October 1992 Strategic Management Conference in London, reported in the May 1993 *Catalyst*—Newsletter of the Centre for Corporate Change, Australian Graduate School of Management, University of New South Wales, Sydney.
2. Report on 'New management patterns: key findings from the MIT 90s research study' at a one-day conference in London on 2 July 1992, jointly sponsored by the Association for Management Education and Development (AMED) and the Strategic Planning Society (both London).
3. Quoted from 'The Top Job', an essay in *Frontiers of Leadership*, Oxford UK and Cambridge USA: Blackwell Limited, 1992.

References

Ackoff, R. (1981) *Creating the Corporate Future*, New York: John Wiley.

Argyris, C. (1993) *On Organizational Learning*, Cambridge, MA: Blackwell.

Beckhard, R. and Pritchard, W. (1992) *Changing the Essence: The Art of Creating and Leading Fundamental Change in Organizations*, San Francisco, CA: Jossey-Bass.

De Bono, E. (1988). 'De Bono's school of thought', *The Australian*, 30 March.

De Bono, E. (1985) *Six Thinking Hats*, London: Penguin.

De Geus, A. (1990) 'Planning as learning', *Harvard Business Review*, March, 1988, quoted in Peter Senge's *The Fifth Discipline*, New York: Doubleday.

Garratt, R. (1990) 'Development and directors', Chapter 1 of *Learning to Lead: Developing Your Organisation and Yourself*, London: Fontana.

Hanford, P. (1983) 'Managing for results', unpublished paper written for the Public Service Board, Queensland State Government, Brisbane.

Hickman, C. and Silva, M. (1984) 'On becoming a strategic thinker', Chapter 2 in *Creating Excellence: Managing Corporate Culture, Strategy and Change in the New Age*, London and Boston: George Allen and Unwin.

Kaufman, R. (1991) *Strategic Planning Plus: An Organization Guide*, Newbury Park, CA: Sage Publications.

Mackay, H. (1993) *Reinventing Australia: The Mind and Mood of Australia in the 1990s*, Sydney: Angus and Robertson (pp. 1–23 describe the 1990s as an 'Age of Redefinition').

Pfeiffer, J. W. Goodstein, L. D. and Nolan, T. M. (1989) *Shaping Strategic Planning*, Glenview, IL: Scott Foresmen and Company.

Weisbord, M. (1991) 'Third wave managing and consulting', part 3 in *Productive Workplaces: Organizing and Managing for Dignity, Meaning and Community*, San Francisco, CA: Jossey-Bass.

Further information on specific strategic thinking tools

Reframing
Bolman, L. G. and Deal, T. E. (1991) *Reframing Organizations: Artistry, Choice and Leadership*, San Francisco, CA: Jossey-Bass.
Six thinking hats
De Bono, E. (1985) *Six Thinking Hats*, London: Penguin Books.
Searching questions to explore[*]
Effective questions to empower
Oakley, E. and Krug, D. (1991) *Enlightened Leadership: Getting to the Heart of Change*, New York: Simon & Schuster.
Holistic thinking model—breadth of your thinking[*]
RAVBA—depth of your thinking[*]
Paradigms and paradigm shifts—RAVBA's cousins
Barker, J. A. (1992) *Paradigms: The Business of Discovering the Future*, New York: HarperCollins.
Types of thinking[*]
Planning perspective—outward, upward and forward
Kaufman, R. (1991) *Strategic Planning Plus: An Organizational Guide*, Newbury Park, CA: Sage Publications
Prerequisites to change[*]
Both/and thinking
Hampden-Turner, C. (1990) *Charting the Corporate Mind: From Dilemma to Strategy*, Oxford: Basil Blackwell.
Mind mapping your strategic challenge
Svantesson, I. (1989) *Mind Mapping and Memory* (especially Chapter 6), London: Kogan Page.
SLIM priority-setting technique[*]
Choices and consequences thinking[*]
Thinking Intentions Profile (TIP)
Rhodes, J. and Thame, S. (1988) *The Colours of Your Mind: Managing Your Thinking Style*, London: Fontana/Collins.
Kinds of thinkers (I_nQ)
Harrison, A. F. and Bramson, R. H. (1982) *The Art of Thinking: Strategies for Asking Questions and Making Decisions*, New York: Doubleday.

Learning styles questionnaire (LSQ)
Honey, P. and Mumford, M. (1989) *Capitalizing on Your Learning Style*, King of Prussia, Pennsylvania, PA: Organization Design and Development Inc.

*These concepts or techniques were developed by Phil Hanford and will be included in his book on strategic management due out in late 1994.

Recommended reading

The following is a carefully chosen few books I heartily recommend to you. They are all top-job oriented, full of wisdom, practical, short and easy to read, and readily available. It would be especially useful for you to read them in the order listed as a study programme, as it were. They will provide you with a very strong knowledge base in strategic management and its implications for you as a leader.

Ackoff, R. (1981) First three chapters of *Creating The Corporate Future: Plan Or Be Planned For*, New York: John Wiley. These chapters on 'our changing concept of the world... of the corporation... of planning' by an acknowledged leader in strategic thinking are classics. Though they were written nearly fifteen years ago, they remain the single best description of the 'big picture' that I have yet come across.

Hickman, C. and Silva, M. (1984) *Creating Excellence: Managing Corporate Culture, Strategy and Change in The New Age*, London and Boston: George Allen and Unwin. Hickman and Silva bring to the table a balanced perspective in that they are both businessmen and consultants with strong academic backgrounds. *Creating Excellence* provides an integrated framework for achieving just that. This is then matched to the stage at which your organization is: start-up, growth, crisis or evolution. Also included are a series of chapters on very practical and specific things that you can do as a leader to increase your personal effectiveness.

Garratt, R. (1990) *Learning to Lead: Developing Your Organisation and Yourself*, London: Fontana. This book is very insightful about the true role of directors and executives as the top team in setting directions for your organization rather than merely solving urgent problems. From that starting point, it goes into your own development as a leader and then onto developing others and the change process and creating a learning organization. All these are top-led initiatives central to remaining a competitive, viable enterprise.

Belbin, M. (1993) *Team Roles At Work*, Oxford: Butterworth-Heinemann. This book by a world leader (some would say *the* leader) in research about teams in an organizational context is full of wisdom and practical advice for directors and executives about the vital, but very tricky, business of top team teamwork and team roles.

Beckhard, R. and Pritchard, W. (1992) *Changing the Essence: The Art of Creating and Leading Fundamental Change in Organizations*, San Francisco, CA: Jossey-Bass. This book is about managing 'fundamental' change, as distinct from incremental change, i.e. changing your organization's essence: its purpose, identity, and key relationships (e.g. with customers, suppliers, etc.). It links together your role in providing leadership, managing change, and building a culture of commitment. Included also are sound pointers on balancing short-term pressures and longer-term organizational health, and the notion of 'operating in a learning mode' where both learning and doing are valued.

11 Strategic thinking in public service

David Wilkinson and Mike Pedler

Introduction

Why write a separate chapter on strategy in the public services? There are a number of factors of special significance in public service management. We argue that effective processes of strategic thinking (as developed elsewhere in this book) are appropriate to public service, but must address the complexities of their context. There are differences *between* the public services, as there are between the public and private domains, but there are also differences between the circumstances, histories and values of individual schools, hospital trusts and local radio stations. Strategic thinking may take place in 'service delivery units' as well as at the 'provider' level of commissioning, regulating and coordinating.

Our purpose is to contribute to the dialogue about the processes of strategizing in public service as leaders struggle to be proactive in the face of change—imposed and otherwise. We want to encourage greater degrees of learning across the different sectors of health, education, social services, police and other government and local government services. Traditionally, many public services have seen themselves as 'different' and special along with the academic and research institutions that have grown to support them. Thus creative work frequently becomes sealed within its sector boundaries *and*, paradoxically, much research takes place within limited and traditional frames of reference.

We offer some future scenarios for public service and conclude that, even if the fragmentation of public governance at local levels continues, effective strategy making, particularly that which crosses 'sector' boundaries, could improve local governance as well as the quality of service delivery. This has implications for leadership. Given the particular requirements in many public arenas to think strategically about organizational change, there is a need for top management development to run in parallel with, and even precede, strategizing.

Key issues of strategy in public service

Is the strategic managerial task inherently different in public service? This is a vexed question, partly because the shape and composition of the old 'public sector' is changing rapidly in the UK and other parts of the world; the pressures for change in the public services are not simply a result of years of Conservative government.

There is a trend towards 'mixed economies' of service delivery through arm's-length units. While most of these remain within the state system, there is a greater use of market testing, internal competition through various forms of user choice, and a wider use of private sector and not-for-profit organizations. Whole swathes of the old public sector have been privatized. What remains covers a wide range of very different activities from enforcement—policing, environmental health, planning—to recreation and leisure. Some services have to deal with great complexities of user expectations, prioritizing and rationing (e.g. education, health, housing and benefits) while others provide *seemingly* simpler but vitally important services (e.g. refuse collection and street cleansing).

We have chosen five key strategic issues which, while not always unique to public service, are often and in combination, those which pose the most difficult strategic questions and dilemmas:

1. User complexity—the 'marketing' problem
2. Governance—increasing complexity demands increasing governance
3. 'New public management'—the pessimistic assumptions of recent reforms
4. Resistance to change
5. Productivity, participation and leadership in public service.

User complexity—the 'marketing' problem

If the first problem of any business is to have enough 'customers', many public services have too many, needing or demanding far too much. The 'marketing' task is *both* to make the public aware of services *and* then to ration the limited supply available of housing, schooling, health care and so on.

Delivery of services in the public domain involves working with a complex series of different interests, stakeholders, user, communities and wide public/political pressures. Some argue that this variety can be reduced to a single 'bottom line'. For example, parents could use vouchers, i.e. pay for the schooling of their children at the school of their choice. But, even if practical, this would surely serve only to push issues of equity and access to a higher level. Even if a government could afford to ignore these potentially explosive local issues, the public *policy* question would still remain to be answered.

Governance—increasing complexity demands increasing governance

Whether a public service is delivered by a public or private organization, and however simple or complex its user interest, it will have been commissioned either within the public arena, or within a statutory framework, and will usually be funded by public money. Whatever the delivery mechanism, vitally important issues of public policy must impinge upon the strategic management of these services.

The increasing use of quasi-markets, competitive tendering and privatization effectively shifts these issues of polity—to the 'higher ' levels of purchaser, client and commissioner. The fact that they may not be adequately dealt with, or that they are outside the political arena, given the increasing use of non-elected quangos, does not mean that they do not exist. They may be ignored but they cannot be delegated away into the marketplace. The complexities, uncertainties and lack of clarity in many areas of public governance frequently add a further and tricky dimension to strategic direction finding (see Osborne and Gaebler, 1992, pp. 43-6 and 101-2).

This is being exacerbated by proliferating variety in service provision. This is not to argue against innovation in provision, but to point out that increasing experimentation of this sort makes the requirement for the 'public overview' and agreed frameworks of governance all the more important.

'New public management'—the pessimistic assumptions of recent reforms

Public services in the UK are being subjected to change, largely via successive government legislation. The driving forces for change—the pressures of rising demand, costs, efficiency and effectiveness, while attempting to control taxation, national spending and inflation—are similar to those in other 'developed' economies worldwide. In the UK, these changes derive largely from an amalgam of 'public choice theory', 'agency theory', and 'classical, Fordist manage-ment'. These ideas share a pessimistic outlook on human nature and potential, and their concoction has been called 'new public management' (NPM) by Hood (1991) and others.

Public choice theory asserts that any group of politicians, professionals or others will subvert the claims of social purpose made by an organization because they always act in narrow self-interest. Hence policy and advice need to be separated. Service delivery should be at arm's length and not inform policy. As much as possible, organization and service delivery should be regulated through specific and tightly monitored contracts. These gloomy assumptions run parallel to those of McGregor's 'Theory X' assumptions about people; that they are fundamentally lazy, work only for instrumental reasons, need close supervision and are motivated simply by money (McGregor, 1960) and can be traced back to their intellectual forefather, Adam Smith:

> By pursuing his own interest he frequently promotes that of society more effectually than when he really intends to promote it. I have never known much good done by those who effected to trade in the public good.

Much of the government's change agenda is framed on the basis of this perspective. Ironically, these assumptions stand in sharp contrast to the philosophy that underpins the drive towards quality improvement and organizational learning that so many private sector, manufacturing and service industries are struggling to bring about.

Resistance to change   On the other hand, supporters of NPM might argue that such brutalism was necessary to break into a self-sealing and backwards-leaning public sector. However, honest supporters might now admit that initiatives such as privatization, purchaser/provider splits, performance-related pay and so on have increasingly become *the answers* rather than possible ways forward to a new vision for service delivery (Newchurch and Company, 1993).

Working towards real change and seeking better service delivery through greater staff involvement and participation requires considerable skills in strategic leadership. This involves understanding the forces underlying the demands from above so that realistic change agendas can be created. This is likely to be extraordinarily demanding because public service leaders are in many cases being asked to stand on the fault line between different managerial mindsets. (Murray, 1991).

In general terms, many public service organizations have been very resistant to change with their vision apparently set firmly on the rearview mirror. This has left them vulnerable to attack from the political right (although it is worth noting that a Labour government in New Zealand used many of these same approaches to initiate public sector change). From the NPM perspective, public sector organizations are 'captured' by self-seeking professionals and other interested parties for their own ends. They then become impervious to external demands for change (Boston *et al.*, 1992).

Without wholly accepting this pessimistic view, and recognizing the many innovations of dedicated people who have sought to experiment, learn and improve services across the public sector, it is arguable that many services are organized in ways that have barely changed over the past fifty years. For example, despite the success of the Open University in open and distance adult learning, few of its pioneering innovations seem to have been translated into the educational mainstream where the development of innovative learning strategies should surely be a strategic priority.

Productivity, participation and leadership in public service

The fifth and final issue is what Drucker (1992) calls 'the new productivity challenge'. Productivity gains in agriculture and manufacturing during this century have been enormous. This pressure is now on professionals, technical, administrative and service workers. Currently, the financial services industry is undergoing massive job losses with the subsequent increase in productivity. As governments seek ways of curbing the expansion of the public sector, these pressures are inevitably coming to the public services.

In services, the search for productivity is about both quantity and quality. According to Drucker, it starts with asking fundamental questions such as What is the task? What do we try to accomplish? Why do it at all? The easiest—but perhaps also the greatest—increases in productivity in such work come from redefining the task and especially from 'eliminating what needs not to be done' (Drucker, 1992, p. 83).

However, the most striking point made by Drucker on the search for service productivity is the need for participation—at all levels—with those involved:

> In making and moving things, partnership with the responsible worker is, however, only the *best* way—after all, Taylor's telling them worked, too, and quite well. In knowledge and service work, partnership with the responsible worker is the *only* way; nothing else will work at all (p. 91)

This is the telling point. Drucker has been making such statements since the 1940s and it is this collaborative approach which was taken up by Deming and others in the pursuit of quality improvement which has had such an impact in areas of Japanese manufacturing.

Drucker's fundamental questions are at the heart of new approaches to 'business process re-engineering' and 'process innovation' involving fully networked information technology (Davenport, 1993, Tapscott and Caston, 1993). One interesting translation of these ideas into the public services is Lathrop's (1993) 'patient focused paradigm' in his study of restructuring health care. This shifts the focus of organization of the hospital around the patient rather than the professional hierarchies or 'smokestacks' of traditional health care.

The search for productivity and quality improvement will be a service imperative. So far, most government interventions for change have been driven from Theory X positions. As Drucker suggests, these are not likely to lead to significant improvements in services to people—which crucially depend upon committed people acting in a tradition of genuine public service—and serve only to re-emphasize the need for public service managers to think strategically about how they go about developing their organizations.

Public sector or public service?

We prefer the term *public service* to *public sector* because the latter implies a clear distinction between public and private. For reasons of history, geography, economic necessity or a particular political outlook, it is difficult to find a service, traditionally delivered in the public sector, that is not delivered in the private sector somewhere in the world—and vice versa. The public sector can also extend into many areas of the economy, including retailing, insurance, mineral extraction, industry and even agriculture; while the private sector can provide even the essential utilities and health, education and social services.

The questions of how efficiently the public sector delivers the more commercial services, or how well the private sector— with its dominant profit motive—can effectively provide social or educational services are likely to remain with us as these distinctions become more fluid. With the movement of services from the public to the private arenas through privatization, competitive tendering and market testing, etc. there is also a growing middle ground of not-for-profit organizations, trusts and other quasi-market arenas.

Hopefully, the question of what is delivered in the private sector, the not-for-profit sector or the public services will become an empirical one based on efficiency, effectiveness, equity and equality of access. In any case, it seems that it is becoming increasingly difficult to draw demarcation lines between public and private, particularly in terms of service delivery.

A new emphasis on the concept of public service shifts attention away from service delivery and refocuses it upon those issues of public policy and governance that remain to be dealt with however small or large the 'sector'. A public service focus may help to re-emphasize broad and crucial issues of policy that have been given scant attention by many local politicians as they have become more and more involved in the 'hands-on' running of the ever-growing giants of recent decades. It could help to shape the new political agendas of the future and perhaps break out of the sometimes sterile bickerings of traditional political divides. There are healthy signs that this is already beginning to happen, with one driving force being the existence of so many 'hung councils'. This should go further, towards a redefinition of governance at local levels; and, in the absence of a national political vision for this, it is likely that the creativity and energy for this will need to be driven locally.

If it is healthy to open the 'ring fence' around the public sector, the same also applies to the many formally sealed boundaries *within* the old public sector. Traditionally, many public services have seen themselves as 'different' and special, along with the academic and research institutions that have grown up to support them. Innovation and research, where they exist, have tended to remain sealed within sector boundaries, with a disposition to reject new ways of thinking from the outside, especially from the private sector—the 'not invented here' syndrome.

As we noted above, this has left many public sector areas vulnerable to the government's attack. In the end, it was only an emerging alliance of teachers and parents, with support from an increasingly concerned business community, that led to the halting of the fast-growing bureaucracy surrounding the National Curriculum and attainment testing in education. In the past, the stronger the professional protest, the more energy has come from government to push the changes even harder. Given the notion of 'capture', and the decreasing regard in government for many public sector professionals, protest was likely to be seen as a signal that the government must be on the right lines—'well, they would say that, wouldn't they!'

If this sort of emerging partnership can produce more balanced policy outcomes, then perhaps they could serve as the new medium for delivering improved services on the ground. For instance, the implementation of community care, taken together with GP fundholding, is encouraging staff at ground level to break out of the old institutional, geographical and professional boundaries. Staff from local authorities, hospitals, community health, and primary care are starting to talk to each other in cross-agency alliances to deliver more relevant, flexible and localized community health care.

These bridge-building, partnership and governance roles are crucial to the re-invigoration of public service. While service delivery can be delegated to 'local mixed economies of provision', this is not true for the central issues of policy, equity, access and regulation. A new public service focus would put these currently low-priority issues at the centre of the new political agenda.

The nature of strategic thinking in the public services

Are the processes of strategic thinking different in the public services? Notions of direction-giving, future thinking, scenario building, dilemma methodology and issues of developments in corporate governance are as relevant here as elsewhere. However, as we have said, it is the *context* in which these thinking tools and processes of learning take place within the public service domain that makes the crucial difference.

As an example, Garratt (1991) argues for a hierarchy of managerial policy, strategy and operations:

> ...The idea of policy has developed as a combined use of wise, sophisticated, and tidy governance, coupled with the definition of the boundaries within which members of a society may exercise their liberties. I argue that the prime job of the direction-givers is to define policy for their organization, i.e. to give the basic rules within which others can plan the allocation of resources and tactics to achieve these broad objectives.

So it is the job of top management to establish the broad brushstrokes of strategy to give direction within the policy framework. This includes the allocation of resources and contracts and ensuring that any political imperatives are met. Garratt continues:

> The essence of the strategist is managing the conjunction of the political world, or 'polity', with the more day-to-day routines of tactics and trying to keep them sufficiently in balance without allowing ossification. It is, therefore, essential for a director to

have the ability to rise above the daily and weekly tactical detail so that he or she can project and direct the business' campaigns. But coping with politicians, pressure groups, and taking overviews are not the normal domains of top managers, especially those promoted from the ranks of the tacticians.

Using these rather optimistic role definitions in local government, politicians would occupy the policy roles, the chief executive and directors would be the strategists and service managers the operational 'colonels'. However, many politicians and senior officers have often been happier working on operational details, solving problems and fighting fires. For elected members—as politicians—being seen to be effective in relation to Mrs Smith's dustbin problem would, and is likely to, receive more favourable attention in the local newspaper. While this is clearly one role for the citizen's representative, the rather more abstract and intractable problems of policy remain unresolved.

Often, officers, frustrated at the lack of both policy and strategic direction, fill the vacuum themselves, and this can lead to conflict when members reassert their authority. In recent years, government has added to the frustration by both devolving greater autonomy to service units, in particular schools while, at the same time, pulling back major powers to the centre. This has led many local politicians and some directors to feel that they have a diminished policy role.

In other public services, such as health and police authorities, political involvement has tended to be less 'hands-on'. Increasingly, however, these roles are being replaced, for example, through the development of Family Health Services Authorities (FHSAs), NHS trusts, and school governing bodies. The sum total of these changes has led to an increasing marginalization of local politicians and also to a whole range of questions surrounding the role of so many newly non-elected appointees to 'non-executive' roles.

An example from the Health Services (Barrett and McMahon, 1990) suggests that policy, strategy and operations are often difficult to disentangle in practice and that, indeed, policies are usually made 'on the hoof' while managers grapple with getting things done. Managers in the NHS

> ...appear to spend much of their time negotiating with individuals and groups which, although part of the organization, seem to have scant regard for its goals, but seem instead to be following their own sectional interests...Although some attention is paid to structures and plans, the managers' overriding concern is to anticipate the tactics that will be employed

against them, and then to develop whole repertoires of possible counter-moves. They spend a great deal of time using their 'network' to establish who is making what deals with whom. They also seem to work hard to keep their team of senior managers loyal to their cause. They do not appear to be in control, but are able to exert influence.... (p. 260)

and '[managers]...are actually holding the ring; managing the network of negotiation and bargaining' (p. 264).

A 'negotiated order' (Strauss, 1979) is reached via trading between groups with different values, interests, stakes, power bases and relative autonomies—where conflict is normal—indeed, endemic. Barrett and McMahon suggest that managers need to develop three types of strategic thought and action if they are to manage well in these conditions: (1) provide a broad but not detailed 'sense of direction'; (2) help people and groups to come to agreements about directions rather than relying on coercion; (3) work with endemic conflict. This approach recognizes the pluralistic nature of organizations in contrast to the unitary assumptions of many top-down attempts at reform. There is a parallel here with the literature on 'federal' organization (Handy, 1992).

Given these realities, can Garratt's separation and hierarchy of policy, strategy and operations survive? Who occupies the strategic roles? What does this imply for strategic thinking at the commissioning levels as well as for service delivery units? In order to address these questions, we need to look at some possible future scenarios.

Future scenarios

Imagine three different pairings of areas: the first, of similar metropolitan areas based on declining manufacturing industries; the second, of similar coastal areas with varied local economies including a small but thriving port and growing tourism; the third, of two market towns linked to smaller ones in extensive rural areas set apart from the metropolitan areas of the UK.

From the vantage point of the year 2001, let us imagine that one of each of these pairings is doing particularly well in comparison with its twin. What has made the difference?

In the successful areas the following has happened:

- Job creation has exceeded job losses, particularly following the cutbacks in service sector jobs in the productivity squeeze of the later 1990s. Many of the new jobs are in new small firms in communications, electronics, specialist manufacturing and services. It is noticeable that some local industries are doing unexpectedly well.

- There is a marked and continuing improvement in educational attainment at all levels and ages with a growing high proportion of young people in higher education. More adults, particularly women, are moving into further and higher education and seeking professional qualifications. Better job prospects, together with improved education opportunities, have become a magnet for both people and firms to relocate.
- There is a slowly improving infrastructure in local transportation, information networks, community-based health-care facilities, etc.
- The health of the population is improving and there has been some slowing of the increase in criminality. Despite improved job prospects and educational attainment levels, there remains a concern about unemployment levels among poorly qualified younger men. The now-accepted connection between unemployment and criminality is the focus of concerted, long-term, cross-agency activity and is less of a problem than it might have been.
- There is a stronger infrastructure of voluntary and leisure activity, groupings and associations of all kinds. Those actively involved now exceed the still-declining membership of the political parties. Increasingly, people are using their voting powers to influence outcomes on particular single issues to which they are committed, and are a significant force in local politics.

Looking back from the year 2001, it was clear that these successes came about as a result of some key developments.

1. By 1994 it was clear that those firms, particularly in manufacturing, which were coming out of recession earlier had done things differently. Surprisingly, during a recession, and in a sharp break from local traditions, they increased their training, research and especially product development, with a marked improvement in quality. They managed to integrate these initiatives in their longer-term business goals and visions in contrast to the 'bottom-line' thinking then prevalent.
2. In the public services, from the early 1990s, there was an increasing realization and acceptance of the need for change irrespective of the political agendas of seemingly endless Conservative governments. A new architecture of service delivery developed as officers, supported by some

local politicians, sought constructive ways of crossing boundaries to provide improved local services. Local government review was used as an opportunity to think forward and seek greater collaboration with both public and private sector partners. The development of health commissioning together with concepts like 'health gain' and 'added value' in education led to a clearer picture of the local effects of economic and social factors.

3. The local authority, particularly through its interactions with the health authority, clarified interlocking commissioning roles. Using initiatives such as CCT (compulsory competitive tendering) and care in the community, it sought an organic approach to achieving the kind of local authority it wanted to become, and to generate locally based initiatives, enterprise and collaboration.

4. The business community, previously fragmented, created a 'forum' to establish its voice and influence and created area-wide future scenarios. DTI (Department of Trade and Industry) 'one-stop shops' and the TEC (Training and Enterprise Council), actively supported by the local authority, encouraged joint working.

5. A key development was the gradual emergence of a consensual long-term vision of the economic and social future of the area. Critically, the emphasis was placed upon the developing strengths, potentials and capability requirements of the area. There was less competition with surrounding areas and more awareness that the main competition came from Europe and one or two other areas in the UK. The social, physical and technical infrastructure had been aligned to create a collaborative climate for the growth of all types of service and manufacturing activities.

6. Education business partnerships grew at a rapid pace. Schools collaborated locally to apply whole school improvement models. The variety, richness and range of teaching learning strategies developed to enhance educational achievement through the new simplified National Curriculum. Collaboration between education and business led to the better identification with the requirement for thinking, learning to learn, and teamwork skills for the future workforce *and* for success in higher education. A noticeable outcome was that many people from outside education, including many business leaders, were considerably more knowledgeable about, and supportive of, the fundamental issues of teaching and learning. This had

spin-offs in improving learning opportunities in other workplaces.

7. The establishment of open-learning networks, and the notion of close buyer–supplier relationships led to 'lean production' systems. For example, the health authority notices that its neighbour, a car components manufacturer, automatically received electronically transferred payments, without the usual paper trails of invoicing, every time a completed car came off the assembly line.

8. The health authority, in alliance with GPs, placed greater emphasis on community and primary care. It also pushed the acute care hospitals towards a more cost-effective and patient-centred approach, in the face of resistance from the hierarchically organized health-care professionals within the hospital. Asserting its 'command' role to change the provision of health care, the authority increasingly saw collaborative ways of facilitating change in its provider units. The evolving mixed economy of provision, together with the purchasing health authority and its local authority partners, began to feel more as though it were part of one organization again. By the late 1990s, newly integrated information systems led to a reduction of the previously much-criticized growth in managerial, financial and administrative staff.

9. Throughout the 1990s, government appeals for innovation in local governance were frustrated partly by its own regional agencies operating in isolation and 'singing from different hymn sheets'. With their longer-term visions and development of cross-boundary links, local alliances are now able to have greater influence with the non-elected regional headquarters of different government ministries, which were themselves brought together in the mid-1990s.

10. There was great innovation in building new forms of public accountability and a wholesale commitment on the part of public services to build links with their users. This led to a new vitality and sense of purpose. The credibility, integrity and honourability of 'public service' was being 're-invented'.

The way ahead? There are many possibilities and influences. National government, always a big, and currently never a bigger, voice in public service policy making, might merge the commissioning role of local authorities with that of the health authorities.

Another government might encourage regional democracy and local public accountability.

Despite the uncertainties, vision building, partnerships, cross-boundary working, the development of learning organizations and learning communities are likely to figure prominently in providing effective public service. Our guess is that those areas which will be relatively less successful in the year 2001 will not move in these directions but will try to respond to change by seeking improvements to the old ways of working. We don't think this will be enough. Something more of a transformation is required. There is no formula: it requires experiment, risk and demanding negotiations; it will need careful bridge building by those who have the initial visions and determination to make something happen.

A final scenario   The public services of the future will be delivered in new alliances of the traditionally separate agencies in a mode of much higher responsiveness to and partnership with users. This will come about partly because of the unremitting demands of 'more for less' but also because of the type of problems now being referred to public service agencies.

These problems are no longer defined within departmental boundaries: it is not a matter of 'building *n* thousand houses' or 'bringing the magic of gas to every home'. Today's problems fall across and between the agencies and utilities. To which department or agency shall we refer demands for reduction in

- Smoking and heart disease?
- Teenage pregnancies?
- Urban river pollution?
- Crime on housing estates?
- Homelessness and poverty?

Such problems require a *horizontal*, cross-agency response to pool know-how, resources, and to coordinate actions and multiple initiatives. At the same time, making services more flexible, responsive, directed to where they are needed and delivered in partnership with users, requires a *vertical* ability to link policy, strategy and operations with user and public 'voice' (Figure 11.1).

This way of working has long been understood and practised by some people and agencies, but it has yet to become the established way of doing things. There is a great need for understanding and a climate of support from

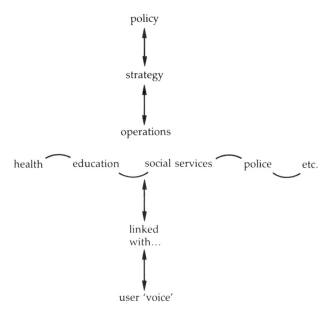

Figure 11.1   Cross-agency working

government and policy makers, not to mention the considerable skills involved in delivering services in this way. This is a
demanding task: examples of *living* user participation and
consultation in service delivery are not widespread. We can
imagine the professional worker needing the perspective of
the community worker, the skills of the counsellor, negotiator
and organizational consultant, and the influencing style and
emotional resilience of the politician!

Nevertheless, the work is beginning. For example, a district
health authority—a 'purchaser' or 'commissioner' of health
care for its local population—is trying the following ways of
accessing and encouraging user 'voice':

- putting an advertisement in the local paper inviting people
  to write in with their opinions
- contacting all known voluntary organizations in the district
  and asking them for their views
- bringing together small groups of people in the homes of
  volunteers for groups discussions
- placing post-paid questionnaires in various public places
  inviting comments.

Even these worthy efforts are likely to be of limited value in
reaching the less socially and politically active citizens, but it is

a start. Moreover, the challenge of cross-agency working with user 'voice' on the pressing social, educational and health-care problems of the day is large enough to excite and tap the commitment of many public service workers.

Back to strategy

What does this imply for the hierarchy of policy, strategy and operational roles? In local government, elected politicians should be encouraged to occupy the policy high ground and a clearer commissioning role would help this. In public services outside local government, board members for commissioning organizations in particular will need to be increasingly sensitive and open to the 'political dimension', to community overview and accountability. Some aspects of policy roles will need strengthening—for example, the ability to think beyond sector boundaries in the search for effective collaboration and partnerships, and setting frameworks for the development of local delivery systems within broad visions.

Non-executive board members are in a particularly difficult position—are they co-opted experts or quasi-representatives? For those committed to the concept of local democracy, this may be far from satisfactory. The injection of people from other backgrounds may be by no means a bad thing but there is no escaping the need for the development of a new local 'polity' to address issues of equity, access and market regulation.

Does this mean that the management of service delivery units is now a purely operational activity? We think not. As suggested earlier, policy, strategy and operations are not so easily separated, nor should they be. The aligning and developing of service organizations within the quasi-markets of the local context will demand strategic thinking as well as operational skill; it will contribute to the making of policy as this emerges. New levels of collaboration between professionals as colleagues are needed for the delivery of 'more for less' services. The individuals in such partnerships will need to be both strategists and leaders. All managers, all public service workers, will need to be proactive in the open, real-time information nets of the public service as a learning organization.

Further, as constructive balances are found between the 'command' and facilitating roles of commissioners in relation to providers, both commissioners and providers should be increasingly drawn into networks of strategic alliances, analogous to the buyer-supplier chains of 'the lean producers' (Womack *et al.*, 1990). The narrow, conflict-based, bureaucratic models of competitive tendering and purchasing that have dominated the 1980s and early 1990s need transcending.

Thus, public service leaders at all levels will need to work with the incremental change in what is currently possible as well as offering visions of transcendence. They are also bound to work within the various constraints and key strategic management issues that we identified earlier. As more private sector leaders engage in public–private partnerships and in the creation of locality-based visions, they will also experience these issues themselves.

In any case, learning to lead strategically in the public services requires special attention to these features, together with a turbulence of change which is unprecedented in the experience of most managers. Some of the more open-ended futures in prospect suggest that development and strategy go hand in hand. From this perspective, leading, learning, action and development become integral to each other.

Final words

One difference between the public services and the private sector has a major effect on matters of strategy. In the private sector, strategy making is overridingly facilitated by what Hampden-Turner (1992) has termed the 'reconciling' function of profit. In public service, there is no such simple reconciler for the many strategic dilemmas to be found:

> Schools cannot decide to stop educating five year olds. The health service cannot refuse to treat patients in Sussex. Yet a private company can easily withdraw from markets, or reduce its product range (Haigh, 1993).

A school may search for ways of serving pupils well but, as part of a wider system of education, it has no desire to see its 'competitors' going out of business. On the contrary, it has every interest in enhancing both itself and the system of which it is a part.

The business of public service is not to make money but to make a difference. Strategy management in public service is 'not for competitive advantage but for social change' (Stewart, 1989, pp. 170-4).

References

Barrett, S. and McMahon, L. (1990) 'Public management in uncertainty: a micro-political perspective of the health service in the UK', *Policy and Practice*, **18** (4), 257-68.

Boston, J., Martin, J., Pollot, J. and Walsh, P. (1992) *Re-shaping the State—New Zealand's Bureaucratic Revolution*, Oxford: Oxford University Press.

Davenport, T. H. (1993) *Process Innovation—Re-engineering Work Through Information Technology*, Boston, MA: Harvard Business School Press.

Garratt, R. (1991) *Learning to Lead*, London: HarperCollins.

Haigh, D. (1993) *Transforming the Dinosaurs*, London: Demos.

Hampden-Turner, C. in Common, R., Flynn, N. and Mellon, E. (1992) *Managing Public Services: Competition and Decentralisation*, Oxford: Butterworth-Heinemann, p. viii.

Handy, C. (1992) 'Balancing corporate power: a new federalist paper', *Harvard Business Review* November-December, 59-72.

Hood, C. (1991) 'A public management for all seasons?' *Public Administration*, **69**, Spring, 3-19.

Lathrop, J. P. (1993) *Restructuring Health Care: The Patient-focused Paradigm*, Booz-Allen Health Care.

Murray, R. (1991) 'The state after Henry', *Marxism Today*, May, 22-27.

Newchurch and Company (1993) *Competitive Tendering with Local Government: A Stuttering Approach*, 12 Charterhouse Square, London, December.

Osborne, D. and Gaebler, T. (1992) *Re-inventing Government*, Reading, MA: Addison-Wesley.

Stewart, J. (1989) 'In search of a curriculum for management for the public sector', *Management Education and Development*, **20** (3), 168-75.

Strauss, A. (1979) *Negotiations*, San Francisco, CA: Jossey-Bass.

Tapscott, D. and Caston, A. (1993) *Paradigm Shift: The New Promise of Information Technology*, New York: McGraw-Hill.

Womack, J. P., Jones, D. T. and Roos, D. (1990) *The Machine That Changed The World*, New York: Rawson Associates.

12 International teams: avoiding the pitfalls and creating a source of international strategy

Sue Canney Davison

The pitfalls in international teams' performance arise from a lack of both courage and cross-cultural team skills. Teams can contribute only if they perform well. A high-performing international team will have consciously worked as hard on their cross-cultural interaction as they did on their task. Very few do. Yet doing so can create the difference between an international team being a block to, or a source of, creative international strategy.

One of the common academic assertions about international teams is that they are more creative than teams of one nationality (Adler, 1986). The assertion has gained some support from experimental research (e.g. Watson *et al.*, 1993). The same research also shows that these teams take longer to get over their communication difficulties than homogeneous teams, so overall performance tends to be the same. Most businesses are creating international teams, not because they may achieve higher creativity *per se* but because they reflect, and are therefore more sensitive to, the business interests in different parts of the world.

As many Western companies have painfully experienced, allowing a team of only Americans and Europeans to devise the strategy for China is likely to create a major problem. The question for businesses is not whether to have representative international teams or not, it is 'having created these teams from necessity, how can we avoid the misunderstandings and, instead, reap the benefits?' The answer lies in actively embodying the necessary skills.

For the sake of this chapter, strategy is defined as the context in which decisions are made (Bower and Doz, 1979). The strategic context highlighted is the embodied mindset of the decision-making managers in the company, rather than the operational, product-driven or technical contexts.

Cultural differences

Experience and research (see Schneider, 1989) has found that a nationally diverse pool of decision makers will embody significantly different approaches towards strategy formulation and implementation. Mintzberg (1987) argues for a balance between 'deliberate strategy where an intended plan is realized' and 'emergent strategy' where a pattern is realized despite or in the absence of an intended plan.

A preference for one or the other can be determined by the cultural attitudes towards uncertainty and power (Hofstede, 1980). It is likely that cultures that prefer to avoid uncertain situations tend more towards deliberate strategy than emergent strategy and vice versa. Organizations in cultures that prefer flatter power structures may be happier to let their managers act pragmatically according to circumstance and allow strategy to emerge. Organizations in cultures which foster strong top-down hierarchies are likely to prefer deliberate strategic formulation and implementation.

Strategy formulation and cultural differences

Different nationalities have also been found to have differing approaches to the sequential stages of strategy formulation. The bases on which individuals will scan, select, interpret, validate and establish priorities is likely to differ profoundly (Schneider, 1989). Schneider describes research where, for instance, the Swiss and Norwegians have been found to scan less than the Dutch, French, Danes, Swedes and North Americans. The Japanese, on the other hand, have been found to be more active, broad and informal scanners.

In selecting the type of information used, some cultures— such as Germany—will prefer formal quantitative information, thinking that it will reduce the risk. Others, such as Arabian Gulf cultures, will prefer informal qualitative information which reflects the relationships and social environment. Schneider points out that, in Japan, 'objective' has been translated as 'the guest's point of view' (Maruyama, 1984).

The Japanese also prefer to source information from many different levels of the organization, while Americans tend to ask the 'wise men' executives. Some cultures may rely more heavily on deduction and logic (United States) rather than intuition and analysis (Japan) to validate their thinking.

So, overall, different national cultures will create different preferences not only for emergent versus deliberate strategy formulation but also for different patterns of preferences in the sequential stages of formulation and implementation. Cultural differences will also influence which teams play a role in creating *and* implementing strategy within the organization. In many Western companies it is the role of top executive teams. In some, such as Shell, specially designated scenario planning teams create alternative strategies for different environmental futures. In others, such as Semco in Brazil (Semler, 1993) and Japanese companies, teams at different levels of the company are involved in generating new ideas and solutions. Some companies may be involved in a mixture of all three, perhaps by importing the Japanese bottom-up style into a US top-down approach and finding a balance as in Honda USA's *waigaya* groups (Pascale, 1990).

Recent in-depth research (Snow *et al.*, 1993) shows that international teams both formulate and implement global strategy in large multinationals. Their strategic contribution is usually focused in one of three areas; increasing global efficiency, increasing local responsiveness, or increasing organizational learning. It was found that the leadership styles, staffing, training and development, job design and rewards and appraisals of each team differ according to the main focus and role. For instance, in the past, Lever Europe has been locally responsible by focusing on country-based operations. Recently, they have combined their European operations across sixteen countries into a brand and business-oriented matrix. The urgent focus is now on acquiring 'global' efficiency. Organizational learning can be expected to emerge as time goes on. Many managers now find themselves as members of multiple international teams. Gaining the necessary skills to create high performance *within* these teams is a top priority. If the teams are not effective, the strategy to achieve regional integration and efficiency will not work. Whatever happens, the degree and rate of learning within the teams will drive future strategy and reorganization.

Pitfalls in the development of international strategy teams

Whether companies are ready for it or not, international teams are now crucial to the success of international strategy formulation and implementation. It is also clear that individuals from different countries will have very different approaches to both the types of, and sequential stages of, strategy formulation. Where, then, are the main pitfalls that occur because the teams are international?

First, dominant sub-groups of managers embodying the norms of the company's original, and perhaps headquarters', nationality tend to suppress the different experiences and ways of doing things of people from other nationalities within the company. Second, the team may not in practice be as nationally diverse as it first seems from the mix of passports. Psychometric testing may show that only people with certain psychological profiles have been selected. Third, the wrong leadership style, prejudices and large differences in common language ability and behaviour of the individual members can destroy meaningful participation and creative interaction.

Elements in the development of effective international strategic teams

1. There are very few truly global companies with an equally balanced spread of activity around the globe. Many large companies act as regional companies with international operations. The boards and top teams tend to be made up of a dominant sub-group of directors from the head-quarters nationality or region and perhaps one or two truly different people from further afield.

   This imbalance often excludes the minority nationalities from effective participation, especially in strategy formula-tion. For instance, an Italian company acquired a US company. Seven Italian top executives made up the executive coordination committee with three Americans. Although the new headquarters was based in the UK, the predominantly one-to-one Italian management style of the CEO who spoke little English alienated the Americans and created in them a detached view towards their jobs. They thought that the committee was for making decisions, but the Italians were clear that it was for sharing the decisions that the CEO was in the process of making. Before remedial action was taken, this team was not using its multiple resources creatively or, equally important, not building commitment to strategy implementation in the US plants.

   Tackling the differences in *how* to create strategy (the strategy-formulation process) is far more threatening for international teams than dealing with differences in content. Sufficient variety in knowledge and expertise has been established as a business necessity. However, the realization that all the people around the table may have a totally different understanding of the best way to formulate strategic content is too much for most managers. Like the Italian CEO, most team leaders subtly, or unsubtly, rely on a habitual way of achieving the task. In this example, the minority Americans believed that some in-depth group discussion should guide any ultimate decision—it was the *how*, not the *what*, that was alienating them.

Imagine the response of a Japanese, personally committed to a bottom-up 'emergent' strategic style when asked to contribute his or her knowledge of what works in Japan to a top-down 'deliberate' strategic process. A normal response is to wait until asked specific questions and do the best possible to tailor the knowledge into something applicable to the context offered. If the rest of the team do not dig deeper by asking probing questions, the team will not work through the process of creating a strategy which is responsive to the best of both approaches. Apart from missing an effective solution, the Japanese team member may well feel that the rest of the team were not really interested, and will be seen to remain 'aloof'.

Both these examples illustrate that not fully involving certain team members is not a neutral position. Bad teamwork can reinforce national and corporate stereotypes and increase levels of frustration and alienation. There may be an argument for not inviting a broad spread of diversity or pushing for higher levels of strategic international integration until the company is ready. If both have already happened faster than learning the skills, a company has no time to lose in actively embodying them.

2. Passports and politically drawn national boundaries are poor indications of ethnic, religious and regional cultural groups and of an individual's commitment to any one national norm. Research can only describe generalities. Individual personality, motivation and past experience can create the opposite influences. For instance, a Japanese who has lived in France for six years may be less committed to some Japanese norms and more to some French norms than six years earlier. Some peripatetic people, who have lived travelling from one country to another, may not be strongly committed to any recognizable national norms. Others respond by sticking even more closely to their original cultures, a few even to the point of parody.

Individual 'starting' positions could be assessed by 'benchmarking' from pre-questionnaires. However, in practice, the extent to which a team member defends or relinquishes his or her normal position can depend entirely on the levels of *trust* and *acknowledgement* reached within the team. It is unpredictable. Moreover, if the team members hold different passports but are all more strongly committed to the national norms that imbue the organizational culture, rather than their own, there will be little national variety accessible to the team. It will not be as 'international' as it first seems.

3. If national diversity is available within the team, then every member needs to participate in a meaningful way in order to access it. This does not mean a rigid one-by-one input. Some people say in a few words what others cannot suggest in many. People differ in how long they like to speak, how much input they like to invite into their argument and whether they prefer the written or spoken word.

For example, in a mixed team of mostly Western Europeans, the South Korean president did not participate much at first and asked to be called 'Mr Lee'. The rest of the team learnt to adjust their behaviour and invite his very positive and brief inputs. However, whenever detailed paperwork was involved, he again ceased to participate. The written word and numbers had a different significance and effect from the spoken one. The South Korean valued the latter higher.

The behavioural norms of many South-east Asian countries mean that individuals will not proffer their alternative point of view unless asked for it. Americans and Western Europeans are usually quite at home interrupting and talking over one another in order to gain entry into the conversation. In any language, it is almost impossible for even fluent second-language speakers to interrupt mother-tongue speakers using idioms at high speed. If these different communication preferences and language skills are not addressed, some people will become excluded. This places a high responsibility for the person chairing the meeting to ensure that non-mother-tongue members are given time to express themselves.

As well as communication and behavioural norms, arrogance and prejudice create major pitfalls in successful teamwork. In many Western companies, especially those that have been used to a colonial past, there is a clear national pecking order. One American CEO of a large financial corporation is brazen that Americans are best, then Britons, the rest of Europe and so on down the ladder, the less each culture is perceived to be like America, the measure of status. In some large European companies, headquarters' nationalities come first, then other Europeans and English-speaking cultures, Arabs and Malaysians are next and Africans are at the bottom. In Saudi

Arabia and Hong Kong, it is the Filipinos who are regularly treated as low in the pecking order. In Japan, it is the South Koreans and Chinese.

Being at the bottom means being seen as less well educated, less intelligent and probably more of a nuisance than an asset on the team, perhaps asking awkward questions (such as 'Why are we doing it this way?'). It often means being talked at, explained to, or simply ignored. Being female in male-oriented societies simply adds to the problem of ranking in the pecking order.

In many established multinationals, the same 'ratings' exist between different levels and functions, for example between 'international' and 'regional' officers. The problem is that it is unfashionable even to describe these pecking orders, let alone bring them to the surface, even though they are still actively exhibited in many international teams. If people are unable to grasp how these prejudices violate fundamental human respect for each other, then perhaps, in the age of multiculturalism and the rising capacities of the Pacific Rim, people can understand that the ignorance demonstrated by these prejudices is a major block to future successful business collaborations and hence their organization's profitability.

Repressing prejudices and ignoring or accommodating differences as low-level compromises fails in the long run. At some point, the team has to actively bring them to the surface to resolve them or face the consequences. In one consortium top team, two very different French and German CEOs sat back to back in the same office. They learnt how to accommodate each other's style in a superficial way but they did not, however, confront or work on the very different underlying priorities. As a result, when the going got tough, the differences emerged and the much-needed partnership between their two companies collapsed, with painful economic consequences.

Effective approaches to developing international strategy teams

To create the optimal strategy and learning, the whole team needs to actively negotiate and craft the best working *process* for that particular team and task. This road to high performance outcomes is seldom taken. It demands investment, training and practise and an awareness of the value of process. The investment starts by creating an effective structure within the team.

In a small marine engineering company, headquartered in Finland, the top team of five has three Finns, one Swede and one Briton. They run the company from four different locations around Northern Europe, meeting once a month for a two-day board meeting to develop and decide strategic issues. The organizational norms are their joint commitment to high-performance goals, an international mindset using English as a common company language, and a sharing of basic business values. Although the CEO sells his own views strongly and dominates the meeting time, all views are listened to, consensus is reached through debate and individual responsibility is taken for strategy implementation. The team has actively worked hard to create the 'discipline, communication, trust and team spirit' needed to span the geographical distances. The result is a high level of synergy and high performance.

What is so noticeable about this team is that its structure and behaviour mirrors the highly interdependent organizational matrix structure created throughout the whole organization and vice versa. The top team can source broad-based input and participation at all levels at the formulation stage and then ensure effective implementation through the devolved nature of the matrix (Galbraith and Kazanjian, 1986). If a company chooses not to create such a 'matrixed' top team, one solution is to create a more intellectually open environment to enable international teams to 'play' with different scenarios, as in Shell's much-discussed scenario-planning teams.

Thinking ahead to implementation when selecting the strategy formulation team can be a canny political move. A Dutch company included an Italian senior finance manager in a very high-profile international task force set up to create and implement a strategy to cut organizational costs. They knew that most of the production cuts would take place in Italy and that, having made key contributions to, and being party to, the decisions, the Italian finance manager would be better prepared to convey the painful news and to do so in the most culturally sensitive manner possible.

Tools and processes for the development of international strategy teams

Once the members of the team have been thoughtfully selected, the team needs to actively craft their working process to suit their task and create meaningful participation from all the team members. Some tools and simple but subtle processes are necessary to achieve this.

The first is to start slowly and finish fast. Instead of 'rushing into structure', interactive tools and skills are most usefully employed at the beginning of the team work.

1. Training in cross-cultural awareness and communication and, in particular, creating a common framework within which it is legitimate to talk about cultural differences. The Western-based frameworks of Hofstede (1980), Trompenaars (1993) and Redding (1990) are easily available and others originating from non-Western writers can be explored usefully. This early legitimization and celebration of international differences is crucial in creating the climate for the development process to succeed.

2. Creating a culturally sensitive way of giving individual and team feedback. In some cultures, positive or negative *personal* feedback causes extreme loss of face. Simple frameworks of learning and behavioural styles can be used to create the neutral territory across which frank and candid feedback about the process can be shared about the group without making it personal.

3. Learning relevant group techniques such as Metaplan, Hexagons or Groupware that can facilitate equal participation and brainstorming by having everyone write down ideas and then collectively discuss and prioritize them.

4. Investing in the relevant information technology to connect the team across geographical distances.

5. Creating a common understanding of, and commitment to, the goals and team objectives.

6. Actively negotiating a culturally workable process. Many teams fall into a pattern within the first few minutes of meeting based on a set of unspoken assumptions. International teams cannot assume that this pattern will access and creatively use their differences. They need to actively negotiate how they are going to approach the task and agree regular and rigorous checks that the process is working.

As the team work progresses, someone in the team needs to:

7. Create the space for meaningful participation from all members. This means slowing down native-tongue speakers and giving room for second-language speakers and different behavioural norms.

8. Summarize, paraphrase, check understanding as the work progresses and keep a visible record of what has been discussed or agreed. Although this is primarily a chairing

role, it is a useful and developable skill for every member of an international team.

9. Ensure that the team uses the allotted time creatively. This means trusting that starting slowly will speed things up at the end and also to keep the discussion positively focused on the goals. To move the team on, similarities and agreements will need to be stressed and celebrated. At other points, the differences need to be used visibly as a source of creativity. There are times for both within the appropriate task method and process, but they have to be managed by the international team.

10. Review and upgrade the interaction and pass on the learning about team process as well as the strategic outcomes to the rest of the organization.

These last four skills can actively improve the fit of the interaction to meet the demands of the task as the team progresses. It is hard to facilitate both the content and the process of a discussion. If the team leader needs to be involved in the content of the discussions, then facilitating these interactive skills can be done by someone else appointed to be a 'process facilitator' or the deliberate handing over of the chairing for that item. In some cultures, such as Latin countries, splitting these 'power' roles may not be possible. It depends upon what the team expects of its leader and the role the leader expects to play. Both need to be stated explicitly.

From observing two teams formulating strategy in an East Asian bank it is clear that the *phases* of the task must also be used creatively. Gathering and sharing the necessary scanned information was not difficult. The problems began as two teams struggled to decide how to structure the information. One team refused to get into a heated debate and focused on staying friendly. The result was that, at this crucial moment, they lost the momentum, were seen by themselves to have 'wasted' an afternoon and never quite recovered. The other team began to develop a heated argument. When the small room started to get uncomfortably 'hot', they went down to the squash courts to open up a brainstorming session on different possible solutions. They came back into the room fired up with eight different strategies and channelled their energies into arguing through the merits of each strategy in light of the information gathered.

International teams are likely to formulate and implement strategy across large geographical distances. Recent research suggests that, when together, the team can best use its time on *value-related* issues and, when apart, it can best use its time creating, sharing and processing *information*. In other words, when together, a successful international team will:

Establish goals
Build relationships and trust
Discover communication and feedback preferences
Resolve differences and conflicts through making values
  explicit
Argue through and come to major decisions
Evaluate and review progress
Jointly undergo some training
If necessary, change behaviours and policies while keeping
  their values and principles.

   When apart, a successful international team will:

Establish regular disciplined information
Find, share and review information
Implement agreed actions and give rapid feedback on the
  consequences
Prepare from joint meetings
Anticipate colleagues' questions and needs.

Best practice in development programmes

At the beginning of this chapter, strategy was established as the context in which decisions are made; the embodied mindset of the pool of decision-making management. How deeply the pool runs down into the organization will be influenced by the national context of that organization.

Whatever the perceived size of the pool, the managers and employees involved need to be skilled in international teamwork. Some Western companies are actively working to develop international team skills and international strategic thinking in combined development projects. Managers work in cross-functional, cross-national teams to develop a specific international strategic issue that is then presented to the board and top management. In the case of GE, the second half of a four-week project actually happens in a difficult cultural context where the company is looking to develop business. For example, the mixed team will develop a strategy to expand the Chinese market by 7 per cent and spend the last two weeks in China facing the gritty reality of their thinking and learning, rapidly, from it.

In Nokia, international telecommunications company, the project work for international team development is spread over four months with two or three workshops on project work, team building, international leadership and strategy interjected during that period. The advantage of this extended time is that the learning has time to sink in between module meetings and is reviewed and upgraded. The contents and findings of the projects are codified and become useful mechanisms for enhancing overall global strategy. The process networks the managers across national and functional borders. At the same time, it instils best practice and experience in international teamwork into the organization's mindset. Instead of acting as sources of pitfalls and expensive mistakes, these international teams become creative sources of both emergent and deliberate international strategy and competent strategic thinking.

References

Adler, N. (1986) *International Dimensions of Organizational Behaviour*, Boston, MA: Kent Business Publishing.

Bower, J. L. and Doz, Y. (1979) 'Strategy formulation: a social and political process', in Schendel, D. and Hofer, C. (eds), *Strategic Management*, Boston, MA: Little, Brown.

Galbraith, J. and Kazanjian, R. K. (1986) 'Organising to implement strategies of diversity and globalisation: the role of matrix designs', *Human Resource Management*, **25**, (1), Spring, 37-54.

Hofstede, G. (1980) *Culture's Consequences*, Beverly Hills, CA: Sage Publications.

Maruyama, M. (1984) 'Alternative concepts of management insights from Asia and Africa', *Asia Pacific Journal of Management*, January, 100-11.

Mintzberg, H. (1987) 'Crafting strategy', *Harvard Business Review*, September-October.

Pascale, R. (1990) *Managing on the Edge*, New York: Simon & Schuster.

Redding, S. G. (1990) *The Spirit of Chinese Capitalism*, Berlin/New York: W. De Gruyter.

Schneider, S. (1989) 'Strategy formulation: the impact of national culture', *Organisation Studies*, **10**, (2), 149-68.

Schneider, S. and De Meyer, A. (1989) 'Interpreting and responding to strategy issues: the impact of national culture', INSEAD working paper No. 89/61.

Semler, R. (1993) *Maverick*, London: Century/Random House.

Snow, C., Snell, S., Canney Davison, S. and Hambrick, D. (1993) 'Developing transnational teams in global network organisations', Executive Summary, ICEDR report, November.

Trompenaars, F. (1993) *Riding the Waves of Culture*, London: Economist Books.

Watson, W., Kumar, K. and Michaelson, L. (1993) 'Cultural diversity's impact on interaction process and performance: comparing homogeneous and diverse task groups', *Academy of Management Journal*, **36**, 590-602.

13 Developing the international manager strategically

Fons Trompenaars

In a global environment, Human Resource Management (HRM) in general, and Management Development (MD) in particular, is increasingly affected by cultural differences. The way HRM is deployed in a multicultural environment is and needs to be part of the larger strategy and, in turn, will shape the organization. The process of developing the international manager reflects, as well as produces, the specific level of internationalization of the corporation. A global MD strategy is unlikely to endure unless it is an aspect of the organization's global concept and vice versa. In a globalizing corporation, the development of the international manager becomes a *strategic* activity, for both the functional level of HRM and for all general management with operative HRM responsibility.

The development of human resources in an internationalizing environment requires some significant additional skills of management. First, we need to acknowledge that the very name 'human resources' already indicates a culturally biased view of the role of human beings in an organization. On the one hand, they can be seen as just instrumental resources for the fulfilment of higher goals determined by the management of a machine-like organization. Next to capital resources, we find human resources in this rather Anglo-Saxon interpretation. On the other hand, in Latin cultures, 'resourceful humans' will better cover its essential meaning and thus 'managing' them is a contradiction in terms. One rather 'guides' resourceful humans which might be one of the reasons HRM in its traditional sense has never worked in Latin cultures.

In the first section of this chapter we will see that the successful international manager has many characteristics of the effective manager operating in a less complex (national) environment. However, he or she needs additional *strategic* talents to reconcile the 'cultural dilemmas' emerging out of the international environment. In other words, awareness of differences is not enough. Second, we will discuss how the organization needs to consider its HR policies and strategies in the context of the ever-growing dilemma of the need for worldwide integration *and*, at the same time, adaptation to local cultural environments. This context is of great relevance because it very much affects the international manager's scope for strategic decision making. Finally, we will go through some elementary HR activities and their organization in the light of cultural variety and the development of international managers. These activities are seen as the major building blocks on which international general managers need to develop their strategic thinking and on which HR policies are developed in international organizations:

1. Recruitment and image
2. Training
3. Staff appraisal and rewards
4. Job evaluation
5. Career development.

However, I will also argue that the placing of human resource issues at the top of the strategic planning process is the key to developing effective international business. It is much too important to be left in the hands of the HR function alone.

The international manager reconciles cultural dilemmas

Dilemmas in relationships with people, time and nature

The internationalization process is ultimately more a matter of people and behaviour than of structure. The effectiveness of the international manager lies essentially in the way one deals with cultural diversity and uses it to strategic effect.

Basic to successfully working with other cultures is the understanding that 'culture' is a series of rules and methods that a society has evolved to deal with the regular problems that face it. They have become so that, like breathing, we no longer think about how we do it. We owe it to Charles Hampden-Turner (1991) to see culture as the way in which people resolve dilemmas that emerge from universal problems. Every country and every organization faces dilemmas in:

- Relationships with people
- Relationships to time
- Relations between people and the natural environment.

While nations differ markedly in how they deal with these dilemmas, they do not differ in needing to make some kind of response. This explains why the successful international manager has to know about the different approaches to be able to subsequently reconcile dilemmas more effectively in line with the organization's strategies and goals.

How does a society deal with rules?

The universal truth versus the particular instance

Universalist societies tend to feel that general rules and obligations are a strong source of moral reference. Universalists tend to follow the rules even when friends are involved and look for 'the one best way' of dealing equally and fairly with all cases. They assume that the standards they hold dear are the 'right' ones and attempt to change the attitudes of others to match. Particularist societies are those where 'particular' circumstances are much more important than the rules. Bonds of particular relationships (family, friends) are stronger than any abstract rule and the response may change according to circumstances and the people involved.

In order to test these extreme definitions, we have asked 15 000 managers worldwide to consider the following dilemma:

> You are riding in a car driven by a close friend who, while definitely going too fast, hits a pedestrian. There are no witnesses. The lawyer of your friend says that, if you testify under oath that the speed was within the limit, it may save him from serious consequences. Has your friend a definite, some, or no right to expect you to protect him? Would you help your friend in view of the obligations you feel you have towards society?

The answers ('Yes'/'No') to the story above, created by Stouffer and Toby (1951), give a measure of universalism against particularism. North Americans and most Northern Europeans emerge as almost totally universalist in their approach to the problem (over 80 per cent voted with 'No'). The proportion falls to under 70 per cent for the French and many Far Eastern nations, including Japan (67 per cent) while, in Venezuela, two-thirds of respondents would like the police to protect their friend.

Time and again in my workshops, universalists respond in such a way that, as the seriousness of the accident increases, the obligation to help their friend decreases. They seem to be saying to themselves, 'the law was broken and the serious condition of the pedestrian underlines the importance of upholding the law'. This suggests that universalism is rarely used to the exclusion of particularism, rather that it forms the first principle in the process of moral reasoning. Particular consequences remind us of the need for universal laws.

In all the six cultural dichotomies we have identified, of which 'universalism versus particularism' is the first, the two extremes can always in a sense be found in the same person. The two horns of the dilemma are very close to each other as it is easy to realize that, as a universalist, the moment you substitute your father or daughter for the friend who is driving the car, the decision you take might be different again.

In fruitful cross-cultural encounters, both sides avoid pathological excesses as all international managers are very often caught in the dilemma of the universal truth—often imposed by his or her headquarters—and the particular or local circumstances which ask for responses that do not fit HQ's demands. The most effective international manager reconciles this dilemma by acknowledging that the particular instances need universal rules in order not to slip into a local pathology. Intuitively, the international manager goes through a cycle *in which the middle is held by his or her talents*. Figure 13.1, devised by Charles Hampden-Turner, illustrates this.

The group versus the self: individualism versus collectivism

Individualism has been described as 'a prime orientation to the self', and collectivism as 'a prime orientation to common goals and objectives' (Hampden-Turner, 1990). Just as for the first of our 'dimensions', cultures do typically vary in putting one or the other of these approaches first in their thinking processes, though both may be included in their reasoning.

To illustrate this, we asked the same 15 000 managers mentioned above to decode which of the following two ways of reasoning is usually best:

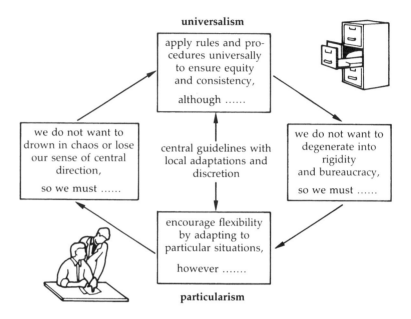

Figure 13.1   Reconciling universalism and particularism

A   'It is obvious that, if one has as much freedom as possible and the maximum opportunity to develop oneself, the quality of one's life will improve as a result.'
B   'If the individual is continuously taking care of his fellow human beings, the quality of life will improve for everyone, even if it obstructs individual freedom and individual development.'

Although results were less sharp in division, one could see clearly that the United States and most European countries prefer the individualistic approach 'A' (United States, 58 per cent; Netherlands, 60 per cent; UK, 55 per cent) while in particular in East Asia (Japan, 47 per cent; South Korea, 41 per ent) a higher degree of collectivism dominates the manager's thinking (Figure 13.2).

Charles Hampden-Turner sees the issue as essentially circular, with two 'starting points'. We all go through these cycles, but starting from different points and conceiving of them as 'means' or 'ends'. The individualist culture sees the individual as 'the end' and improvements to collective arrangements as the means to achieve it. The collectivist culture see the group as 'the end' and improvements to individual capacities as a means to reach it.

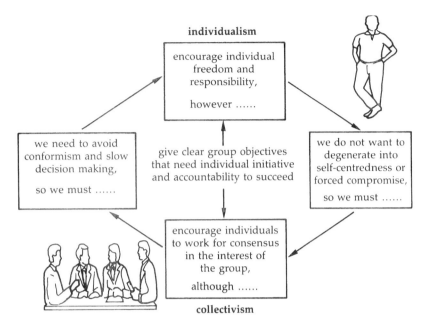

Figure 13.2   Reconciling individualism and collectivism

The effective international manager is convinced that individualism can find its fulfilment in service to the group. In order to define group goals which are of demonstrable value to individuals, these individuals have to be consulted and asked for participation in the process of developing them. Reconciliation is not easy, but it is possible. It is a key objective of the strategic thinker to create an organizational climate which enhances these possibilities.

Do we display our emotions? Affective neutral versus affective relationships

In relationships between people, reason and emotion both play a role. Which of these dominates will depend upon whether we are affective, i.e. show our emotions, in which case we probably get an emotional response in return, or whether we are emotional neutral in our approach.

Typically, reason and emotion are, of course, combined. In expressing ourselves we try to find confirmation of our thoughts and feelings in the response of our audience. When our own approach is highly emotional, we are seeking a direct emotional response ('I have the same feelings as you on this subject'). When our own approach is highly neutral, we are seeking an indirect response ('Because I agree with your reasoning or proposition, I give you my support'). On both occasions, approval is being sought but different paths are being used. The indirect path gives us emotional support contingent upon the success of an effort of intellect. Alternatively, the direct path leads to an emotional affirmation regarding the rightness of one's intellectual proposition.

Overly affective or expressive cultures facing overly neutral cultures often have problems relating with each other. The neutral person is easily accused of being ice-cold with no heart; the affective person is seen as out of control and inconsistent. When such cultures meet, the first essential for the international manager is to recognize the differences and to refrain from making any judgement based purely on emotions, or the total lack of them. The effective international manager does make this reconciliation almost intuitively through the virtuous circle shown in Figure 13.3. This is of particular importance for strategic thinkers as they strive to balance content and process in international teams.

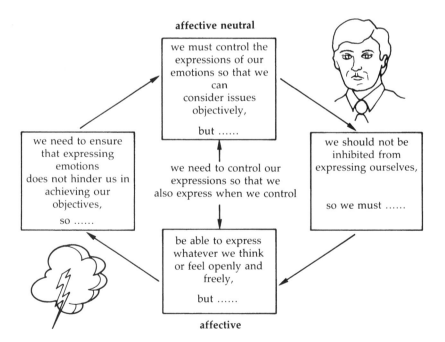

Figure 13.3   Reconciling affective neutral and affective

How far do we get involved? Specific versus diffuse cultures

Closely related to whether we show emotions in dealing with other people is the degree to which we engage others in specific areas of life and single levels of personality, or diffusely in multiple areas of our lives and at several levels of personality at the same time (Figure 13.4). In specific-oriented cultures, a manager segregates out the task relationship she or he has with a subordinate and insulates this from other dealings. But, in some countries, every life space and every level of personality tends to permeate all others. This range is illustrated well by responses to the question of whether a subordinate—although he does not feel like it at all—will help his boss to paint his house when asked.

Asking our managers again, about 65 per cent of all British, Dutch, Swiss, French and US respondents do not feel at all inclined to assist. As one Dutch manager observed, 'House painting is not in my collective labour agreement'. Germans, Italians and Japanese still side with the specific approach with over 56 per cent. The diffuse votes gain ground in countries like Hong Kong and Singapore (52 per cent), Spain (51 per cent) and Venezuela (44 per cent).

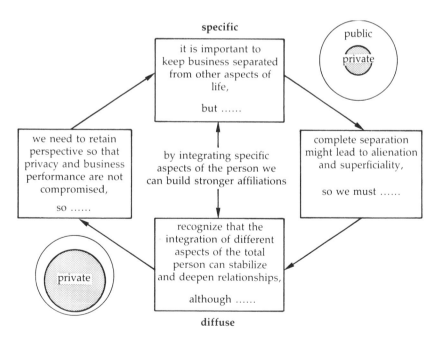

Figure 13.4   Reconciling specific and diffuse

It is important for the international strategist to keep in mind that diffuse cultures tend to have lower turnover and employee mobility because of the importance of 'loyalty' and the multiplicity of human bonds. They tend not to 'head-hunt' or lure away employees from other companies with high salaries. Takeovers are rarer because of the disruption caused to relationships and because shareholders (often banks) have longer-term relationships and cross-holdings in each other's companies and are less motivated by the price of shares.

Of our six dilemmas, this is perhaps the one in which *balance* is most crucial, from both a personal and a corporate point of view; recognizing that privacy is necessary, but that complete separation of private life leads to alienation and superficiality; that business is business, but stable and deep relationships means strong affiliations; and that these will determine the range of strategic possibilities open to the top teams.

Do we work for our status or is it given? Achievement versus ascription

All societies give certain of their members higher status than others, signalling that unusual attention should be focused upon such persons and their activities. While some societies accord status to people on the basis of their factual achievements, others ascribe it to them by virtue of age, class, gender, education, etc. While 'achieved' status refers to doing, 'ascribed status' refers to being (Figure 13.5).

In the organizational context, achievement-oriented organizations justify their hierarchies by claiming that senior persons have 'achieved' more for the organization; their authority, justified by skill and knowledge, benefits the organization. Ascription-oriented organizations justify their hierarchies by pointing out that people with high status—resulting in personal authority, influence, but also in the high expectations that society has of him or her—should also have the 'power-to-get-things-done' as this serves best the effectiveness of the organization.

To measure the extent of achieving versus ascribing orientations in different cultures, we used the following statements, inviting participants to mark them on a five-point scale (1 = strongly agree, 5 = strongly disagree):

A   The most important thing in life is to think and act in the way that best suits the way you really are, even if you don't get things done.

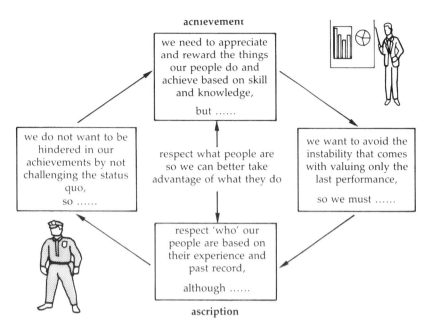

Figure 13.5   Reconciling achievement and ascription

B   The respect a person gets is highly dependent on their family background.

While a high number of Western European and US participants disagreed with both statements by 60–65 per cent, Japan and the Southern Europeans were about 55 per cent. In comparison, ascription orientation is still much stronger in less industrialized or former Communist countries (Poland, 47 per cent; Russia, 42 per cent; Venezuela, 36 per cent).

Despite far greater emphasis on ascription or achievement in certain cultures, they do, in my view, develop together. Those who 'start' with ascribing usually ascribe not just status but also future success or achievement and thereby help to bring it about. Those who 'start' with achievement usually start to ascribe importance and priority to the persons and projects which have been successful. It is, once again, a question of where a cycle starts.

How do we organize our Time? Past, present or future orientation

When managers need to coordinate their business activities, they require some kind of shared expectations about time. Just as different cultures have different assumptions about how people relate to one another, so they approach time differently. This orientation is about the relative importance cultures give to the past, present and future. Furthermore, it makes a big difference whether our view of time is sequential—a series of passing events—or whether it is synchronic—with past, present and future all interrelated so that ideas about the future and memories of the past both shape present action.

The methodology used to measure approaches to time comes from Tom Cottle (1900), who created the 'Circle Test'. Managers participating were asked to think of three circles of equal or different size—representing past, present and future—and to draw and arrange them in the way that best showed how they felt about the relationship of the three (Figure 13.6).

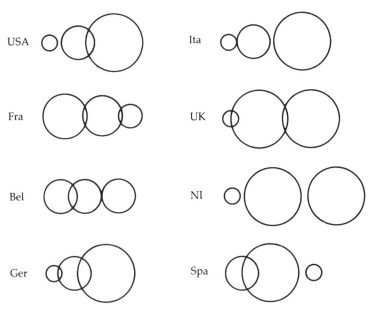

Figure 13.6   Past, present and future (from left to right)

The international strategic manager is often caught in the dilemma of the future demands of the larger organization, needing visions, missions and managing change towards it and past experiences of local populations. The time dilemma and a possible reconciliation are shown in Figure 13.7.

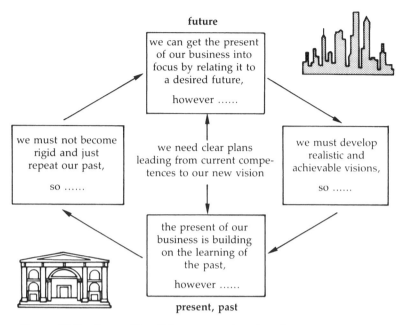

Figure 13.7 Reconciling future, present and past

Reconciliation of cultural differences as the major human talent of international strategic management

The international strategic thinker strives toward riding the waves of intercultural differences rather than ignoring them or trying to reduce them to one specific culture. (This chapter draws heavily on my book, *Riding the Waves of Culture* (1993).) Almost all our problems, and their solutions, are recognizable all over the world. Whichever principle internationally thinking and operating managers start with, the circumstances of business and of organizing experience require them to reconcile the *dilemmas* we have been discussing.

One can only prosper when as many particulars as possible are covered by rules, yet exceptions are seen and noted. You can only *think* effectively if both the specifics and the diffuse wholes, the segments and the integrations are covered. Whether you are at heart an individualist or a collectivist, your individuals must be capable of organizing themselves and your collectivities are only as good as the health, wealth and wisdom of each member. It is crucial to give status to achievers, but equally crucial to back strategies, projects and new initiatives from people who have not yet achieved anything, in other words, to ascribe status to these in the hope of facilitating success. Everyone should be equal in their rights and opportunities, yet any contest will produce a hierarchy of relative standings. Respect for age and experience can both nurture and discourage the young and inexperienced. Hierarchy and equality are finely interwoven in every culture. It is true that time is both a passing sequence of events and a moment of truth, a 'now' in which past, present and future are given new meanings.

In the final analysis, culture is the manner in which these dilemmas are reconciled, since every nation seeks a different and winding path to its own ideals of integrity. It is my position that businesses will succeed to the extent that this reconciliation occurs, so we have everything to learn from discovering *how* others have travelled to their own position and to build this into our strategic thinking to create an effective international organizational culture.

The organizational context of the international manager's activities

The international manager might have significant talents in reconciling cultural differences but his or her effectiveness is also dependent on the larger environment in which he or she needs to operate. There are some significant dilemmas to solve on the macro scale which involve both effective strategic thinking and policy formulation.

Centralization versus decentralization

The main dilemma which strategic thinkers across cultures confront is the extent to which they should centralize, thereby keeping up a certain type of cultural control but imposing on foreign cultures rules and procedures that might affront them. Alternatively, they could decentralize, thereby letting each culture go its own way without having any centrally viable ideas about improvement since the 'better way' is a local, not a global, pathway.

Nevertheless, centralizing and decentralizing are, like all the other dimensions introduced in this chapter, potentially reconcilable processes. A biological organism grows to higher levels of order and complexity by being more differentiated *and* more integrated. The more departments, divisions, functions and differentiated activities a corporation pursues, the greater the importance of coordinating all this variety in its 'central nervous system'. It is because we are all different that we have so much to exchange with each other. In matters of culture, as in the relationship of the sexes, the difference can be the chief source of attraction. Italian design and Dutch engineering can lead to conflicts, as we have seen; they could also lead to a product 'Made in Heaven'.

One way of reconciling the dilemma of the centralization versus decentralization debate on the cultural level is to articulate an explicit philosophy of company values world-wide. Management then needs to build on these and develop subtle mechanisms which balance local needs and global necessities. Different policies on the corporate level and on the micro level of the internationally operating manager are not an exception. This dilemma comes on two levels.

On the one hand, there is the attraction to the old universalistic idea of a highly integrated approach to company policies: 'Why don't we do it similarly every-where?' On the other, recent developments show that the international (HR) manager is becoming increasingly aware of the particularistic need for differentiation and local adaption: 'We are becoming acquainted with the effects of too rigid centralization. At our local operations in France and in Central Africa, we find it leads to an advanced form of "corporate dancing". A lot of dancing, but hardly any rain.'

The error-correcting international manager

Other cultures are strange, ambiguous, even shocking to us. It is unavoidable that we will make mistakes in dealing with them and feel muddled and confused. The real issue is how quickly we are prepared to learn from mistakes and how bravely we struggle to understand a game in which 'perfect scores' are an illusion and where reconciliation only comes after a difficult passage through alien territory.

We need a certain amount of humility and a sense of humour to discover cultures other than our own; a readiness to enter a room in the dark and stumble over unfamiliar furniture until the pain in our shins reminds us where things are. World culture is a myriad different ways of creating the integrity without which life and business cannot be con-ducted. There are no universal answers but their are universal questions and dilemmas, and that is where we strategic thinkers need to start.

How to develop the international manager

The development of the international manager is not an easy and unidimensional task. Many levers can be pulled to increase the likelihood that a manager will become more effective in the international arena. This final section will focus on some of these levels, particularly those which will allow the strategic thinker to set the organizational climate and context in which their people will develop. From those, the implementation of their strategic thinking will be made either easier or significantly more difficult.

Recruitment and image

The development of the international manager starts with the way the recruitment process is designed. Even for established international companies, it is essential to define the fundamental requirements of people and relate these to the recruiting process. The recruitment process again increasingly depends on the image the organization has in the labour market. This dependency increases with the ambitions for internationalization of the organization.

First, it is simplistic to think that one can achieve the goal by employing personnel with a cosmopolitan flair. It seems increasingly that the recruiting process needs to start by presenting an image of the company as an international organization. This image is needed to attract and employ the right candidates. One should be careful here, though, because a too international profile or one which does not emphasize the international nature of the company enough is dangerous. When a Shell HR manager was interviewed, it was noted that Shell had a problem at the end of the 1980s in keeping its best graduates because some of them were disappointed by the relative lack of international careers it could offer in the short run. Other companies felt the reverse problem because locally recruited staff could not be moved to start an international career since they were not prepared for it initially and neither was their family.

Furthermore, it seems that the image of the large international companies has not changed enough over the last twenty-five years to accommodate the great changes in expectations of potential junior employees. A quarter of a century ago, a young student had a desire for power, to some degree stimulated by his or her parents. With some patience, this goal could be reached. Nowadays, it seems that, in the UK at least, the young 'eager beaver' has a greater need for autonomy than for power.

In other words, career planning is still done but it can be assumed that career makers will do this themselves, instead of leaving it up to the firm's guidance. The image of the big multinational companies is still tainted, though, with the expectation: 'Just be patient and you will automatically become a powerful manager.' Therefore, the images of many of the large corporations no longer always impress talented potential employees. The problem is not how to devise criteria for the selection of top candidates but 'How do we attract the best candidates when we can no longer control their careers?'

Knowing this, it is necessary to do some sophisticated and strategic image research on how your organization is perceived. It might reveal the degree of perceived globalization, the extent to which mobility is an essential characteristic, as well as international experience. Is the organization seen as a Dutch company that happens to operate outside its frontiers or a global company that happens to operate also within the Netherlands? Is this picture consistent or do opinions differ? Note that the lack of a clear or a too divergent image can be more harmful than a sharp one that is not desired. These issues need to be clarified first and then addressed in order to be able to work towards a future workforce that supports the organization's international strategy.

Within the recruitment process, one can make use of a variety of very effective 'message carriers' sub-strategies to generate the image desired. One way to attack a not clearly defined company image within the labour market is to promote the use of visiting lecturers and professors from acknowledged teaching institutions. This seems to be an effective tool to influence the image of the representing organization in academia. The guest lecturer can also appear proactive by pushing the image in a desired direction. From the organizational point of view, this means that one has to proceed selectively in the choice of whom we select to voice our message. If a more international image is our goal, the choice of a guest lecturer whose experience is limited only to Manchester or Lyon and surroundings might well prove to have disastrous consequences for the company's image.

A second sub-strategy is to hire professionals who take care of the contacts with the labour market. An example of this is a public relations person who keeps contacts with educational facilities. It is important to keep these facilities updated on the future requirements of the business community and of our firm in particular.

A point that needs attention, because it seems to be important in the image-creating process, is related to the actual recruiting process itself. The effect of the manner in which, and by whom, staff are selected must not be underestimated. Surely a local recruiting process enhances the company's image in that country, particularly if its operations are based elsewhere, or if no clear profile has yet been established? Many European enterprises have, regardless of this, chosen an international recruiting process.

Two methods are normally used. First, there is the internationalization of the recruiting panel. Apart from creating a more international image, the multicultural selection team is crucial in recognizing potential expatriate staff. A varied number of perspectives usually improves the judgement of a candidate's qualifications. Second, the invitation of candidates to non-local venues is an important symbolical step in the process of building up an international image. Although it is indeed more expensive, the positive effect on the academic circuit is beyond price.

In the organizational context, one should seriously consider whether the subsidiaries will have influence on the local recruitment process, including the selection of future international managers. Many international companies allow this last category of managers to be selected in a different country, preferably where the headquarters are situated. Final selection processes in a country different from that of the candidate's origin do not only offer the advantage of enhancing the company's international image; it should also not be forgotten that people who make decisions as to which candidates are to be attracted often recruit after their own image. In this sense, the recruitment process is an advanced form of 'cloning'.

At this point it is necessary to proceed very selectively in our choice of recruiters and their own image (self-projection). It is, therefore, logical that internationally effective managers are best selected by currently effective international managers. Recruitment processes are quite different across cultures. Intercultural teams are seen by most companies as contributing much to enhancing the degree of cultural awareness of candidates.

For instance, take Schlumberger. They have chosen a recruitment approach according to their different business areas. Some recruiters work within a geographical area of their business—no panel interviewers but Egyptian recruiters who recruit French people for a Dutch company in a certain business area. Recruiters within the same business area maintain a relatively informal network to see if they can help each other out. It is a very hands-on approach where the cultural background of the recruiter doesn't play a role and, as a result, culturally dependent criteria will be challenged. This goes a long way to helping define the specific corporate culture, and international balance, they require.

Training

A recent study within an internationally operating organization has shown that a very large proportion (92 per cent) of all training effort was still directed towards the development of technical skills. Much less attention was devoted to non-technical and behavioural programmes. Furthermore, it was found that the latter type of training was given mostly to employees who had almost reached the apex of their professional career.

In other cases, though, interviews showed that, in order to teach cultural sensitivity from the start, an increasing number of companies chose to give young employees a more general intercultural training. In the early 1970s, Shell started to bring general cultural concepts to the attention of employees who had just graduated and who had received a predominantly technical education. Many companies such as AKZO, Heineken, Eastman Kodak, Q8 and TRW are organizing these 'awareness' courses in a less emphasized way, namely as part of a more general training process. For young highly trained employees, a general culture introduction programme seems very effective. In addition, there should be specific training courses for those who are preparing a project in a certain country or for those who will be transferred.

Again, the decision where and by whom training is being carried out can be a powerful tool in the internationalization process, not only in terms of effective international MDs but also regarding the image the company is building up in academic and training institutions. This image is fundamental to being able to reinforce existing, and develop new, strategies.

Staff appraisal and rewards

Appraising and rewarding are essentially cultural processes. Both try to influence the motivation of people. A couple of years ago, Apple in California, a beautiful example of the small professional culture, did limit the staff appraisal to the administration of one sheet of paper. On one side, you would find the question 'What did you change last year?' and, on the reverse side, 'What will you change next year?'

While this is an extreme example of very little complexity and detail, the other extreme approach is found in predominantly engineering organizations where the ignorance of a detail is seen as a deadly sin. Shell and Philips, for example, use very detailed and internationally valid systems, specifying exactly against what criteria employees worldwide should be appraised. ICI Pharmaceuticals, on the other hand, just tells its management to appraise every subordinate once a year. The way it is done is left to the manager.

However, a quality that is experienced as very important in the United States is perhaps seen differently in other cultures, as there is no system that can avoid being value-, and meaning-, full. As an example, a French manager from Elf Aquitaine complained about the fact that, in France, a real leader needs to be able to discuss intelligently a variety of subjects in such a way that a real contribution of content can be given to the task at hand. Conversely, an American manager will only be seen as a leader if he or she can follow the discussion and draw conclusions from it for the next decision for action. It's the classical difference between the 'father of the family' and the 'manager' in the more task-oriented culture.

Rewarding people is just as sensitive to culture as appraising them. For the development of the international manager, it is very important to install reward systems that clearly signal what qualities are particularly sought after. For instance, local operations and international mindsets are, to a certain extent, incompatible. Given the growing necessity of 'thinking globally and acting locally', some companies check yearly the mobility of people and their families, the development in their language abilities and their successes in international projects. Bonuses in return could be seen in non-financial rewards such as free cross-cultural seminars, language training or (international) moves within the organization. In some companies, this is the best symbol of success.

On a more structural level, we see that culture affects the effectiveness of reward systems. It is entirely reasonable that a person in a collectivist culture should seek to reward his or her team members for his own successful efforts. They get the money he or she helped to generate, he or she gets the respect, affection and gratitude—not such a bad bargain. That the high performer in an individualistic society might like to attract rewards away from colleagues is also entirely reasonable. The solution is for the collectivist and individualist cultures to distribute group and personal rewards in accordance with their own judgements and results. In a truly international or transnational corporation, every nation would have the universal rule that 'success must be rewarded commensurate with its size', yet the international manager is charged with finding optimal mixes between personal and group rewards.

Job evaluation

Worldwide, the job-evaluation system is perceived as a process which helps the international managers assessing the relative values of jobs as well as a rank order in salaries both within and across cultures. A job is a job and culture can hardly intervene there. Therefore, a universally applied job evaluation system is quite often seen as one of the tougher and effective measures to harmonize worldwide differences across managers and employees in general. Many HR managers emphasize in their interviews that the evaluation system (quite often the Hay system) allows them to depoliticize discussions where culture is taken as an alibi for overpaying managers in some parts of the world. The success of companies like Hay Consultants has been a reflection of that mode of reasoning.

However, it seems that job-evaluation systems have not lived up to all their expectations. Shell was one of the first industrial companies that introduced the application of a sophisticated job-evaluation system on a worldwide scale some thirty years ago. In the middle of the 1980s, the first cracks in its universal applicability appeared. Several functions, R&D in particular, and several regions stopped hiding their reservations against the sturdiness of the system. Although the positive contributions were acknowledged, Shell decided that much more freedom to alternative uses should be allowed.

Career development

As effective international or even global managers are the essential resource of the international corporation, how to best raise them becomes a vital question. While the term 'career' has different meanings across societies—in particular, with view to the competencies the young recruit builds up over time—companies have chosen different approaches to the career development (CD) of their international staff.

Common to their views, though, is the conviction that the development of the global managers is, with no exception, international. There is no substitute for line experience in three or four countries to create a global perspective. Shell, for instance, takes international experience so seriously that one refusal for an international assignment is accepted; a second means the end of your career in Shell.

For some companies, much attention is given to the development of international skills at the initial stages of the graduate career. ICL and Daimler-Benz, for example, designed a specific 'Young Graduate Programme' in which newly appointed graduates receive international exposure and training in a highly selected group. Group members are spanning the globe in their regular meetings, learning about the international aspects of business and management.

At ABB, people are very much encouraged to work continuously in mixed nationality teams. According to its CEO, Percy Barnevik, people are forced to move around and to create personal alliances across borders: 'Global managers are made, not born. We are herd animals. We like people who are like us . . . you rotate people around the world.'

To foster this transnational approach, ABB has defined some general guidelines for coordinating its career development policies. Karl Schmid (VP, International Assignments, ABB) has summarized them as follows:

- Speed up the flow of managers across organizational border lines
- Increase scouting for internal talents
- Strive for aggressive and bonus-oriented management compensation
- Apply incentive systems which are heavily oriented towards the bottom line and are also desirable on lower levels
- Base salary revisions should be highly differentiated
- 'Givers' will be rewarded.

Still, ABB prides itself not to create nor to impose any central CD policy. This is left to the individual countries.

Many international companies are heading towards an approach advocated by Paul Evans (1990):

- Recruiting locally from the local university marketplaces
- First five to eight years of career focused on technical and function development
- Monitoring for generalist potential
- Developing selective international group by central management
- Reviewing development of this group by specialized management review committees.

Evans, Lank and Farquhar (1989) have observed patterns of career development that are significantly different across cultures. Let us look at different approaches in the Anglo-Dutch, Germanic, Japanese and Latin cultures.

The Anglo-Dutch approach is typical for cultures in which recruitment does not need to be aimed at the elite. The selection is actually done in the first five to seven years in the company in specific technical or functional jobs. Assessment centres (both formal and informal) are the ways the incumbents are checked if they service the goals of the company. The potential is assessed in these initial years and is carefully monitored in later stages of the career. The management development is taken seriously and is formalized whenever possible.

If one did the same in the more role-oriented German society, much energy would be lost without much benefit. To prepare management for their important functional role, much attention is given to the first two to three years. At Daimler-Benz, a special programme for the 'Nachwuchs-Gruppe' is developed, where an international group of young graduates receives a tough training programme combined with some in-company jobs and special assignments. In their first years, much job rotation is combined with the intensive training programme. In later stages, this deepening development programme, which enables the candidates to come out of too much specialism from university times, is taken over by purely functional careers. Competition in this type of culture is based purely on functional expertise. It is interesting to see that many of the German top managers have—and carry with pride—the title of 'Doktor' or 'Professor.'

The Latin model of career development fits the main characteristics of the 'family'. The entry to the largest international companies is very elitist (think of the 'Grandes Ecoles' in France). This is not only because of the competencies needed for the tough jobs in top management. It is also required because the organization is essentially a political system in which much status is given to ascribed characteristics such as formal education. Status is given to people for the title as such, not so much as a predictor of mastery in a function role but of mastery in the social web of relationships. It is very enlightening that the family model has no genuine objections against careers that are made through the knowledge of important people, so-called 'mentors' in the organization, including (extended) family members.

Summary and recommendations

First, we have discussed characteristics of the effective international manager. Obviously, an international manager has all the characteristics of a good local manager. However, he or she needs additional talents to deal with cultural diversity and to reconcile the dilemmas that cultural variety imposes upon management. These have a highly positive effect on their strategic thinking.

Second, we have discussed the issue of the context of the international manager, i.e. the organizational set-up. How can we possibly develop international management in firms that have subsidiaries in other countries, while all management methods seem to be inappropriate for exportation beneath the dividing lines of culture? These give the continuing dilemmas for strategic thinkers.

Companies make choices among three alternatives.

- First, those that proceed with centrally imposed methods for the development of a 'corporate identity' or 'corporate culture'. This means that the application of doctrines, methods and instruments is frequently ineffective and used only as rituals in a 'corporate rain dance'.
- Second, companies that impose no central methods and give up the idea of a 'corporate identity' and synergy.
- Third, those looking for strong centralistic guidelines and common objectives. Within the framework of these premises, there needs to be sufficient room for subsidiaries to develop their own 'culture-fitted' applications in the five major areas of the development of international staff: recruitment and image, training, staff appraisal and rewards, job evaluation and career development. Realization of this third alternative poses many problems, but they are worth tackling!

Culture heavily affects processes as well as the meaning of content. Considering policies and programmes in a multicultural environment can lead to more successful implementation, provided the group ensures that it allows for differences in the way people from different cultures feel comfortable contributing to the process. However, a pattern is emerging in how to best approach the dilemmas it raises in the process of internationalization. A key starting point for many companies is placing human resource issues at the top of the strategic planning process. Development of international managers is not just the domain of the HR function. It is the key to developing successful business strategy.

References

Cottle, T. 'The Circle Test—an investigation of perception of tempered relatedness and dominance', *Journal of Projective Technique and Personality Assessment*.

Evans, P. (1990) 'International management development and the balance between generalism and professionalism', *Personnel Management*, December.

Evans, P., Lank, E. and Farquhar, A. (1989) 'Managing human resources in the international firm: lessons from practice', In Evans,

P., Doz, Y. and Laurent, A. (eds), *Human Resource Management in International Firms: Change, Globalisation, Innovation*, London.

Hampden-Turner, C. (1990) *Charting the Corporate Mind.*

Hampden-Turner, C. (1991) *Corporate Culture*, London: Economist Books.

Stouffer and Toby (1951) 'Role conflict and personality', *American Journal of Sociology*, **VI**, 395-406.

Trompenaars, F. (1993) *Riding the Waves of Culture—the importance of understanding cultural diversity in business*, London: Economist Books.

14 Helicopters and rotting fish: developing strategic thinking and new roles for direction-givers

Bob Garratt

The old organizational myth that the people at the top do not know where they are or where they are going may well be true. Prominent amongst recent surveys of top team members is one from the Institute of Directors in London called 'Development of and for the Board' (1990). This shows that over 90 per cent of the large sample of those at the top of their organizations—the directors and vice-presidents—had no induction, inclusion or training to become a competent direction-giver of their business. My experience shows that this percentage seems to hold good in Europe, East Asia, Australia, New Zealand and the United States. It goes a long way to explaining the failure of many organizations to deliver quality products and services effectively and efficiently in both the private and public sectors.

Blockages to the direction-giving role

My Chinese colleagues use an old saying 'that the fish rots from the head'. I am unsure as to the physiological correctness of this but I do know that it is a powerful metaphor for viewing direction-giver development. People in organizations know instinctively that there are always problems at the top yet there is little common language to describe the issues. Instead, stories and metaphors evolve through the organizational folklore. However, work is under way to understand the issues and provide robust developmental processes for those, whether 'directors' or 'vice-presidents', who have to give direction to their organizations. This chapter attempts to map this emerging field of study and practice with particular emphasis on strategic thinking.

There are two distinct types of blockages from which most directing problems start:

- A failure to understand the roles of direction-givers in the organization
- A lack of any systematic training and development processes to get the direction-givers into their roles.

To begin to understand how such key organizational issues may be overcome it is important to make a simple assertion—there are fundamental differences between the processes of *managing* and *directing*. Because this fact is usually not acknowledged in organizations little priority in terms of time and money budgets is given to the development of the directors. The working assumption is that somehow on being given the job title of 'director' or 'vice-president' the newly promoted manager becomes omniscient. They will suddenly know everything about everything, need no help in sorting information from data, can take farsighted decisions every time, while keeping an active social life, being perfect parents, and staying in full health. No one needs to accept responsibility for the development of a new direction-giver (by definition, they will pick it up as they go along) and they will quickly be accepted by the other top team members. The organizational folklore view that the top team is a collection of powerful individuals whose only obvious connection are the central heating pipes is obviously a canard. Unfortunately, it is not. What can be done about it?

Coming to terms with the direction-giver's role: the learning board

First, a clear statement of the direction-giver's role within the specific organization needs to be given either on promotion to the role or, even better, before. Second, the chairman or president must be responsible as coach and mentor for ensuring that the newly promoted direction-giver gets into the role quickly and effectively as a member of the top team.

There are problems with even finding a clear statement of the direction-giver's role. While in the area of 'corporate governance' this is being clarified slowly around the world—the director knows what is expected of him or her by the legislators and regulators, especially the national stock exchange—once we go beyond this area of 'strategic conformance', then the picture blurs rapidly. I have been working in companies with a model that suggests four key direction-giving activities and, importantly, a *rhythm* to a board's, or executive committee's, year (Figure 14.1). This identifies two short-term, conformance-related, processes—*accountability* and *supervision of management*—and two long-term, performance-related processes—*policy formulation* and *strategic thinking*.

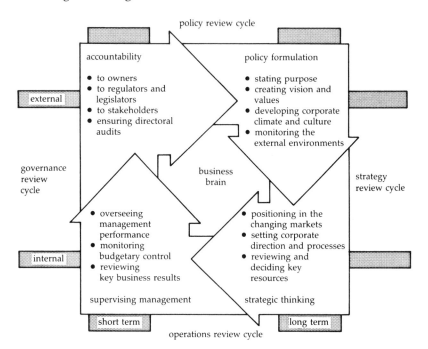

Figure 14.1   The learning board

Because people promoted to the direction-giving role come from a long managerial career if they develop at all into the direction-giving role, they tend to stay close to the conformance-related roles of supervision of management, and accountability. This is understandable. They will take some comfort in relating to the management issues even if they are often scared witless by the onerous corporate and personal liabilities they must contract to when becoming a director. In fact, one of the big developmental issues on the conformance side is to stop newly appointed direction-givers sliding back rapidly into their old managerial roles. I will discuss later why this happens when we look deeper at how the director development process fails.

The most difficult step for new direction-givers is to cast aside their old managerial role to make that key step into becoming comfortable with the *strategic performance-related* aspects of giving direction—*policy formulation* and *strategic thinking*. This involves a massive change in attitude, styles of thinking and the budgeting of time for direction-givers. It means that, whether the new role is full or part-time, executive or non-executive, owner–director or hired hand, a significant amount of time will need to be spent *thinking* about the organization's possible futures rather than coping with the present. Effective chairmen and presidents understand this and ensure that there is some sort of organizational 'rite of passage' for new direction-givers. This says that from now on this person must spend significant time designing the future, away from operational crises, if there is to be a long-term effective and efficient organization. It also signals to others in the organization that this means an entirely different use of time by the newly appointed director. Whereas in their managerial career time had been fragmented and attention spans short, now as a director they must give priority to such thoughtful processes as creating time to reflect on environmental trends, competitor analysis and organizational effectiveness, and have the capacity to reframe them in such a way that they can create a sustainable competitive edge. In the early stages of director development this usually proves highly unnerving for someone who has made their way up the action-orientated managerial career path.

Blockages to direction-giver development

One can understand how newly appointed direction-givers can easily be sucked back down the black hole of managing—it is known, busy, demanding, and comfortable. If one looks at the induction-to-transition development process (Figure 14.2) it can be seen that most senior managers on promotion to the direction-giving role at the end of typically a twenty- to thirty-year managerial career fall at the first hurdle. As the IOD survey shows, there is rarely any induction process for them. There is no one to greet them as they cross the great divide between 'managing' and 'directing'. There was no organizational rite of passage to mark this crucial developmental step and little (if any) knowledge imparted as to what the new job entails. In a quoted company one might be given the rules about how to behave in relation to the local stock exchange but even that cannot be taken for granted. It is very rare for newly appointed direction-givers to have to sign their acceptance of the local exchange rules, or for the chairman or chief executive to have to sign that they have explained them to the new recruit. It seems curious that for most

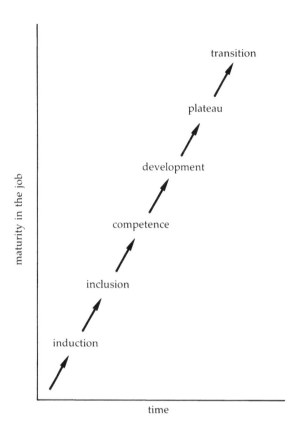

Figure 14.2   The induction to the transition development process

organizations around the world the norm is to appoint people to the key jobs in the organization and then trust to luck that they pick it up as they go along, with help from no one. Direction-giving seems to be a curious 'profession'. One gets the job title first, then might just think about becoming competent. Competence is not seen as necessary, and is seldom measured.

Matters are made worse by the lack of any reasonable Inclusion process. This is the social and psychological process by which any line manager ensures that a new member of a work group is bonded socially with the other group members. It is a process that needs regular but almost homeopathic doses of coaching from the line manager. If it is not done in the first two to four weeks of arrival then that newcomer may never fully be integrated by the group. If inclusion does not happen then, however notionally 'competent' the newcomer was at selection, they can never reach true competence in this work group because they are not integrated into the group's unique culture.

This powerful inclusion, and exclusion, process is particularly strong at the top of an organization. Here 'inclusion' is both more blatant and simultaneously more subtle. It is binary in its effects. One is either 'in' or 'out' regardless of job title. Board members can be nominal, and often are, while the real business of direction-giving is left to one or two powerful individuals. Inclusion may be partial with the 'real' inclusion being held out as a prize for those who conform to the dominant power players' views and values. Such prizes can, for example, be being asked to join a prestigious club or association; having the ability to use the directors' box at football or the opera; or in one classic case of being given a special cheese from the chairman's own farm at Christmas. Here even those directors given a cheese last Christmas may not get one this, so the board's behaviour from the autumn onwards tends to become highly conformist — members wish to be seen to be 'in'. This is the directoral equivalent to 'having the key to the executives' washroom' and people will do some personally demeaning things to get such prizes. In my experience this is true across all national and organizational cultures.

If the developmental stages of induction and inclusion are not acknowledged and acted upon, then the newly appointed direction-giver will not reach the necessary level of competence for that board. They will have suspected this personally for some time. They will have found their attendance at board or executive committee meetings mechanical. They will have been encouraged not to ask discriminating, or intelligently naive, questions. They will have been encouraged not to rock the boat, to leave it to the experienced power players, and to accept their new job title as a reward for long managerial service rather than as the start of a new career stage. To avoid the personal stress their felt incompetence brings they then become very human and, some time between months six and nine, they seek a position of comfort away from the current challenges. While keeping the job title, new car, performance bonuses, stock options, and service contract, their behaviour changes. Rather than seek to become a competent direction-giver (the climate is felt not to be there ever to allow that) they unofficially return to their old managerial job, or its nearest equivalent. They feel great again. They can do this job—that's why they were promoted. Things do not seem so bad after all.

There are two major organizational problems for a top team member who does this. First, returning to your old job when someone has replaced you means that much heat, and little light, is generated as the two job holders (one official, one unofficial) fight it out. The confrontation usually sets up a knock-on effect down the organization as people who were promoted find they have to drop back, unofficially, again to their old job. This knock-on effect causes both a major developmental block in the organization and a very unhealthy, non-learning climate. This can be measured as part of an Organizational Climate Survey. If people are reporting that they are being paid at a level one or two above the job they actually do, then you have a developmental problem starting at the top. The fish is rotting.

Second, the key competencies of direction-givers will be defined only by the dominant power players on the top team. If they too have had no training and development then we are in danger of creating 'Bourbon organizations' which, like the Bourbon kings, learn nothing and forget nothing.

Developing strategic performance-focused direction-givers

While needing always to strike a balance between the conformance- and performance-related aspects of the direction-giver's role, my experience has been that it is the performance side which is least understood and developed. This means taking the *policy formulation* and *strategic thinking* aspects of the Learning Board model as worthy of investment and development. It is interesting to note that the Latin root of the word 'development' comes from *volupe*, which means both bringing out the richness within and in making manifest what is there. That could be a good job description for an organization's chairman or president role in developing their board and their organization.

Moving from the 'conformance' focus of a board or executive committee's role to a 'performance' focus takes time and is uncomfortable. Creating time to think critically about the past, present, and especially the future is unsettling for most managers. The realization that thinking strategically is an *intellectual* activity comes as a shock to many successful managers. Breaking the bonds of the action-fixated activity of managing even for a small amount of time seems threatening. What would one do with such a vacuum? Phones would not ring, adrenaline would not flow, debate and reflection rather than orders and crisis would be possible. Most worrying would be the risk that one would be seen to be wanting in exercising one's critical faculty in what at first sight looks like fuzzy-edged speculation of the possible changes in the future environment. Direction-giving does not look like a 'proper job' to many managers. No wonder it seems threatening.

A three-stage approach

I have found it necessary to have the board, or executive committee, agree that three parallel streams of development are required to achieve a healthy organizational brain and heart—the core of the direction-givers' role:

1. An organizational development process
2. A board development process
3. A personal development process.

These must be set in the context of the agreed business development process.

Organizational development

The organizational development process sets the organizational processes and structures in which the other two processes occur. I will not go into detail in this chapter as it is well covered elsewhere (Garratt, 1994). I use the idea of the Learning Organization linked to action learning processes to release the energy and learning of the people working in the hour-to-hour, day-to-day operational cycles of the business. This delegation of significant problem-solving authority to the workforce reduces the number of managers significantly and focuses those remaining on ensuring the maintenance and development of the operational systems. It also makes it more difficult for the direction-givers to intervene randomly in the operational cycles as it forces them to budget significant amounts of time to focus on their core roles in the policy and strategy cycles of learning in their organization.

Board development

This is where an agreed board development process is necessary. It takes the organizational development process as its context and asks the board to concentrate on becoming a *learning board*. To start the board development process the four functions of the learning board are spelled out and a series of AwayDays arranged at which agreement is reached about the specific roles for this board, and the inputs which each member brings to that board. There is no selection process implied. I work with what I am given. It is necessary to map, usually using psychometric inventories, what resources and competencies we have in this board. Of particular interest is the *diversity* that the members bring. One knows from the classic studies of symptoms of corporate collapse (Argenti, 1976) that one of the main reasons for the fish rotting from the head is that too many of the same type of people get to the top. This corporate cloning leads to little critical thinking, little debate, virtually no constructive dissent, and a whole raft of issues which become undiscussable by the board. In these conditions there is not sufficient variety for rigorous strategic thinking to be done.

My experience is that matters are made worse by most boards being composed of power players more interested in their own ego stimulation than in the development of an effective and efficient business (Belbin, 1981). Moreover, they are often strongly driven by their values underpinned by logic and rationality both of which are essentially past-orientated thinking processes, rather than by the present facts and future possibilities (see Chapter 7). None of this creates a calm and reflective atmosphere in which one can debate the strategies needed to achieve the organization's purpose and vision.

Once the board's psychometric maps are displayed then there are a range of well-established group development methods which allow the issues to be acknowledged and a process agreed for their resolution. Then the board can begin the process of being the brain, and heart, of the business— creating the climate and structures, in which the operational side can get on with its proper work of delivering quality products and customer service. In doing so they can learn how to get into the four key roles of the learning board.

Personal development of directors   Once the board is clearer about its roles and is seen to be working towards their view of competence (Institute of Directors, 1994) then the developmental focus can be changed to the personal development of each of its members. To get maximum return for the investment of time and money here, this should be run in parallel with the board development activity. The psychometric maps used before can now become a focus for measuring gaps between the individual's capabilities and those needed for the four learning board roles. These gaps can be prioritized and made into a personal development plan. In many of the corporate and national cultures in which I work these are handled confidentially with an external consultant acting as a coach to help the individual to reach effective board performance quickly.

My experience is that it is the strategic thinking processes themselves that most intimidate the new direction-giver. They have invested some twenty to thirty years of their life in becoming specialized in their technical and managerial fields. That is why they were promoted to director in the first place. But direction-giving feels a very fuzzy discipline. A lot of it seems intangible. If one is monitoring changes in the political, physical, social, economic or technological environments then there is often little immediate action one can take, except and to refine one's thinking about them. Matters are made worse by disruptions from the environment which are of such magnitude that one feels helpless—changes in interest rates, changes of government, hurricanes wiping out key commodities, etc.—allow for little immediate action, except some damage limitation and a lot of thinking about what this does to future plans and scenarios.

The realization that it is not just the quantity but also the *quality* of strategic thought that makes the competitive difference here often does not occur. If the board is committed to the idea that this is the difference which makes the difference—the development of their unique and sustainable competitive edge—then it is to the development of their thinking *processes* to which they need turn.

Four strategic thinking styles

Four distinct thinking styles need to be addressed. Most managers and technical people have been educated using analytical thinking only. This *convergent thinking* is helpful in reducing uncertainty around problems but in doing so it does reject most alternative possibilities and places a high priority on creating certainties. As most of the directoral work, except supervising management, deals with uncertainties this is not a helpful preferred thinking style. If too many convergent thinkers come together at the top of the business, they will generate 'analysis paralysis', and censor ideas at too early a stage. The rot starts.

What needs to be developed first is a capacity for *divergent thinking* which enjoys and uses the different possibilities of a given idea or problem. This thinking is the sort in which architects, designers, and open-systems software people are trained. It synthesizes differences into a new and richer whole. Most managers find it very difficult at first because it goes against all they have learned. Take a simple example. How many uses can you think of for a household brick? The convergent thinker will come up with perhaps four or five. The divergent thinker will come up with perhaps thirty. The latter do not suffer inhibitions and self-censoring of ideas. They get the ideas out first before applying their critical faculties to them. Only later do they stop diverging and apply criteria which allow them to begin to converge to a solution. I see this as one of the two key directoral thinking skills. It allows the director to begin to enjoy and use the ambiguities and diversity of the uncertain future to achieve higher-quality thinking and solutions than any convergent thinker could ever attain.

Second, and running in parallel with divergent thinking, is the uninhibited use of *intelligent naivety*. This uses the paradox of the undoubted intelligence of the direction-givers, individually and collectively, to ask naive, profound questions of areas about which they know little. A key direction-giving skill is learning to have the confidence to ask and continue to ask until you are satisfied, 'why?' 'how?' etc. of people you suspect of using technobabble to intimidate directors to push through a doubtful proposal. Once learned, it helps a board to get over the well-known phenomenon of them taking a stupid decision collectively which their intelligence would not have allowed them to take as individuals.

The third key directoral thinking skill is being able to break out of 'binary thinking' — something is either right or wrong, good or bad, etc. — and use *both ... and* thinking. 'Both ... and' is a synthesizing process which avoids a reductionist thinking approach by seeking higher-level solutions which combine often apparent contradictions. These higher-quality resolutions, or reframing, of existing problems have another advantage. A major problem of binary thinking is that it can quickly grow into a personalized conflict—either he is right or I am. This reinforces the power politics of the board. 'Both ... and' thinking can help to raise both warring parties' eyes to the overarching *issue* and dilemmas which rises above the interpersonal squabbles and allows the energies to be diverted from debilitating personal squabbles towards high-level organizational issue resolution.

The fourth key directoral thinking skill is that of being able to take the *helicopter view*. This uses the idea of rising above the immediate problems and is derived from the work of the US brief therapists on 'second-order change' (Watzlawick *et al.*, 1974) and Chris Argyris's work on double-loop learning. It is often found in the selection criteria for future direction-givers. It demands the intellectual ability to rise above the immediate problems and see them in differing contexts through having the ability to change the perspectives from which problems are viewed. This allows for more critical debate and dissent in the top team and allows them to develop *scenarios* rather than rush into planning and budgets. Others have written more elegantly than I about scenarios in this book (see Chapters 8 and 9) so I will not go into them here except strongly to encourage their use. I will stress that the development of the helicopter view allows issues to be seen from many heights and angles. The ability to tolerate and use these different perspectives is a key direction-giving thinking skill and is fundamental to scenario building. It helps to sensitize direction-givers to spotting the 'weak signals' in a mass of dynamic and contradictory data in the external environment, and allows them to visit many possible futures in a risk-free way before they happen. This builds confidence in the direction-givers that they have debated and considered many alternative actions *before* the future unfolds itself.

I have discussed the four styles of strategic thinking here. Chapter 7 in this book takes a detailed look at each piece of thinking which can build effectiveness in this intriguing area (see also Mintzberg, 1994).

The ten steps of strategic thinking

Let me demonstrate a sequence by which a board can develop its strategic thinking skills through a ten-step process: I assume that the board must always have a dynamic picture of their SWOT analysis (the Strengths and Weaknesses, Opportunities and Threats) in front of them. This forms the frame into which they add their pieces of mosaic to create their world view, using the types of techniques listed below:

1. *Prepare a SWOT analysis*   This is the key picture that the Board must keep in its collective mind. The SWOT analysis forms the dynamic background against which all the internal and external changes are viewed. It needs to be revisited by the board regularly and rigorously, at least once very six months, for debate and dissent. The framework in which the SWOT is formed is usually helped by using the acronym PPESTT. This denotes the changes in the following environments:
   Political
   Physical (Green)
   Economic
   Social
   Technological
   Trade.
2. *Analyse added value (e.g. the value chain)*   This Michael Porter analytical tool is helpful in getting the board's intellectual helicopter off the ground. The focus is on the internally orientated competitive advantage generated by

specific added value of your company compared with one's competitors. It would be normal to find only one or two areas in which you add significant value added compared with your known competitors. It encourages the use of 'both...and' thinking.

3. *Analyse competitive positioning (e.g. the five-forces model)* This Michael Porter model gets the board higher off the ground and further away from the comfort of the managerial world. It looks at the external forces of the threat of new entrants, threat of new products or services, economic power of suppliers, economic power of customers, and the churning (repositioning) of existing competitors, and the interaction between them as well as barriers to entry (costs of entry) to existing markets. It encourages the use of the helicopter view and divergent thinking.

4. *Agree the key environmental variables* The board needs be aware of the key external factors which, if carefully monitored on a regular basis, allow them to focus their search for environmental changes. These are their key trend lines, or ratios, which give the corporate mindsets. If they do not do this they will go mad trying to make sense of all the irregular and uncertain changes occurring around their organization. Such changes could, for example, be interest rates, discretionary spending levels, lifestyle changes, governmental spending patterns, etc. This encourages the use of intelligent naivety and 'both...and' thinking styles and sensitizes them in their search for 'weak signals'.

5. *Develop more than two scenarios* This is the point where many managers initially feel airsick. What we are not trying to do is simply prepare a 'best-case' and a 'worst-case' picture. It is more subtle than that. One is trying to prepare the board's thinking over time to have debated all sorts of combinations of environmental variables. Then as the future is revealed one can gain competitive advantage in three ways. First, the board is more confident in coping with the necessary change as they are likely to have visited it in their corporate mind previously. Second, they are more sensitized to monitoring the external environment and are thus more likely to spot the 'weak signals', which often presage major change, long before their competitors. Third, they develop the ability to identify key dilemmas caused by the external environment, and build their confidence in resolving the seemingly intractable. In this book Charles Hampden-Turner and Bill Weinstein have

written elegantly about scenarios (Chapters 8 and 9) so I will not go into them in depth here. The only thing I will do is add a caveat. Scenarios are *not* predictions. They are a key tool for developing the intellectual capacity of the direction-givers but are not meant to allow direction-givers to turn such thoughts immediately into plans and budgets. Henry Mintzberg's excellent book *The Rise and Fall of Strategic Planning* (1994) develops this point well and shows the fallibility of the previous strategic planning systems.

6. *Review the strategic implications and dilemmas for the business of each scenario through board, and in-company debates and discussions.*
7. *Take decisions on the policies and strategies of the organization.*
8. *Take decisions on the strategic allocation of resources to achieve these policies and strategies.*
9. *Start the planning process*   Note that it is only now that planning begins.
10. *Install the feedback processes so that the strategies, plans and environmental changes are linked into a Learning Organization system.*

This may seem a lot of time to spend when the board wants to get down to the 'real' business of plans and budgets. Remember, that these may be very real to managers but that direction-givers have other realities, prime among which are understanding the changing dynamics and patterns of the many conflicting external environments in which their organization exists.

This ability to tolerate and use ambiguity and uncertainty, of valuing diversity and learning, and of budgeting time to create a helicopter view in the chaotic environments of today's business seems to differentiate the effective direction-givers from the also-rans. All these skills are developable in direction-givers. I encourage you to do so. It is so much more energizing than having the smell of rotting fish about you at the end of an apparently successful managerial career.

References

Argenti, J. (1976) *Corporate Collapse: Causes and Symptoms*, New York: McGraw-Hill.
Belbin, M. (1981) *Management Teams: Why They Succeed or Fail*, London: Heinemann.
Garratt, R. (1994) *The Learning Organization*, London: HarperCollins
Institute of Directors (1990) *Development of and for the Board*, London.

Institute of Directors (1994) *Good Practice for Boards of Directors*, London.

Mintzberg, H. (1994) *The Rise and Fall of Strategic Planning*, New York: Free Press.

Watzlawick, P., Weakland, J and Fisch, R. (1974) *Change: Problem Formulation and Problem Resolution*, New York: W. W. Norton.

Index

ABB, 238
Accountability, 13, 14, 15, 16, 22, 24, 73, 76, 176, 199, 200,
    202, 244
Action Learning, 169, 249
Aesthetics, 50
Agency Theory, 16
AKZO, 235
Apple, 59, 235
    Apple Powerbook, 48
Architecture, 47, 60
Attitudes, 75, 76, 77

Baker Perkins (APV Group), 54
Baby, 73, 75, 78
Beliefs, 72, 73, 74, 76, 77, 78
Benchmarking (*see also* Organisational Climate Survey),
    127–130, 209
Bifurcation, 39
Black and Decker, 54
Blind Spot (*see also* Scotoma), 73
Board of Directors, 11, 12, 13, 14, 16, 18, 71, 77, 78
    development of, 4, 6, 8, 11, 25, 27, 242, 249–250
    committees, 16, 17, 21, 26
    structure of, 16, 17, 18–19
Braun, 48, 49
    Dieter Rams, 57
BP, 163
Brain
    left, right, 49, 55–56, 58
Brunel, Isambard Kingdom, 61
Business brain, 6, 8, 250
Business system, 48, 50

Canon, 54
CEO (Chief Executive Officer), 11, 13, 14, 16, 17, 18, 20,
    21, 22, 25, 26, 27
Chairman, 3, 4, 11, 15, 16, 17, 18, 21, 22, 25, 26, 243, 245,
    247, 248
Change, 30, 32, 35, 37, 39, 45, 71, 74, 75, 77, 91, 228
    prerequisites to, 177
    resistance to, 162, 163–164, 190–191
Colour code, 86
Colours, 82, 85
Commitment, 5, 69, 139, 141, 145, 161, 165, 171, 172, 186,
    198, 202, 208, 209, 212, 213
    emotional, 75

    to design, 57
Committees, Board (*see* Board)
Competence of direction-giver, 157–186, 246–247, 248,
    250
Competition/competitors, 6, 8, 20, 23, 31, 32, 47, 67, 78,
    81, 125, 127, 167, 253–254
Conceptual mapping, 83, 85, 92
Conformance, 15, 16, 17, 19, 20, 21, 24, 243, 244, 248
Consumer behaviour, 54
    connections between consumer behaviour and
    technology, 54
Corporate collapse
    symptoms of, 250
Corporate governance, 6, 11, 13, 16, 188, 243
Corporate hierarchy, 48
Creative thinking, 70, 136
Creativity, 6, 56, 78, 82, 102, 103, 136, 172
Cross-cultural examples
    Africa, 211
        Central Africa, 231
        South Africa, 12
    Anglo-American, 12, 133
    Anglo-Dutch, 238
    Anglo-Saxon, 110
        compared with Latin, 218
    Arabian Gulf, 206
    Arabs, 211
    Argentine, 100
    Asia, 5, 6, 12, 23, 24, 112
        East Asia (Far East), 6, 100, 102, 103, 106, 109, 111,
        118, 132, 136, 214, 221, 222, 242
        South-East Asia, 5, 48, 109, 210
    Australia, 7, 12, 17, 118, 242
    Belgium, 108
    Brazil, 207
    Canada, 12, 100, 118
    China, 5, 23, 29, 100, 102, 103, 106, 109, 111, 114, 117,
        118, 205, 211, 215, 216, 242
        Overseas Chinese, 136
    Communist, 32, 122, 227
        collapse of Communism, 102
    Denmark, 206
    Egypt, 234
    Europe, 21, 32, 48, 56, 100, 102, 105, 106, 107, 110, 111,
        114, 117, 118, 205, 207, 210, 222, 233, 242
        East,

Europe (*continued*)
North, 220
South, 227
West, 227
EU, 125
Finland, 68, 69, 212
France, 108, 123, 205, 209, 211, 221, 225, 231, 235, 239
Germany, 18, 99, 100, 103, 104, 106, 107, 108, 118, 123, 127, 132, 206, 211, 238, 239
Holland (Netherlands), 108, 206, 211, 222, 225, 234
Hong Kong, 5, 6, 12, 100, 136, 211, 225
India, 12
Indonesia, 106, 111, 136
Italy, 108, 208, 212
Japan, 12, 23, 48, 54, 99, 100, 102, 103, 104, 105, 106, 109, 110, 111, 112, 113, 114, 117, 118, 123, 125, 127, 128, 132, 136, 206, 207, 209, 211, 221, 222, 227, 238
Shinto influence, 132
Korea, 106
South Korea, 100, 136, 210, 211, 222
Latin, 218, 238, 239
Latin America, 103
Malaysia, 100, 106, 111, 112, 136, 211
Mexico, 103
New Zealand, 12, 191, 242
North America, 100, 102, 103, 114, 206, 220
Norway, 206
Pacific Rim, 211
Philippines, 211
Poland, 227
Russia, 227
Saudi Arabia, 211
Singapore, 12, 100, 136, 225
Spain, 225
Sweden, 107, 108, 206, 212
Switzerland, 206, 225
Taiwan, 106, 136
UK, 8, 15, 17, 18, 22, 25, 26, 100, 102, 104, 106, 108, 111, 117, 118, 212, 222, 225, 222
public service, 187–204
USA, 2, 11, 13, 18, 48, 54, 100, 102, 103, 104, 105, 106, 107, 108, 109, 110, 111, 112, 113, 117, 118, 122, 206, 207, 208, 210, 222, 225, 227, 235, 236, 242
Venezuela, 221, 225, 227
Western
aspirations, 113
capitalism, 100
companies, 205, 207, 210, 215
cybernetics, 130
economies, 113
ideology, 12, 111
managers, 2
world, 1
Customers and citizens,
distinction between, 8

Daimler-Benz, 237, 239
Debate, 4, 6, 7, 86, 92, 212, 213, 252, 253
Deere & Co, 48, 49, 57
Delta Group
Lord Caldecote, 26

Design
decay, 48
engineering, 47
industrial, 47, 48, 50, 52, 54–55, 56, 61
as operational weapon, 47
as strategic weapon, 47
infusion, 58
paradoxes, 48
pioneers, 48
product, 47
Design-based incrementalism, 55
'Design mix'
(performance, quality, durability, appearance/cost/ feel/character/integrity), 51
'Design person/policy/strategy/permeation' model, 57
Designers
T-shaped, 58, 59
U-shaped, 59
Developing competencies in strategic thinking
basic facts, 160–161
blocks to development, 164–166
complacency about developing competencies, 162–163
framework for development, 169–170
why important, 161–162
Developing international managers, 231–232
Differentiation, 47, 126
skin-deep, 62
real, 62
Digital equipment, 54, 56
Dilemmas, 7, 100, 120–136, 219–220, 252, 254
innovation and designed strategy (top-down) versus emergent strategy from the grass roots (bottom-up), 120–122
political nationalism versus economic nationalism, 122–125
competition versus co-operation, 125–127
systematically raising quality standards and benchmarking versus mutual indulgence of latent needs, 127–130
correcting defects from our expectations versus amplifying possible deviations and useful exceptions, 131–132
celebrating the sovereignty of markets (short-term) versus converging towards future rendezvous (long-term), 132–136
dilemmas (cultural), 218–219
universalist versus particularist, 220–221
individualism versus collectivism, 221–223
affective neutral versus affective relationships, 223–225
specific versus diffuse, 225–226
achievement versus ascription, 226–227
past, present or future orientation, 227–229
organizational context of the international manager's activities
centralisation versus decentralisation, 230–231
error-correcting international manager, 231
Directing
as an intellectual activity, 4, 6, 248, 252, 255
different from managing, 1, 25–27, 75, 158, 243, 245

Direction-givers/direction-giving, 1, 2, 4, 5, 6, 7, 8, 72, 74, 75, 76, 79, 101, 137, 140, 143, 146, 148, 194, 242–256
  blockages to, 242–243
Director
  and old managerial job, 244, 247–248
  decisions and risks, 7
  induction, 164, 242
  liabilities, corporate and personal, 244
  rite of passage, 245
  roles/job of, 2, 6, 12, 15, 16, 22, 243–245
  training and development, 6, 11, 25, 26, 242, 243
  title, 2, 4, 5
Disjointed incrementalism, 35
Diversity, 252, 255
  of board members, 249–250
Dominant image, 72, 74, 75
Double-loop learning, 42, 45, 80, 175, 252

Earl, Harley, 62
Eastman Kodak, 235
Education, 1, 25
  conventional, 60
  designers', 60
Effective board, 20–22
Effective organizations, 1, 5
Effective questions to empower, 172
Elf Aquitaine, 236
Emergent strategy, 32, 34, 40, 44, 45
Emotion, 74
Emotional, 75
Engineering, 47
  design, 47
  concurrent, 51, 52
  human, 30
  integrated, 51, 52
  simultaneous, 51, 52
Entrepreneurship, 40, 41, 42
Environment, 8, 14, 15, 23, 30, 33, 35, 36, 37, 38, 40, 43, 99, 140, 141, 142, 143, 144, 145, 146, 149, 150, 151, 152, 153, 154, 156, 162, 164, 207
  disruptions from, 6, 251
  key environmental variables, 254
  monitoring, 6, 15, 251, 254
  scanning the surrounding world, 91, 101, 151
Environmental knowledge, 53
Envisioning, 72
Egonomics, 53
Espoused Theory, 30
External Orientation, 14–15, 33

Five Forces Model, 254
Ford, 48, 54, 57, 62
  Don Peterson, 56–57
  Taurus, 48
  Taurus/Sable project, 56
  'Team Taurus', 56
Future(s), 2, 5, 6, 14, 24, 31, 39, 99, 139–156, 245, 250

Gatt Agreement 1993, 1, 2
GE, 215

Generic, 88, 89
Gestalt, 91
  Gestalt switch, 39
Goal, 74, 75, 76, 77
Groupware, 213

Habit, 75, 76, 77
Hard and Soft, 83
  (*see also* McKinsey & Co; *and* Processes)
Harmony
  innate quest for, 57
Harvard Business Review, 6, 122
Harvard Business School, 54
Harvey-Jones, Sir J, 162–163
Hay evaluation system, 237
Heineken, 235
Helicopter view, 68, 89, 159, 167, 171, 252, 253, 255
Hexagons, 213
Holistic thinking model (breadth of your thinking), 173–174
Honda, 36
Human Resource Management (HR), 218–219

IBM, 11, 48, 49, 57
ICI, 235
ICL/International Computers, 162, 237
IDEO, 56, 57
Imagination, 59–61, 93
Implementation, 5, 6, 29–30, 33, 34, 139, 148, 157, 167, 206, 207, 212
Inclusion, 242, 246–247
Induction, 27, 242, 244, 245
Information Age, 78
Ingenuity, 2, 5, 103
Insight, 41–42, 56, 59, 92
Institute of Directors, 242, 245, 250
Institutional investor, 18
Integrator
  designer as, 82
Integrity, 37, 38
  organizational, 51
  product, 51, 54
Intelligence, 82
Intelligent naivety, 247, 252, 254
Internal orientation, 14–15, 33
International manager
  appraisal and rewards, 235–236
  career development, 237–239
  job evaluation, 236–237
  organizational context of activities, 230–231
  reconciles cultural dilemmas, 219–230
  recruitment and image, 232–234
  strategic talents, 218–219
  training, 234–235
International teams
  as sources of international strategy, 205–217
  different behavioural norms in, 210–211
  dominant sub-groups in, 208–209
  effective structure of, 212
  examples of best practice in training, 215–216
  lack of diversity in, 209–210

International teams (*continued*)
    tools and processes for developing international
       strategy teams, 212–215
Intrapreneurship, 32, 35–36, 40, 43, 44, 45
Intuition, 6, 36, 37, 40, 41, 42, 56, 67

Jobs, Steve, 57
    Apple, 57
    next computer, 57
Joint ventures, 12, 13, 22, 27
Judgement, 5, 19, 90

Keiretsu, 111, 125
Komatsu, 36

Law of Requisite Variety, 37, 38
Leadership, 20, 22, 26, 78, 162, 163, 181, 190
Learning Board, 6, 8, 26, 243, 244, 248, 249, 250
Learning Loop (*see also* Strategic Cycle), 101, 116
L≥C, 4, 37
Learning Organization, 39, 41, 185, 200, 202, 249, 255
Learning styles questionnaire (LSQ), 182
Lever, 207

Management development, 7, 29, 30, 32, 37, 43, 44, 45
Managers, 1, 7, 12, 18, 25, 29, 30, 43, 44, 45, 76, 77, 139,
    151
    involvement and development, 155–156
    product, 47
    programme, 47
    project, 47
Map, mapping, 5, 83, 84, 85, 89, 94, 95
    cognitive, 83
    conceptual, 85, 92
    mind, 83, 178–79
    strategic process, 84
Marketing, 47
    imagination, 55
    myopic, 48
    '4 Ps', 48
Meaningful distinction, 47, 54, 61
Mental faculties, 82
Mental muscles, 6, 82
Mental operations, 82, 91
Mental processes, 85
Mental vocabulary, 89
Mentors
    of new board members, 26–27, 243
Meta-learning, 42, 43
Metaplan, 213
Microsoft, 11
Mind mapping
    your strategic challenge (*see also* Maps), 178
MIT, 161–162
Model of mind, 82
Moggridge, Bill, 56, 57
Monitoring and supervising management, 7, 14–15, 18,
    19, 24, 244
Motorola, 103
Multilinguality, 56

Multinational companies, 47

McGregor's Theory X, 190, 192
McKinsey & Co, 50, 58, 73
    7S framework, 58
    'hard' S, 58
    'soft' S, 58

Next computer, 57
Non-executive directors, 17, 18, 19, 25, 27, 195, 202

Olivetti, 48, 49, 54, 56, 57
Opinion, 73, 76
Organization climate survey, 248
Organizational efficiency and effectiveness, 1, 8, 193,
    242
Outside directors, 13, 16, 18, 19, 21
Owner-manager, 12, 19

Paradigm shifts, 174–175
Parallel development
    benefits of, 52
Past orientation, 14, 67, 250
Pattern making, 33
Performance, 14, 15, 16, 17, 18, 19, 20, 21, 24, 248
Perrow's typology, 42
Peter principle, 75
Philips, 48, 52, 54, 235
Philosophy, 82
Planning perspective, 176–177
Policy, 1, 5, 8, 14, 15, 16, 21, 194, 202
Policy making/formulating, 15, 16, 21, 24, 244, 245, 248
Policy, strategy, operations, 8, 202, 249
    review of cycle, 244–245
Political will (purpose), 2, 5, 6, 37
Polity, 192, 202
Possibility thinking, 72
PPESTT (with SWOT analysis), 4
Predictions
    fallibility of, 141–143
    need of, 140–141
Preparing for more than one future, 146, 151
Printed circuit, 76
Processes
    'hard', 49, 56
    'soft', 49, 56
Process vs data, 86, 88, 89, 94
Process re-engineering, 30, 192
Product development
    new, 51, 54
    parallel, 49
    sequential, 49
Product design, 47
Product differentiation, 47
Product integrity, 54
Profile, 83
Psychometric testing
    of directors, 249, 250
    of international teams, 208
Public sector, 8

Public service
  business process re-engineering, 192
  buyer-supplier chains, 202
  capture, 193
  commissioning, 189, 201, 202
  cross-agency working, 194, 200, 201
  cross-boundary working, 200, 202
  future scenarios, 196–199
  governance, 189, 193, 194
  growth of various forms of provision, 192–193
  learning organizations, 200
  local politicians (members), 193, 195
  mixed economy of service delivery, 188, 194
  new public management, 189–190
  non-executive roles, 195, 202
  officer roles, 195
  patient-focused paradigm, 192
  policy, 194, 202
  polity, 194, 202
  private sector, 203
  productivity, participation and leadership, 191
  public choice theory, 189
  public policy issues, 193
  public sector and public service (distinction between),
    192
  purchasing, 189, 201
  resistance to change, 190
  sector barriers, 193
  strategic alliances, 202
  strategic thinking in strategy, 187–204, 194, 202
  strategy, key issues, 188–192
  user complexity, 188–189
  user voice, 201
  vision building, 200, 203

Q8, 235

RAVBA (depth of your thinking), 174
Reframing, 8, 170–171, 184, 242, 252
Regulators, 13, 14
Rover cars, 48

Scenarios, 4, 6, 7, 39, 90, 100–114, 196–199, 200–202, 207,
    212, 252, 254, 255
  a workable version, 140, 155–156
  as expressions of uncertainty, 143–144, 145
  as hypothetical alternative futures, 143
  as means of anticipating impact of change, 144
  as means of sharpening awareness of assumptions,
    145
  as pre-planning strategic thinking, 146
  distinguished from contingency planning, 145–146
  how they are made, 148–151
  results in identifying future challenges, 146–147, 151
  the need to revise them, 153
  their scope, macro and micro, 154–155
Scenario thinking
  as alternative to predicting, 142
  as compatible with decisiveness, 147–148
  as mental preparation for uncertain future, 143
  contrasted with contingency planning, 145–147

Schlumberger, 234
Scotoma (*see also* Blind spot), 73, 75, 77
Second order change, 252
Self worth, 76, 77
SEMCO, 207
Seven Ss of management, 58
Shareholders, 11, 12, 14, 15, 19
Sharp, 54
Shell, 154, 161, 207, 212, 232, 235, 237
Short term vs longer term, 158–160
Silicon valley, 47
Situational matching, 81
Six thinking hats, 171–172
Skills
  of designers, 49, 50, 53, 55, 56, 59, 60–61
  of directors/direction-givers, 2, 5, 11, 18, 19, 22–25, 26,
    31, 33, 40, 78, 94, 158, 163, 166, 167, 168, 169, 170,
    190, 198, 201, 218, 235, 237, 252, 253, 255
  of international teams, 205, 207, 210, 213–214
SLIM priority setting technique, 179
Smith, Michael (APV-Baker Perkins), 56
Sony, 48, 54–55, 57
  my first Sony, 54
  Sony camcorders, 54
  Sony Profeel, 54
  Sony Walkman, 54, 55
  Sony Watchman, 54
Stakeholders, 13, 188
Stephenson, George, 61
Stories
  need for, 152–153
Strategic alliances, 12, 19, 20, 23, 202
Strategic cycle (*see also* Learning loops), 117, 118, 119,
    137, 249
Strategic decision-making, 11, 16, 18, 139, 219
Strategic design, 57, 122
Strategic direction, 13, 18, 21, 24, 33, 36, 37
Strategic environment, 14, 15, 33
Strategic intent, 30, 32, 36, 37, 40, 41, 43, 44, 45
Strategic logics, 101, 114, 116
Strategic options, 32–37
Strategic planning, 2, 3, 4, 18, 31, 32, 33, 35, 37, 40, 43, 44,
    50, 72, 139, 146, 219
Strategic repertoire, 6, 41, 45
Strategic thinkers, 2, 5, 8, 67, 68, 69, 99, 223, 224, 229, 230,
    231, 232
Strategic thinking (*see also* Thinking)
  developing competencies in, 160–166, 169–170
  process of, 8
  purposes of, 157–158
  as 'seeing' (ahead, behind, above, below, beside,
    beyond), 7, 67–70
  ten steps of, 253–255
  vs operational thinking, 158–159
Strategic thought, 24, 30, 90, 251
Strategist, 15, 29, 30, 31, 43, 45, 61, 68, 69, 89, 90, 91, 94,
    99, 101, 194, 195, 202
Strategy
  culturally different approaches to different types and
    stages, 206
  definition, 205

Strategy (*continued*)
    emergent, 32, 34, 40, 44, 45, 119, 120–121, 209
    formulating/formulation, 1, 14, 15, 16, 18, 20, 21, 23,
        24, 29, 30, 45, 80, 81, 85, 86, 88, 90, 91, 92, 93, 94,
        206–207, 208, 212, 244, 248
    and cultural differences, 206–207
    intended, 34, 40, 44
    realised, 34, 40, 44
    translated into policy, 14
Styling, 51, 54
Subconscious, 73, 76
SWOT analysis, 3, 253
System, 89, 91

Teams
    (*see also* International teams)
    integrated, 49
    multidisciplinary, 47
    'team rugby' 51
Technology, 54
Teleological, 74
Texas Instruments, 54
Theories in use, 30
Thinkers
    board level, 24
    both/and, 178, 252, 254
    choices and consequences, 180
    convergent, 4, 251
    divergent, 4, 251
    either/or (binary), 7, 144, 252
    operational, 158, 159
    possibility, 72
    strategic, 1, 2, 3, 4, 5, 6, 7, 8, 11, 18, 23, 24, 25, 26, 27, 31,
        50, 67, 71, 72, 75, 77, 78, 79, 80, 89, 146, 157–160,
        163, 194–196, 219, 230, 232, 239, 244, 248
    types of, 143, 175
Thinking faculties, 83
    intentions, 82
    intentions profile (TIP), 5, 180–181
    map, 84
    operations, 81
    processes, 88, 89
    style, 81, 251–253
    tasks, 84
Thought experiments, 90
Thought plan, 89

Thought-requirements, 81
Thunks, 82, 83, 84, 85, 86, 87, 88, 89, 90, 91, 92, 93, 94
Time, 182
    allocation of, 16, 248
    demands of boards, 21, 94
    dilemma, 228
    orientation (past, present, future), 227–229
    time to think vs time urgency, 165–166
    to reflect, 8, 245
'Tools for thinking strategically' (TTS)
    design, 169–170
    duration, 168–169
    further information, 182
    objectives, 167–168
    overview, 166–167
    range of strategic thinking tools, 170–182
Training, 4, 11, 22, 25, 234–235, 242
Trends, 8
    cultural, 53
    social, 53
Triad Design, 54
Trust, 11, 36, 74, 77, 94, 209, 210, 215
Truth, 73, 75, 77, 78
TRW, 235
Turbulence, 27, 30, 31, 32, 33, 35, 36, 37, 38, 39, 40, 42, 43,
    45, 99
Turf warfare, 49

'Unchaining' product designers, 47, 48
Unisys, 57

Value chain, 48, 50, 53, 253
Virtuous circle, 119, 122, 123, 127, 129, 132, 135, 136, 137,
    224
    vicious circle, 119
Vision, 2, 5, 36, 69, 71, 72, 77, 78, 79, 89, 91, 92, 93, 95,
    139, 189, 190, 193, 197, 198, 199, 200, 202, 203, 219
    design, 55
    product, 55
    team, 52–53
Visualization, 59–61

Yamaha, 54

Xerox, 57

Index of authors

Abegglen, J. and Stalk, G., 115
Ackoff, R., 183, 185
Adler, N., 205, 216
Andrews, K., 115
Ansoff, I., 31, 37, 45
Argenti, J., 255
Argyris, C., 30, 42, 45, 130, 183, 252

Barker, J. A., 184
Barrett, S. and McMahon, L., 195–196, 203
Bateson, G., 130
Beckhard, R. and Pritchard, W., 183, 196
Belbin, M., 185, 250, 255
Berle, A. and Means, G., 28
Boisot, M., *xi*, 5, 7, 39, 46
Bolman, L. G. and Deal, T. E., 184
Boston, J., Martin, J., Pollot, J. and Walsh, P., 191, 204
Bower, J. L. and Doz Y., 205, 216
Business Week, 61, 63
Buzan, T., 83, 179

Cadbury Committee (UK, 1992), 16, 18, 28
Canney Davison, S., *xi*, 8
Clark, K. and Fujimoto, T., 51, 62
Cottle, T., 228, 240

Davenport, T. H., 192, 204
De Bono, E., 73, 120, 171, 183, 184
De Geus, A., 6, 119, 161, 183
Deming, W. E., 115, 192
Design Management Institute, Boston, 54, 62
Doi, T., 115, 128
Dreyfuss, H., 61, 62
Drucker, P., 191, 192
Dumas, M. and Mintzberg, H., 57, 58, 62

Evans, P., 238, 240
Evans, P., Doz, Y. and Laurent, A., 240–241
Evans, P., Lank, E. and Farquhar, A., 240

Friedman, M., 115

Galbraith, J. and Kazanjian, R. K., 212, 216
Galton, F., 60–61, 62
Garratt, B., *xi-xii*, 15, 28, 183, 185, 194–195, 196, 204, 249, 255

Haigh, D., 203, 204
Hamel, G. and Prahalad, C., 36, 46
Hammer and Champy, 115
Hampden-Turner, C., *xii*, 7, 184, 204, 219, 221, 222, 241, 254
Hampden-Turner, C. and Trompenaars, F., 101–102, 115, 117–118
Handy, C., 196, 204
Hanford, P, *xii*, 7, 184
Harrison, A. F. and Bramson, R. H., 184
Hayek, F., 44, 46
Hickman, C. and Silva, M., 184, 185
Hilmer Report (Australia, 1993), 17, 28
Hilmer, F. and Tricker, R. I., 28
Hofstede, G., 206, 213, 216
Honey, P. and Mumford, A., 185
Hood, C., 189, 204

Institute of Directors, 242, 250

Johnson, C., 115
Juran, J., 115

Kakabadse, A., 115
Kaufman, R., 184
Kotler, B. and Roth, G. D., 51, 62
Kuhn, T., 39, 46

Laszlo, E., 39, 46
Lathrop, J. P., 204
Levitt, T., 54, 55, 59–60, 62
Lindblom, C., 35, 46
Lorenz, C., *xii-xiii*, 7, 54, 56, 57, 62

McCormick, J., 115
March, J. and Simon, H., 45, 46
March, R. M., 115
Maruyama, M., 115, 132, 206, 216
Michel, D., 119
Mintzberg, H., *xiii*, 2, 7, 30, 33, 34, 46, 56, 57, 58, 62, 115, 206, 216, 253, 255, 256
Morita, A., 115, 127
Murray, R., 190, 204

Newchurch and Company, 190, 204
Normann, R. and Ramirez, R., 115, 137

Oakley, E. and Krug, D., 184
Ohmae, K, 23, 28
Osborne, D. and Gaebler, T., 189, 204

Pascale, R., 39, 46, 207, 216
Pedler, M. and Wilkinson, D., *xiii, xv*, 8
Perrow, C., 41, 42, 46
Peters, T. and Waterman, R., 57, 62
Pettigrew, A., 115
Pfeiffer, J. W., Goodstein, L. D. and Nolan, T. M., 184
Pinchot, G., 35, 37, 46
Porter, M., 31, 46, 50, 51, 62, 107, 115, 125, 253, 254
Prestowitz, C. V., 115
Prigogine, I., 39, 46

Quinn, J., 35, 46

Redding, S. G., 213, 216
Rhodes, J., *xiv*, 5, 7, 82, 95, 184
Rhodes, J. and Thames, S., 82, 95, 184
Ross Ashby, W., 37

Sanderson, S. W. and Uzumeri, V., 55, 62–63
Schneider, S., 206, 216
Schneider, S. and De Meyer, A., 216
Scott, B., 124
Semler, R., 207, 216
Senge, P., 115

Simon, H., 45, 46
Smith, Adam, 190
Snow, C., Snell, S., Canney Davison, S. and Hambrick, D., 207, 216
Stewart, J., 203, 204
Stouffer and Toby, 220, 241
Straus, A., 204
Sun, General, 15, 23
Svatesson, I., 184
Sworder, C., *xiv*, 6, 7
Systems Dynamics Group, 115

Tapscott, D. and Caston, A., 192, 204
Taylor, B. and Tricker, R. I., 28
Thom, R., 39, 46
Thoreau, H. D., 166
Tricker, R. I., *xiv*, 6, 28
Trompenaars, F., *xv*, 8, 115, 213, 217, 229, 241

Vogel, E., 115

Watson, W., Klumar, K. and Michaelson, L., 217
Watzlawick, P., Weakland, J. and Fisch, R., 252, 256
Weick, K., 43, 46
Weinstein, B., *xv*, 7, 254
Weisbord, M., 184

Womack, J. P., Jones, D. T. and Roos, D., 204